PENGUIN BOOKS

AQUINAS

F. C. Copleston was born near Taunton in 1907. He was educated at Marlborough College and St John's College, Oxford. In 1930 he entered the Society of Jesus and after philosophical and theological studies was ordained in 1937. In 1939 he was appointed Professor of Philosophy at Heythrop College, Oxfordshire, a post which he held until 1970 when he was appointed Principal of the college. After the war he lectured in Germany, Italy, Spain and America and spoke on philosophical topics in the Third Programme. In 1952 he was appointed Professor of Metaphysics in the doctorate course at the Gregorian University, Rome, where he lectured during the first semester until 1968. From 1972 to 1974 he was Dean of the Faculty of Theology and Professor of the History of Philosophy in the University of London. On his retirement in 1974 he was appointed an Emeritus Professor at the University of London. He was then Visiting Professor at the University of Santa Clara in California (1975) and at the University of Hawaii (1976) and was Gifford Lecturer at the University of Aberdeen for 1979–80. He was elected a Fellow of the British Academy in 1970 and was made an Honorary Fellow of St John's College, Oxford, in 1975. He received honorary doctorates from the universities of Uppsala (1983) and St Andrews (1990). F. C. Copleston died in 1994.

He is the author of works on Schopenhauer and Nietzsche, as well as of *A History of Philosophy* in nine volumes, *A History of Medieval Philosophy* (1972), *Religion and Philosophy* (1974), *Philosophers and Philosophies*, a collection of essays (1976), *On the History of Philosophy* (1979), *Philosophies and Cultures* (1980), *Religion and the One* (1982), *Philosophy in Russia* (1986) and *Russian Religious Philosophy* (1988). His publication *Contemporary Philosophy* contains papers on such topics as positivism, the function of metaphysics, and existentialism.

AQUINAS

F. C. COPLESTON

PENGUIN BOOKS

PENGUIN BOOKS

Published by the Penguin Group
Penguin Books Ltd, 80 Strand, London WC2R 0RL, England
Penguin Putnam Inc., 375 Hudson Street, New York, New York 10014, USA
Penguin Books Australia Ltd, 250 Camberwell Road, Camberwell, Victoria 3124, Australia
Penguin Books Canada Ltd, 10 Alcorn Avenue, Toronto, Ontario, Canada M4V 3B2
Penguin Books India (P) Ltd, 11 Community Centre, Panchsheel Park, New Delhi – 110 017, India
Penguin Books (NZ) Ltd, Cnr Rosedale and Airborne Roads, Albany, Auckland, New Zealand
Penguin Books (South Africa) (Pty) Ltd, 24 Sturdee Avenue, Rosebank 2196, South Africa

Penguin Books Ltd, Registered Offices: 80 Strand, London WC2R 0RL, England

www.penguin.com

First published in Pelican Books 1955
Reprinted in Penguin Books 1991
18

Copyright © F. C. Copleston, 1955
All rights reserved

Printed in England by Clays Ltd, St Ives plc
Set in Linotype Pilgrim

www.greenpenguin.co.uk

Penguin Books is committed to a sustainable future
for our business, our readers and our planet.
The book in your hands is made from paper
certified by the Forest Stewardship Council.

Contents

Prefatory Note

AQUINAS was a university professor and teacher, and his works bear the impersonal and objective stamp which one naturally associates with writers of his profession. There was no obvious drama in his life comparable to that for which Socrates is always remembered. Nor was he one of those strange, lonely figures like Nietzsche, whose personalities exercise a constant attraction for biographers and psychologists. The main facts of his life can therefore be narrated very briefly.

The exact date of Aquinas' birth is uncertain, though it probably took place in or about 1225. He came of an originally Lombard family and was born at the castle of Roccasecca near the small town of Aquino which lies between Naples and Rome. At a very early age he was sent to the abbey of Monte Cassino for elementary schooling, and in about 1239 he went as a student to the university of Naples, which had been founded by the Emperor Frederick II in 1224. While at Naples he entered the Dominican Order, and this action aroused opposition on the part of his family, who shut him up for a time under guard. On regaining his freedom he went north to pursue his studies under Albert the Great, also a Dominican, at Paris and Cologne. After returning from Cologne to Paris in 1252 he lectured according to custom first on the Scriptures, from 1252 to 1254, and then on the *Sentences* of Peter Lombard, from 1254 to 1256. In the medieval university the practice of explaining and commenting on a text occupied a prominent place, and the *Libri quattuor sententiarum (Four Books of Opinions)*, a mainly theological work compiled by Peter Lombard in the twelfth century, continued to be used as a textbook until the end of the sixteenth century. The leading theologians and philosophers of the thirteenth and fourteenth centuries, including Aquinas, Duns Scotus, and William of Ockham, lectured and wrote commentaries on it.

In 1256 Aquinas became a regular professor of theology, occupying one of the two chairs allotted to the Dominicans at Paris, though it was not until the following year that his appointment was fully recognized by the university, the reason for this delay being the dispute between the secular clergy and the new religious Orders. From 1259 to 1269 he was in Italy, where he taught successively at Anagni, Orvieto, Rome, and Viterbo. In 1269 he resumed his lecturing at Paris, but in 1272 he went to Naples to organize the Dominican house of theological studies. Two years later he was summoned by Pope Gregory X to take part in the Council of Lyons, but he died on the way on March 7th, 1274. A rather wandering life of this kind can hardly have been altogether congenial to a scholar and thinker; but his unremitting application to study and writing in all possible circumstances enabled him to produce an astonishing number of works in his short life of some forty-nine years. He was, we are told, somewhat absent-minded, in the sense that his absorption in his thoughts led him sometimes to forget his surroundings. But he was noted for his kindness, and in spite of his devotion to study he found time for regular preaching. As a priest and friar he was in every way exemplary, and at any rate towards the end of his life he enjoyed mystical experience. In December 1273, after an experience while saying Mass, he suspended work on the third part of his *Summa theologica*, telling his secretary that he had reached the end of his writing and giving as his reason the fact that 'all I have written seems to me like so much straw compared with what I have seen and with what has been revealed to me'. He was canonized on July 18th, 1323.

The best-known works of Aquinas are the two systematic treatises, the *Summa contra Gentiles* (*A Summary against the Gentiles*) and the *Summa theologica* (*A Summary of Theology*). The commentary on the *Sentences* of Peter Lombard was an early work; in his commentaries on Aristotle

Aquinas was primarily concerned with explaining the text; and the commentaries on Scripture do not concern us here. It is in the two *Summas* that we find his mature thought. There are, however, other writings in which Aquinas develops special themes, and some of these are invaluable for a study of his philosophy. Some of them like the *De veritate* (*On Truth*), the *De potentia* (*On Power*) and the *De malo* (*On Evil*) are what are known as *Quaestiones disputatae* (*Disputed Questions*). These were the results, formulated by the professor, of regular disputations held at intervals throughout the year. In addition to these ordinary disputations or discussions there were *Quaestiones quodlibetales* (*Questions about any Subject*), disputations held at Christmas and Easter, in which a variety of subjects might be discussed; and we have a number of Aquinas' *Quaestiones quodlibetales*. Finally, there are the opuscula, some of which, like the *De ente et essentia* (*On Being and Essence*), an early work, are of considerable importance from the philosophical point of view. One can mention also the *De regimine principum* (*On the Rule of Princes*), the authentic parts of which were written in Italy, and the *De unitate intellectus* (*On the Unity of the Intellect*), which belongs to Aquinas' second period at Paris.

Of the two *Summas* the *Summa contra Gentiles* was written first, the first book being written at Paris and the other three in Italy. According to tradition it was composed at the request of St Raymond of Peñafort to help those engaged in the conversion of the Moors in Spain; but no very profound inspection of the work is required in order to see that it is very far from being simply a manual for missionaries. The 'Gentiles' whom Aquinas had in mind were not so much the ordinary devout Mohammedans as those whose outlook was imbued with a naturalistic philosophy. And the purpose and aim of the book must be seen in the context of the confrontation of Christianity with the apparently naturalistic interpretation of reality represented by Greco-Islamic philosophy. One of Aquinas' aims was to show that the Christian faith rests on a rational foundation and that the principles of philosophy do not necessarily lead to a view of the world which excludes Christianity either implicitly or explicitly. But he was not writing only for those who already shared with Christians a certain number of beliefs; for in the second chapter he expressly mentions the 'pagans' as well as the Jews and the Mohammedans. This fact makes it less surprising that he devotes considerable attention to subjects like the existence of God. In the first book he treats of the divine existence and nature, in the second book he considers creation and the human soul, its nature and its relation to the body, and in the third book he goes on to deal with the final end of man. He starts the work with a consideration of truths which, he was convinced, can be proved by reason alone, while in the later chapters of the third book and in the fourth book he comes to specifically Christian doctrine.

The *Summa theologica* was written, Aquinas tells us, as a systematic and summary exposition of theology for 'novices' in this branch of study. Most of it was composed in Italy and during Aquinas' second period at Paris. He was working on the third part during the final years at Naples, but, as I have already mentioned, he did not complete it. The work is divided, then, into three parts; but the second part is itself divided into two parts, known respectively as the *Prima secundae* (the first part of the second part) and the *Secunda secundae* (the second part of the second part). The first part is devoted to the subject of God and creation, though it includes a treatment of human nature and man's intellectual life. In the second part Aquinas considers man's moral life, dealing in the first sub-part with man's final end and general moral themes and in the second sub-part with particular virtues and vices. Finally, in the third part he comes to Christ and the sacraments.

It will be seen that neither *Summa* can be called a philosophical treatise; for even the *Summa contra Gentiles* contains a good deal of matter which does not fall under the heading of 'philosophy'. And this is true not only according to post-medieval ideas of the nature and scope of philosophy but also according to Aquinas' own delimitation of the frontiers of philosophy and dogmatic theology, which will be outlined in the course of the first chapter. Moreover, even though the commentaries on Aristotle and certain other works like the *De ente et essentia* can be called purely philosophical works, it would be a mistake to suppose that the *De veritate*, for example, must deal with purely philosophical topics. Some of it does indeed treat of philosophical topics like logical truth, conscience and free will; but it also deals with themes which belong specifically to Christian theology, such as Christ's knowledge and divine grace. And this absence from Aquinas' writings of any systematic philosophical treatise in the post-medieval style makes it rather difficult to advise a person who wishes to begin studying his philosophy in his own writings but who at the same time does not wish to concern himself with themes belonging specifically to Christian theology. However, one way of beginning such a study would be to take a book of selections, several of which are mentioned in the Bibliographical Notes at the end of this work, and use this as a key to Aquinas' writings. Another way which can be recommended would be to take the *Summa theologica* and study it with the aid of *A Companion to the Summa* by Walter Farrell, O.P., which is also mentioned in the Bibliographical Notes.

Finally, the methods of reference which I have employed in this book stand in need of explanation.

As has been stated, the *Summa theologica* consists of three parts (to which a Supplement was added), the second part being itself divided into two sub-parts. Each part is again subdivided into 'questions', and most of the questions contain several 'articles'. The numbering of the questions starts again with each part (including the second half of the second part), and the numbering of articles begins afresh with each question. In each article Aquinas firsts cites objections against the doctrine which he wishes to propose. He then exposes his doctrine or theory in what is known as the 'body' (*corpus*) of the article. Finally he replies to the objections in turn in the light of the doctrine which he has explained. In the references to the *Summa theologica* the reference is always to the 'body' of the relevant article, unless a phrase like '*ad* 1' or '*ad* 2' is included, in which case the reference is to the reply to the objection in question. *In corpore* means that the relevant quotation is taken from the body of the article last referred to. Thus the reference '*S.T.*, I*a*, 16, 3' means that the quotation is taken from the first part (*pars prima*) of the *Summa theologica*, question 16, article 3, in the body of the article. The reference '*S.T.*, II*a*, II*ae*, 98, 2, *ad* 1' would mean that the quotation had been taken from the second sub-part of the second part of the *Summa theologica*, question 98, article 2, in the reply to the first objection.

Quaestiones disputatae like the *De veritate*, *De potentia*, and *De malo* are divided into questions and articles, though in some cases, as in that of the *De anima* (*On the soul*), there is only one question. The structure of the articles is similar to that found in the *Summa theologica*. The reference '*De potentia* 6, 4, *ad* 2' would mean therefore that the relevant quotation had been taken from the fourth article of the sixth question of the *De potentia*, in the reply to the second objection.

The title of the *Summa contra Gentiles* has been abbreviated in references to *S.G.* The work is divided into books and chapters. The reference '*S.G.*, 2, 4' would mean therefore that the relevant quotation had been taken from the fourth chapter of the second book of the *Summa contra Gentiles*.

The opuscula are divided in different ways. For example, the *De ente et essentia* and the *Compendium theologiae* (*A Compendium of Theology*) are divided into chapters, while the *De regimine principum* is divided into books and chapters, and the commentary on Boethius' work about the Trinity (*In librum Boetii de Trinitate expositio*) into questions and articles. Inspection of the relevant work should make clear the meaning of the reference numbers.

Aquinas' commentaries on the writings of Aristotle are divided into books, chapters and *lectiones* (lectures). The reference '*In Metaph.*, I, c. 1, *lectio* 1' would mean that the relevant quotation had been taken from the first *lectio* of Aquinas' commentary on the first book of Aristotle's *Metaphysics*, and that this *lectio* dealt with the first chapter of Aristotle's text or with part of it.

CHAPTER ONE

Introductory

NOBODY would be prepared to maintain that in studying the development of political society in Europe we could profitably omit all consideration of the Middle Ages. For it is clear that they were an important formative period in this development and that the latter cannot be properly understood without reference to them. And I do not think that any well-informed person would now deny that an analogous statement can be made about the rôle of medieval philosophy in the general development of European philosophical thought. It would certainly be extremely foolish to pretend that there was simply an unbroken continuity, without the emergence of any new factors, between medieval, Renaissance, and post-Renaissance philosophy. The general cultural transition from the medieval to the post-medieval world had its repercussions in philosophy; and the scientific developments of the Renaissance were powerfully influential in stimulating new ways of thought. But though there was novelty, there was also continuity. It is a great mistake to take simply at their face-value the claims advanced by writers like Descartes to have achieved a radical break with the past and to have inaugurated a completely new philosophical era. And the customary abusive allusions to Aristotelians and Scholastics which occur fairly frequently in the writings of Renaissance thinkers can be very misleading if they are taken to mean that in actual fact an entirely new start had been made without any connexion with what had gone before. Even though, as Descartes warns us in his own case, we have to be on our guard against supposing that a post-medieval thinker who uses a term which occurred in medieval philosophy is necessarily using it in the same sense in which it was used by medieval philosophers, it remains true that writers such as Descartes and Locke cannot be fully understood unless one has some real knowledge of medieval philosophy. For example, a thorough understanding of Locke's theory of the natural moral law and of natural rights demands a knowledge not only of the fact that it was partly derived through Hooker from medieval theory but also of the way in which it differed from the theory of a philosopher such as Aquinas. Even if one decides to look on medieval philosophy as being little more than a preparatory stage in the development of European thought, it is still true that it was a stage, and an important one, and that it exercised an influence far beyond the confines of the Middle Ages.

The historical importance of medieval philosophy is indeed far more widely admitted now in this country than it was even some thirty years ago. It is recognized not only that there is such a thing as medieval philosophy but also that there was in the Middle Ages a great variety of philosophical outlooks and ideas, ranging from abstruse metaphysical speculation to empiricist criticism of metaphysics, and from a spiritual view of the primary function of philosophy to a devotion to the niceties of logical analysis. And at least two British universities, of which Oxford, an important centre of philosophical thought in the Middle Ages, is fittingly one, have instituted lectureships in medieval philosophy. The subject is at any rate regarded as a legitimate field for historical research and as affording material for doctorate theses.

At the same time it still seems to be considered a reasonable procedure in practice that the student of European philosophy should jump from Aristotle, who died in 322 B.C., to Francis Bacon and Descartes, who were born respectively in A.D. 1561 and 1596. And I think that the fundamental reason for the persistence of this neglect and by-passing of medieval philosophy is the conviction, whether explicit or implicit, that the medieval philosophers have little of value to offer us. It is not denied, of course, that many of them were men of outstanding ability and intelligence. But it is widely felt that their general outlook and their general ways of thinking about the world are obsolete and that their philosophical systems have passed away with the culture to which they belonged. And in view of the fact that some readers may approach a book on Aquinas with the implicit assumption that we cannot expect to find in the writings of a medieval philosopher any valuable contribution to present-day philosophical discussion I want in this chapter to make some general remarks which may help to make such readers more prepared to give Aquinas a hearing. Within the compass of this book I cannot, of course, discuss at length different conceptions of the nature and function of philosophy. Nor, in a book devoted to Aquinas in particular, can I undertake to defend medieval philosophy in general. This would be in any case an absurd undertaking. For one could no more defend simultaneously the positions of, say, Duns Scotus and Nicholas of Autrecourt than one could defend at the same time the philosophies of F. H. Bradley and Rudolf Carnap. For the matter of that, I am not primarily concerned with 'defending' even Aquinas. It is not my opinion that the philosophy of Aquinas consists of a body of true propositions which can simply be handed on and learned like the multiplication tables; and in any case whether the reader agrees or disagrees with Aquinas' ideas is for himself to decide. But at the same time I am convinced that a great deal of what Aquinas had to say is of permanent value; and I want at least to make it easier for the reader to consider sympathetically his style of philosophizing and his interpretation of the world.

Some objections against medieval philosophy are connected with features which are more or less peculiar to the intellectual life of the Middle Ages. For example, the fact that most of the leading philosophers of the Middle Ages, including Aquinas, were theologians easily gives rise to the conviction that their philosophizing was improperly subordinated to theological beliefs and interests and that their metaphysical arguments were not infrequently instances of what we call 'wishful thinking'. But on this matter I must content myself with the observation that if we take any given line of argument in favour of some belief or position the relevant question from the philosophical point of view is whether the argument is sound rather than whether the writer wished to arrive at the conclusion at which he did in fact arrive or whether he already believed in that conclusion on other grounds. For example, it is possible for a man who has believed in God from childhood to ask himself whether there is any rational evidence in favour of this belief. And if he offers what he considers to be rational evidence, it ought to be considered on its merits and not dismissed from the start on the ground that it cannot be anything more than an instance of wishful thinking. Whether or not we come to the conclusion that his arguments were in fact probably examples of wishful thinking, we should not assume that they were simply on the ground that the man already believed in God. As regards Aquinas' view of the relation between philosophy and theology, I shall outline it in a later section of this chapter.

Other objections against the medieval metaphysicians are so closely connected with a particular philosophical system that they cannot easily be handled in a short work devoted to the system of another philosopher. If, for example, one accepts the Kantian philosophy, one will necessarily consider that the notion of the medieval metaphysicians that they could obtain knowledge by metaphysical reflection was misguided. But though some of what follows would be relevant to a discussion of Kant's position, the Kantian philosophy as such cannot be discussed here. It may, however, be as well to remark that Kant's specimens of metaphysical reasoning were taken from the Wolffian School rather than from Aquinas, of whom he knew little. And in my opinion some of the strongest points in Aquinas' philosophy are those in which his attitude differs from the attitudes of the philosophers of the seventeenth and eighteenth centuries whom Kant attacked.

But it is unlikely that the reader who tends to assume from the outset that a metaphysician like Aquinas cannot possess for us more than an historical interest bases his

assumption on a previous acceptance of the critical philosophy of Kant, considered as such, or on the fact that
Aquinas was also, and indeed primarily, a theologian. It is,
I think, much more likely that it is based on some general
ideas about metaphysics and metaphysicians which are pre-
valent in this and in certain other countries. Some of these
ideas are connected with one of the most important features
of the post-medieval world, namely the rise and development of the particular sciences. It is widely felt, and by no
means only by professional philosophers, that the particular
sciences in the course of their development have wrested
from philosophy one after another of the fields which it regarded as its own. Cosmology has given way to physics, the
philosophy of life to scientific biology, and speculative psychology is in process of surrendering to exact science as scientific psychology gradually comes into being. The sciences,
it is true, do not treat of theological problems or of 'ultimate'
metaphysical questions. But metaphysicians have never succeeded in showing that they have a method whereby these
questions can be answered. Metaphysicians have tried to explain the world or to render the world intelligible. But even
when we can understand what they are trying to say, there
does not seem to be any recognizable way of verifying or
testing their speculations. It looks as though the only understanding of the world which we can attain is that provided
by the sciences. Everything points to the conclusion that
just as philosophy took the place of theology, so has science
taken the place of philosophy, at least of all speculative
philosophy. The philosopher must content himself with the
task of clarifying propositions and terms; his business is
with analysis and clarification, not with system-building or
with the attainment of truth about reality. It was indeed
natural enough that in the Middle Ages, when science was in
a very rudimentary state of development, people should
look to theologians and philosophers for knowledge about
the world; there is no question of blaming the medievals for
this. But we cannot be expected to pay much attention to
writers who admitted claims on behalf of philosophy which

are now disputed. Hence while we can admire the work which Aquinas accomplished within his own historical context, we cannot believe that he has much of permanent value to offer us.

Since, however, this attitude towards metaphysics may seem to be associated too closely with those who would rule it out altogether, the following point of view can be outlined. Metaphysicians seem to fall into two groups, though they are not mutually exclusive in the sense that a philosopher cannot have a foot in either camp. Some have supposed that they had an *a priori* method of their own whereby they could obtain factual information about the world and even transcend experience, giving us information about transcendent reality or realities. But if their claims are justified, why is it that they give mutually incompatible pieces of information? It would appear that they cannot at any rate provide us with any certain knowledge by the methods which they employ. At best their theories can be regarded as no more than hypotheses. And they can be regarded as hypotheses only if something can be indicated within the field of experience which tells for or against the hypothesis in question. Other metaphysicians, however, have been more given to enunciating general propositions about the things given in experience than to making the attempt to transcend experience. But in so far as these propositions purport to give information about the essential structure or about essential characteristics of things, analysis shows either that they are no more than familiar trivialities expressed in a rather pompous form or that they are completely vacuous propositions which give no information whatsoever. The only form of metaphysics which has any chance of survival is the construction of hypotheses which are of wider generality than scientific hypotheses, in the sense that they may cover a wider field than that covered by any particular science, but which must be in some assignable way empirically testable. In other words, metaphysicians, if they want to be taken seriously, must come to terms with empiricism; and their theories must take the form of empirical hypotheses. Medieval metaphysicians, however, believed that they were capable, not merely of constructing empirical hypotheses which are subject to revision, but of attaining certain and final knowledge by means of metaphysical reflection. Hence, while their philosophies may be of some interest, they cannot be taken very seriously from the purely philosophical point of view. Fossils can be of interest; but they are none the less fossils.

Now, these attitudes towards metaphysics are quite understandable. And the problems involved are real problems. Furthermore, they cannot, in my opinion, be settled by appeal to the authority of any philosopher. For one thing, problems which have been rendered acute by the growth and development of the particular sciences can hardly be adequately settled by appeal to the authority of a man who wrote before the scientific Renaissance and who consequently could not discuss the problems in quite the form in which they appear to us. In the next chapter I shall say something about Aquinas' views on the relation of philosophy to the particular sciences, and I think that the attitude implicit in what he says is sound. But it would be an anachronism to look to a thirteenth-century philosopher for a treatment of this question which could be called adequate in face of the modern situation. For another thing, Aquinas was the last man to think that philosophical problems can be settled by appeal to great names. 'Argument from authority based on human reason is the weakest' (*S.T.*, Ia, 1, 8, *ad* 2). In other words, an argument in favour of a given philosophical or scientific position is the weakest sort of argument when it rests simply on the prestige attaching to the name of an eminent philosopher or scientist. What counts is the intrinsic value of the argument, not the reputation of someone who has sponsored it in the past.

But though the problems which arise in connexion with the nature and function of metaphysics cannot be settled by an appeal to the authority of Aquinas or of any other thinker, it seems to me that Aquinas' general outlook and conception of philosophy are of permanent value. The number of philosophers who today draw inspiration from his writings is considerable, though his influence is stronger in France, Belgium, Germany, and Italy, and even in the United States of America, than it is in England. And though his positions doubtless need development, a theme to which I shall return in the last chapter, they are by no means irrelevant to modern problems about philosophy. For he stands as a representative of a particular type of philosophizing and of a wide conception of the scope of philosophy, which spring from a natural tendency of the human mind, the desire to understand the data of experience, man and the world in which he finds himself, in the completest possible way. The desire to understand is obviously not confined to philosophy, but if it is given free play it inevitably leads to philosophy and even to metaphysics. Whether the attempt to attain a unified interpretation of reality as known to us, and still more whether the attempt to understand the existence of finite things and to obtain clarity about the general situation which makes all particular situations possible, is an attempt which can meet with success, is not a question which can be answered *a priori* and in advance. But the desire to make the attempt is natural enough. There seems to be an ineradicable tendency in the human mind to reduce multiplicity to unity, to seek for explanations and hypotheses which will cover an ever wider range of facts and events. We can see this tendency at work in the sciences, and it can also be seen in metaphysics. It is true that if the language of science is taken as the one norm of intelligible discourse, it follows that metaphysical language tends to strain the meaning of terms to breaking-point, but it is also true that the impulse towards unifying the variety of events and phenomena is present both in science and in metaphysical philosophy. Neither the scientist nor the metaphysician is content to accept a purely chaotic multi-plicity of heterogeneous and unrelated events: we are far from doing this even in ordinary life. And though it is possible both in science and in metaphysics to slur over important differences in an over-hasty attempt at unification, the impulse towards unification seems to be involved in the process of understanding. For Aquinas at any rate the metaphysician is concerned, in part at least, with understanding the existence of finite things; and that there is anything to understand in this connexion depends on there being features of finite things, considered as such, which give rise to the relevant question or questions. If we assume that there are such features, the process of coming to understand will involve the relating of finite things to a metafinite ultimate reality, however it may be conceived. And it is most unlikely that the human mind will ever finally abandon the search for 'ultimate explanations' and the raising of questions about 'ultimate reality'.

One of the reasons why this is unlikely seems to be that metaphysical problems are prompted by the obvious facts of change and impermanence, of instability and dependence, which are encountered in our experience of ourselves and of other things. Spinoza spoke for many human beings when he remarked on the search of the mind for the permanent and abiding, for an infinite reality transcending the flux and instability which appear to characterize all finite things. And metaphysics, when it does not degenerate into the mere repetition of traditional formulas or into arid logomachy, expresses this impulse at a particular level of intellectual life and reflection. The expression of this impulse within the field of academic philosophy is indeed more apparent at one time than another; but when it is banished from the field of academic philosophy it shows itself outside this field. Further, it tends to return within the field itself, and, to judge by historical analogies, its banishment is temporary. Doubtless many thought that Kant had finally interred speculative metaphysics, but this did not prevent the rise of German idealism. And the discrediting of Hegel has not prevented the development of other types of metaphysical philosophy. We have only to think of Jaspers, for example, in Germany or of Whitehead in America.

But though metaphysics tends constantly to recur, there have been and are different conceptions of its nature. Some philosophers have talked as though by a purely deductive and quasi-mathematical method we could not only deduce the general system of reality but also make new factual discoveries. This attitude, however, which we generally associate, in part at least with justice, with the 'rationalist' metaphysicians of the seventeenth and eighteenth centuries, is now rejected. And one of the things which I want to show in this chapter is that it was not the attitude of Aquinas. The latter did not believe that there are innate ideas or principles from which we can proceed to deduce a metaphysical system on a mathematical model. But the question arises whether, if we reject the method of Spinoza and the dreams of Leibniz, the alternative is to admit that metaphysical theories can be no more than empirical hypotheses which are inherently subject to revision simply because they are hypotheses. This is obviously a possible conception of metaphysics. And if we decide that certainty can be attained only about the truth of propositions which are in some sense 'tautologies', it is perhaps the only conception of metaphysics left to those who admit metaphysics. In order to be able to claim that certainty is obtainable, at least in principle, in metaphysics, it would have to be shown that the mind can apprehend as necessarily true propositions which are based in some way on experience and which do say something about things and not exclusively about words. In other words, it would have to be shown that 'empiricism' and 'rationalism' do not exhaust the possibilities and that we are not forced to choose either the one or the other. And I think that in Aquinas' philosophy we find an example of another possibility which is well worth examination. I do not mean to suggest that his philosophy can simply be taken over as it stands without development and without prolonged examination of his fundamental positions. I mean rather to suggest that it is an organism which is capable of growth and development of such a kind as to reconcile on a higher plane the sharp antitheses which have emerged in the subsequent history of philosophic thought.

It may seem that the notion of 'certainty' in metaphysics

ought to be rejected out of hand in view of differences between philosophical systems and in view of the fact that no
one system has won universal and lasting acceptance. But
in the first place the notion of certainty need not be linked
with the notion of a static and fossilized system. And in the
second place there is perhaps more agreement among metaphysicians than is at first sight apparent. For instance there
is a considerable measure of agreement among both Western
and Eastern metaphysicians about the existence of infinite
being, transcending finite things. In some cases at least sharp
divergences begin to arise when a philosopher tries to go
beyond the limits of the human mind and to penetrate into
a sphere from which the conditions of our knowledge exclude us. I think that the reader will find that Aquinas' conception of the competence of the metaphysician in this
respect was modest and moderate.

In the succeeding sections of this chapter I propose to discuss some general points about Aquinas' philosophy which
may serve as an introduction to his thought and which may
at the same time help to show the reader that his philosophy
deserves respect and serious consideration. In the rest of the
book I shall confine myself mainly to exposition and explanation of what Aquinas says without constant reference
to possible criticism, for the discussion of which space does
not suffice.

*

The first point which I wish to make is that it is a miscon-
ception to suppose that the fundamental rôle of sense-perception in human cognition was a discovery of the classical
British empiricists. It had already been stated, and emphatically stated, by Aquinas in the thirteenth century. It is true
that the latter was not the first to state it; for the doctrine
was already present in Aristotle. But among the thirteenth-
century metaphysicians it was Aquinas who laid most
emphasis on it. While certain writers, such as St Bonaventure (d. 1274), maintained a theory of what we may call
virtually innate ideas, a theory which bears some resem-

blance at any rate to the theories put forward at a later time by Descartes and Leibniz, Aquinas stressed the experimental foundation of human knowledge. It was his constant and frequently expressed conviction that the mind does not start off with any stock of innate ideas or of innate knowledge; and he reaffirms Aristotle's statement that the mind is initially like a wax tablet on which nothing has yet been written. 'This is clear from the fact that in the beginning we understand only potentially, though afterwards we understand actually' (S.T., Ia, 79, 2). That is to say, the mind is initially a capacity for knowing things; but we should have no natural actual knowledge of the world at all except through experience of things. And the primary form of experience is sense-experience, that is, contact with material things through the senses. It is the senses which first set the mind in contact with existent things and which supply it with the materials for the formation of ideas. We do not, for instance, first have the idea of man and then later discover that there are men: we first become acquainted through sense-perception with individual men and we are thus enabled to form the abstract idea of man. Sense-perception is ultimately presupposed by all our knowledge whether of existent things or of abstract ideas or meanings. Indeed, Aquinas does not hesitate to say that the 'proper' or proportionate object of the human mind in this life is the nature of the material thing. 'The first thing which is known by us in the state of our present life is the nature of the material thing, which is the object of the intellect, as has been said above many times' (S.T., Ia, 88, 3).

Although he does not express himself in this way, we can say that for Aquinas we cannot know the meaning of a word which signifies a material thing unless we have learned the meaning either ostensively or by definition or description. For example, even if I have never seen a skyscraper, either in reality or in a photograph or picture, I can still learn the meaning of the word if I am given a definition or description of it by means of words like 'building', 'storey', 'tall', and so on. But it is obvious that I cannot understand the description

unless I know the meaning of the words occurring in it. And
in the long run I shall arrive at words the meaning of which I
must have learned ostensively, that is, by having my attention drawn to instances of what they stand for. I can, of
course, learn the meaning of the word 'skyscraper', without
knowing that there are skyscrapers, that is, that there is
anything to which the definition or description of a skyscraper applies. But I could not learn the meaning of the
word without some experience of actually existent entities.

Furthermore, in a sense Aquinas laid more stress than did
the classical British empiricists on the part played by sense-
perception in human cognition. For while not excluding introspection or reflection as a source of knowledge, he did
not mention sense-perception and reflection as parallel
sources of knowledge. He did not think that introspection or
reflection is an initial source in the same sense in which
sense-perception is. His point of view was that I become
aware of my existence as a self through concrete acts of
perceiving material things other than myself, inasmuch as
I am concomitantly aware of these acts as mine. I do not
enjoy a direct intuition of the self as such : I come to know
myself only through acts directed towards things other than
myself. I not only perceive a man, for example, but I am
concomitantly aware that I perceive him, that the act of
perception is my act. And this awareness involves the awareness of my existence as a self. 'The soul is known by its acts.
For a man perceives that he has a soul and lives and exists
by the fact that he perceives that he senses and understands
and performs other vital operations of this kind. . . . No one
perceives that he understands except through the fact that
he understands something, for to understand something is
prior to understanding that one understands. And so the
soul comes to the actual realization of its existence through
the fact that it understands or perceives' (De veritate, 10, 8).

To prevent misunderstanding of this passage it should be
added that Aquinas draws a distinction between my awareness of the existence of the self and my knowledge of the
nature of the self. To know that I have a soul or that there

is in me that by which I perceive, desire, and understand is one thing: to know the nature of the soul is another. For the latter knowledge deliberate reflection, 'second' reflection, is required; but the reflection by which one is aware of the self in a very general sense is not a deliberate reflection, and it is common to all human beings. It must not be confused therefore with philosophic reflection: it is automatic in the sense that I cannot perceive without an implicit awareness that I perceive. And the point is that my awareness that I perceive is dependent on my perceiving something. I can indeed reflect consciously and deliberately on my interior acts; but this presupposes a non-deliberate or automatic awareness of my outwardly-directed acts (of seeing, hearing, desiring, and so on) as mine. And this in turn presupposes the fundamental rôle of sense-experience or sense-perception. Aquinas believed that man does not consist of two juxtaposed substances, the operations of which are independent one of another, but that he is a unity, the soul being naturally united with a body. And because of the intimate union of soul and body the mind is naturally dependent on the senses for the acquisition of ideas and of knowledge.

*

From what has been said it is evident that Aquinas did not believe that the philosopher can deduce an informative philosophical system from certain innate ideas or principles. For he did not admit any innate ideas or principles. He did, however, admit self-evident propositions which in some sense give information about reality. He believed, in other words, that there are propositions which are necessary and yet at the same time give information about reality; and he called them *principia per se nota* (self-evident principles). They can be said to be analytic if an analytic proposition is defined as a proposition which is seen to be necessarily true once the terms are understood. But if an analytic proposition is understood as one which says nothing except about the use of symbols, Aquinas would not admit that his *principia per se nota* are analytic in this sense: at least he would not admit that they are all analytic in this sense. For he was convinced that there are necessary propositions which do say something about reality.[1] I shall return to this subject later. For the present I want to show first how Aquinas reconciled the admission of these propositions or principles with the above-mentioned doctrine that all our natural knowledge depends on sense-perception and secondly how their admission does not mean that they were for Aquinas the source from which information about reality could be deduced in a quasi-mathematical manner.

Aquinas distinguished two types of self-evident principles. The first type consists of those propositions in which the predicate 'falls under the definition of the subject', that is, in which the predicate gives the whole or part of the connotation of the subject or is contained in the intention of the subject. Definitions are of this type, and purely formal propositions like A is A. The second type consists of those propositions in which the predicate is an attribute or property which belongs necessarily to the subject. Analysis reveals that the predicate belongs necessarily to the subject. And there can be no doubt, I think, that Aquinas looked on the principle of efficient causality, if stated in a metaphysical form (for example, 'everything which begins to exist begins to exist through the agency of an already existent extrinsic thing'), as a self-evident principle of this second type. He was well aware that 'relationship to a cause does not enter the definition of a being which is caused' (*S.T.*, Ia, 44, 1, *ad* 1); and it is as well to realize that he was aware of it. But he maintained that analysis of the nature of a thing which begins to be reveals its relationship to a productive agent which we call 'cause'. He would not admit that the principle

1. Nowadays propositions which are claimed to be both necessary and informative are frequently called 'synthetic *a priori* propositions'; synthetic as giving information about reality and as not being purely formal, *a priori* as being necessary and universal. This term seems to me to be a convenient one. But it is apt, because of its historical association with the philosophy of Kant, to give a misleading impression. Hence I avoid the use of the term here.

of efficient causality could ever be refuted, but he certainly thought that it gives information about the nature of being which begins to exist.

Now, if the doctrine that all our natural knowledge depends ultimately on sense-experience meant that the process of acquiring knowledge about reality was simply a passive process of receiving sense-impressions and that the mind was simply a passive recipient, recognition of these principles would not be possible. But Aquinas did not think that the mind is purely passive. As we shall see in the first of the two chapters on Man, he was convinced that even on the level of our knowledge of visible things mental activity, a process of active synthesis, is involved. Moreover, nobody else really supposes that the mind is no more than a passive recipient of sense-impressions. If it were, not only metaphysics would be impossible, but also the scientific work of a Newton or an Einstein. It is clear that the whole scientific process of forming hypotheses and deducing confirmable or testable conclusions involves mental activity, an activity of synthesis and interpretation. The doctrine of the fundamental rôle of sense-perception in the acquisition of knowledge by no means demands the conclusion that we are confined to immediate and uncoordinated experimental data. And Aquinas could quite well have endorsed Kant's famous statement that 'though all our knowledge begins with experience, it by no means follows that all arises out of experience' (*Critique of the Pure Reason*, introd., 1), provided that the statement is taken in itself and apart from Kant's theory of the *a priori*.

According to Aquinas we first have experience of, for example, actual things coming into being and of causal agents. The concepts of a thing which comes into being and of a causal agent are thus experimentally grounded. But once we have the concepts and understand the terms, analysis reveals a necessary connexion or relation which is affirmed in the relevant judgement, in this case the proposition expressing the principle of efficient causality. In other words, from a psychological point of view our knowledge originates in sense-perception and presupposes it, even when it extends beyond its immediate reach. But from the logical point of view the nexus or connexion between subject and predicate in a self-evident proposition is affirmed as necessary, not because the terms connote objects given in sense-experience, even when they do this, but because analysis of the terms reveals the necessary connexion between them. It must be added, however, that this is not for Aquinas a purely verbal analysis when there is question of the type of self-evident principle to which the principle of efficient causality belongs. As we have seen, he recognized that relationship to a cause does not 'enter the definition' of a being which begins to exist. Analysis here means reflection on the objective meaning of the terms, on a concrete instance or concrete instances, bearing fruit in insight into the relationship between them. Aquinas believed that without experience we should have no idea of a thing beginning to exist; but he also believed that experience of concrete instances of things beginning to exist through the agency of an extrinsic thing yields insight into the fact that a thing which begins to exist must necessarily do so through the agency of an extrinsic and already existent thing. Thus once we have had the requisite experience we can know *a priori* that if at any time something begins to exist it does so as the result of an already existent extrinsic thing. This theory is certainly not empiricism; it is indeed incompatible with developed empiricism. But Aquinas did not consider that it contradicted the 'empiricist' element in his own philosophy. 'Once the mind knows what is a whole and what is a part, it knows that every whole is greater than any one of its parts; and the case is similar in regard to other self-evident principles. But it cannot know what is a whole and what is a part except through ideas derived from images. . . . And so the knowledge of principles comes to us from sense-perception' (*S.T.*, I*a*, II*ae*, 51, 1). The fact that Aquinas makes frequent use of this example of the whole being greater than any one of its parts renders even more acute the objection to the theory of necessary and informative propositions, that if they are necessary they are linguistic and not factually informative

33

statements. But I leave aside this question for the moment, in order not to interrupt the line of thought.

Though Aquinas admitted self-evident principles which in some sense give information about reality, he did not think that we can deduce a whole system of philosophy from these abstract propositions. It is true, of course, that for him we should not recognize the principle of efficient causality unless we had had experience of causal relations. Hence, if we take into account the psychological genesis of our recognition of these principles, we can say that recognition of the principle of efficient causality shows that there are causes. But we cannot begin with the principle and deduce by sheer logic that there are causes in the world. It is necessary that if a thing begins to exist it does so through the agency of an already existent extrinsic thing; but it is not logically necessary that there should be any thing which has begun or begins to exist. The principle can be expressed hypothetically. If there is any thing which begins to exist, it does so through the agency of an already existent extrinsic thing. And the same is true of other self-evident principles. Aquinas admitted one and only one self-evident and necessary existential proposition, namely the proposition 'God exists'. But as he went on to insist that although this proposition is self-evident 'in itself' it is not self-evident for any human being, we can say for all practical purposes that according to him there are no self-evident and necessary existential propositions as far as we are concerned. Hence we cannot deduce the system of existing reality from any set of definitions or axioms or from any set of metaphysical principles. For the matter of that, we cannot start with what Aquinas calls the first principles of the speculative order, like the principle of contradiction, and deduce all other self-evident principles. When he talks about 'reducing' some self-evident proposition to the principle of contradiction, he is referring to the activity of showing that to deny the proposition would involve one in a contradiction. In this sense it is said to be 'reducible' to the principle of contradiction and 'founded' on it. But it does not necessarily follow that the proposition in question can be deduced from the principle of contradiction.

We cannot therefore construct a purely deductive system of self-evident propositions. And even if we could, we still could not deduce that any entities exist. And this is a point of some importance. For it shows that Aquinas' conception of the philosopher's activity does not involve the claim that he has a special method of his own whereby he can perform the task of the particular sciences. The philosopher cannot deduce from the principle of efficient causality the particular causes of particular events. He cannot, for example, tell us what are the causes and conditions of cancerous growths. Nor from the general statement that every material thing possesses an intelligible structure or 'form' (a theory to be considered in the next chapter) can he deduce that material things are physically composed either of the four elements of ancient tradition or of atoms and electrons. We cannot deduce from purely metaphysical premisses the hypotheses and conclusions of the sciences.

This point can be made clearer by anticipating to a certain extent and drawing attention to Aquinas' general conception of the metaphysician's activity. The latter is concerned with interpreting and understanding the data of experience; and to this extent the root-impulse of his mind is common to himself and the scientist. But the metaphysician concerns himself primarily with things considered in their widest and most general aspect, namely as beings or things. For Aquinas he directs his attention above all to things as existing: it is their existence on which he rivets his gaze and which he tries to understand. And this is one reason why Aquinas says, as we shall see later, that the whole of metaphysics is directed towards the knowledge of God. At the same time the metaphysician first considers the intelligible structure of things regarded precisely as such and the fundamental relationships between them. He concerns himself, we may say, with the categorical structure of empirical reality. And Aquinas considers, for example, the categories of substance and accidents and the distinction in every finite thing between act and potentiality, themes which will be discussed in the next chapter.

Now, in all this Aquinas was concerned with the structure of things considered on a much wider level of generality than they are considered in the particular sciences. He was quite well aware that by saying, for instance, that every finite thing is composed of potentiality and act, that it is something definite but not yet all that it can be, he was not saying what are the concrete potentialities of this or that definite thing or what precise shape its development takes. And he was aware that in saying that a living organism is a developing unity in which we can distinguish 'matter', that which it has in common with all material things, and 'form', that which seals it, as it were, as a thing of a definite type, he was not telling us anything about the concrete physical structure of a daffodil as distinct from a daisy. For a knowledge of the physical structure of this or that type of organism or of this or that type of inorganic thing we have to turn to the relevant science. Similarly, metaphysical insight into the nature of relations does not tell us, and cannot tell us, what concrete relations are to be found in the world. Metaphysics is not the same thing as empirical science; nor can we deduce the latter from the former. As will be seen in the next chapter, there is no very clear distinction in Aquinas' writings between philosophy and the particular sciences. Nor could a clear-cut distinction be expected at that period. But he said enough, I think, to indicate the exigencies of his system with regard to the development of this distinction. The purification of science from metaphysics, in the sense of not allowing metaphysical propositions to do duty as concrete scientific hypotheses, and the preservation of metaphysics from being interpreted as a kind of primitive physics seem to be both demanded by his general point of view. Metaphysics does not stand in the way of the development of the sciences; it leaves room for their development, and indeed demands their development, that concrete content may be given to the bare bones of categorical generality. On the other hand, the development of the sciences does not render metaphysics superfluous. The fact that we grow in knowledge of the concrete structures of definite types of things does not make it any the less true to say that every material thing has a structure. This latter type of knowledge is indeed 'useless' if we mean by this that it cannot be used in precisely the same way that a scientific hypothesis is used. But it is not useless for those who are animated by the desire to know explicitly the general categories and structural principles of being as proportionate to the human mind.

Aquinas does indeed imply that metaphysics gives the general heuristic principles which the scientist employs. But he does not mean that the scientist need consciously accept heuristic principles from the metaphysician. It is rather that the scientist, like anyone else, grasps implicitly, for example, the distinction between a thing and its relations and thinks in these terms. What a metaphysician does is not to dictate to the scientist but to isolate and analyse abstractly the most general principles and categories which in Aquinas' opinion the scientist, as anyone else, necessarily uses in practice, not because the human mind is determined or conditioned by purely subjective forms or categories but because every mind apprehends them implicitly in experience. Metaphysical analysis, provided that its metaphysical character is preserved in its purity, can attain a certain state of finality; but scientific knowledge can go on increasing. And increasing scientific knowledge does not necessarily involve a revolution in metaphysics. For their functions are different.

I conclude, therefore, that in so far as a general attitude of mistrust towards metaphysics is based on the notion that metaphysics necessarily involves the claim that the philosopher can deduce the system of the world from *a priori* principles, it is misdirected to the extent that it includes Aquinas' philosophy in its object. It is true that some Aristotelians of a later period shut their eyes to the scientific advance of the Renaissance and to all intents and purposes confused metaphysics with physics. And it is true that some post-medieval metaphysicians talked as though philosophy could be turned into a purely deductive system akin to pure mathematics. But I think that Aquinas would repudiate the attitudes of these groups. But this obviously does not answer the question whether when Aquinas enunciated propositions about things as things he was really saying anything at all. Nor does it answer the question whether when he went on to talk about God he was not attempting to transcend experience in a way which was quite incompatible with his view of the fundamental rôle of sense-perception in human cognition. And I want now to discuss briefly these two topics.

*

As regards the consideration of things as things or beings and the analysis of them when considered in this way, the objection can be raised that, though this procedure may be legitimate in the sense that no *a priori* prohibition can be issued against indulging in it, it leads to no more than the enunciation of trivialities and really provides no information. Mention has already been made of the distinction made by Aquinas between act and potentiality, between a thing's actuality, its being actually this or that, and its capability of change, of acquiring fresh accidental characteristics or even, in the case of material things, of becoming a different kind of thing. And it is immediately evident that in one sense at least the statement of the distinction provides no new information at all. The fact, for example, that the ordinary man – the man, I mean, who is innocent of philosophy – puts wood or coal on his fire in winter shows clearly enough that he is well aware that wood or coal are capable of undergoing change, that they possess potentiality. Similarly, the ordinary man has no doubt about events having causes. If someone is found shot, the ordinary man simply takes it for granted that the dead person either shot himself or was shot by someone else, whether intentionally or accidentally. Even if the cause of the person's death cannot be determined, the ordinary man does not dream of doubting that there was a cause. Hence if the metaphysician comes along and announces that finite things are metaphysically composed of act and potentiality and that every event has a cause or causes, he gives the impression of enunciating in terms of unnecessary solemnity truths of which everybody is already aware.

In my opinion, this is a point of considerable importance. But I do not think that it would disturb Aquinas. It is true that people in general are well aware that this or that particular thing is capable of change, and they are well aware in practice that events have causes. And this awareness finds expression in the concrete propositions of ordinary speech. But the so-called man in the street does not consciously advert to or 'notice' structural characteristics of the things which enter into the field of his experience, since these characteristics are so familiar in practice that they are taken for granted. And because he does not consciously advert to them and reflect upon them he does not apprehend reflectively their connexion with finite being as such. Nor, though he has a practical awareness of the causal relation and though he doubtless often investigates the particular causes of particular events, does he attempt to analyse the nature of the causal relation. The metaphysician, however, pays attention to what is so familar that it is customarily taken for granted, and he attempts to analyse in an abstract way characteristics and relations of which all possess an implicit and unreflecting awareness. And when he analyses, for example, the causal relation, he is not conveying to people the fresh piece of information that there are causal relations; for they know this already. Still less is he telling them what is the particular cause of this particular event. He is analysing what it means to say that X is the cause of Y and Y the effect of X.[1] For the matter of that, does not a great deal of philosophy in general consist of a clarificatory analy-

1. I suggest that much of what is now called 'linguistic analysis' does not differ fundamentally from what Aquinas would have thought of as metaphysical analysis. The descriptive names may differ; but what is done seems to be often much the same sort of thing. The results of the analyses of Aquinas and of a modern analyst may often be different. But this is another matter.

sis of what is in some sense already known? For example, people did not have to wait for Socrates in order to be able to distinguish between good and bad and in order to say correctly that one action was objectively just, another unjust. The ordinary Athenian certainly had some knowledge of moral values. But it does not follow that he could have provided definitions of justice, courage, and so on. All he could have done was to do what was so often done by those whom Socrates questioned, namely to point to concrete instances. The ordinary Athenian's knowledge of moral values was implicit and practical rather than explicit and theoretical or abstract. And he was doubtless often confused in his ideas. What Socrates tried to do was to make clear what was confused and explicit what was implicit. But we do not on that account say that Socrates' activity was useless. Nor, when the metaphysician analyses the causal relation or draws attention to the essential structure of finite being, is there any reason for saying that his activity is useless, unless we are prepared to say that philosophy in general is useless.

Perhaps the matter should be carried a little further in connexion with Aquinas' *principia per se nota* or self-evident principles. But I had better make it clear at once that we shall not find in Aquinas an explicit treatment of the question how far these self-evident principles are 'informative'. And to attempt to find all possible problems and their answers in any given philosopher is, I consider, a silly practice. Nevertheless Aquinas says enough to suggest that he might not be so put out at the observations of some modern critics as one might at first be inclined to suppose.

Let us take the statement that a finite whole is greater than any one of its parts.[1] It is often pointed out that this proposition is true, and necessarily true, in virtue of the meaning of the terms. Once given the meaning of the terms, the proposition cannot be anything but true. And it is inconceivable

1. I say 'finite' whole because I am not concerned with the special problems arising out of infinite sets in mathematics.

that any instance could be adduced which would lead us to say that the proposition is after all false or that it admits exceptions. For if our attention were drawn to any alleged contrary instance, we would say, 'that is not what is meant by a whole' or 'that is not what is meant by a part'. But though the proposition is true it does not tell us that there are in the world any wholes or any parts. What it does, it may be said, is to elucidate the use of words or symbols: it gives no factual information. It may be said that the proposition does not concern words alone; for it affirms an objective relationship between that to which the word 'whole' is applied and that to which the word 'part' is applied. If the conventions of the English language required the use of 'part' where we use 'whole' and 'whole' where we use 'part', then it would be true to say that the part is greater than any one of its wholes and false to say that the whole is greater than any one of its parts. But the objective relationship affirmed would be the same as the objective relationship affirmed by the proposition expressed according to actual English usage. And this shows that it is not simply 'a matter of words'. But the retort can be made, of course, that though this is true no 'information' is conveyed by the proposition, however it is expressed, since everyone already knows that what is called a 'whole' is greater than what is called its 'part'.

It seems to me, however, that Aquinas would admit this. He distinguished between self-evident propositions, the meaning of the terms of which are very easily understood, so that the proposition can be said to be immediately obvious to practically everybody, and self-evident propositions, the meaning of the terms of which are not easily understood, so that the truth of the proposition is by no means obvious to all. What constitutes a self-evident principle is not the number of people who understand the terms and see the necessary truth of the proposition but the necessary connexion itself between subject and predicate, which may or may not be clear to all. Now, the proposition 'the whole is greater than any one of its parts' is given as an example of the first type. It is a proposition, the meaning of the terms of which are so easily understood that the truth of the proposition is naturally known to practically everyone. Though people are not accustomed to say to themselves 'the whole is greater than any one of its parts', they know it already if they are normal persons. And I do not think that Aquinas would have any hesitation in admitting that if one announced solemnly to an ordinary man that the whole is greater than any one of its parts, one would not be giving him any factual information about the world, if to give information to someone means to tell him something which he did not know before.[1] For Aquinas clearly supposes that every normal person is well aware that the whole is greater than any one of its parts. What he does is not to suggest that the proposition gives new information but to offer it as an admitted instance of an indubitable proposition. And if it is said that it is necessarily true in virtue of the meaning of the terms, this is what Aquinas also says. He would doubtless add that an objective relationship is affirmed; but he was not so stupid as to suppose that this relationship is unknown until one has formulated or heard formulated the abstract proposition.

The principle of efficient causality, however, is different. We could hardly define 'whole' without mentioning 'part' or 'part' without mentioning 'whole'. But as Aquinas himself observed, relationship to a cause does not enter the definition of a thing which begins to be. Unless we state the principle of causality in a frankly tautological form ('every effect has a cause'), the principle is not 'tautological' in the sense in which 'the whole is greater than any one of its parts' has been called 'tautological'. It has indeed sometimes been said that the principle of causality, expressed in the form 'every event has a cause', excludes nothing and so asserts nothing. But there are some people who deny the principle; or rather there are people who deny that the prin-

1. I do not mean to imply by this that those who say that propositions of this kind are not informative do so on the ground that they do not provide 'new' information.

ciple is universally and necessarily true. And if it can be denied, it is at least not thought to be vacuous by those who deny it. For it excludes what is asserted by the people who deny it. But if it can be denied in such a way that the denial is not purely verbal, a difficulty arises in connexion with the claim that it is 'self-evident'. Is it an empirical hypothesis or is it an instance of what might be now called a 'synthetic *a priori* proposition'? Aquinas certainly understood it in the latter sense. But I do not want to discuss this problem, important as it is. What I want to do is to make the point relevant to the present discussion, namely that all act on the supposition that all events have causes and that most people would be prepared to say that they 'know' that all events have causes, even though they may not be able to say anything more about the matter. Hence the formal enunciation of the principle of efficient causality cannot come to them as a piece of information in the same sense in which one gives a man information when one tells him that there is a cobra under his chair, this being a fact of which he was ignorant. Yet the principle does say something. It says something about things which begin to exist, if there are such things, and it excludes from the class of things which are necessarily caused a thing which does not begin to exist, supposing that there is such a thing.

We can see therefore that for Aquinas the philosopher as such has no privileged access to a sphere of experience from which non-philosophers are debarred. His insight into the intelligible structure of the world presented in experience is the result of reflection on data of experience and of insight into those data which are in principle data of experience for everyone, whether he is a philosopher or not. William James declared that scholasticism, which he spoke of as 'common sense's college-trained younger sister', was nothing but common sense rendered pedantic. This was not intended exactly as a compliment; nor would James' verdict be accepted by everyone. But there is, I think, some truth in the remark. For Aquinas, to confine one's observations to him, did not think that the philosopher enjoys private access to a sphere of reality from which ordinary people are excluded. The ordinary man apprehends in some sense the fundamental metaphysical principles, though he does not formulate them in the abstract way in which they are formulated by the philosopher. It is so often the case that the philosopher makes explicit what is implicitly known by people in general. For example, the ordinary man uses universal terms correctly, and he can be said to know, in some sense of the word 'know', that there are no existent universals 'out there'. For he would never dream of looking behind the hedge or taking a telescope to see if there is a universal called 'horseness' existing out there in addition to horses. But he would probably be at a loss, were he asked to give a logical analysis of universal terms. Hence when a philosopher like Aquinas says that there are no universal entities existing independently 'out there', he is not giving the ordinary man a brand-new piece of information. On the other hand, his analysis of universal terms is not superfluous.

*

This is all very well, it may be said. Whether we agree or not with Aquinas' analysis of causality or of act and potentiality, it is clear that in this particular field he is not working on the assumption that he has privileged access to a sphere of reality from which the ordinary man is excluded. It is clear, in other words, that in some at least of his metaphysical analysis he does not pretend to play the part of an explorer, bringing us back news about the existence of things which were hitherto entirely unknown by ordinary mortals. But it has already been pointed out in this book that for Aquinas the whole of metaphysics is directed towards the knowledge of God. And does he not here pretend to be able to transcend the sphere of ordinary experience and to bring back news of the existence of a being which lies outside the scope of normal human cognition?

It is necessary to understand Aquinas' point of view as a metaphysician. With centuries of theism behind us we naturally have some notion of God; and if we are doubtful

more space for
your
thoughts

about the truth of theism, we inevitably tend to put the following sort of question, 'Is there a God?' or 'Does God exist?' or, if we are more sophisticated, 'Is it the case that there is a thing, and one thing only, which is infinite, omniscient, omnipotent, etc.?' And once the question has been put in this way, it is natural to go on to say that before we try to answer it we ought to find a method whereby such questions can be answered. But though this way of approaching the matter is perfectly understandable, and though the question could have been put in this way in the thirteenth century, since men like Aquinas also had an idea of God before they asked whether there is any rational evidence in favour of belief in God, Aquinas' actual approach was rather different. For it is plain that for him attentive reflection on the objective meaning of, say, coming into being and passing away discloses the relation of dependence of things which come into being and pass away on something other than themselves which does not come into being or pass away, and cannot do so. His conviction was that if a man does attend (which he may not do, of course) to the metaphysical structure of things as things, their existential dependence on something which transcends them becomes apparent. And the function of the arguments for God's existence is to give explicit statement to the process of metaphysical analysis and reflection. Thus the objective existence of a completely independent being on which the things which fall within the field of our natural experience depend existentially forces itself upon the mind which carries through an analysis of the metaphysical structure of these things. In this sense we can say that for Aquinas the proposition affirming God's existence is not so much an answer to the question 'Is there a God?' as an answer to the question 'What are things considered simply as beings?' For him the mind is first acquainted with material things. It can consider these things from a metaphysical point of view. If it does so, it will be led, he is convinced, by the process of analysis to see them as dependent on 'something' beyond them. And the question then arises what sort of being is this 'something'. Aquinas' affirmation of God's existence is not offered as an empirical hypothesis to explain, say, religious experience; still less is it grounded on some personal incommunicable experience. His proofs of God's existence constitute a prolongation of the reflection on things as things to which attention has already been drawn. He is thus prepared to say that 'all cognitive agents know God implicitly in everything they know' (*De veritate*, 22, 2, *ad* 1). And this is the point which I am trying to make. When the metaphysician affirms God's existence, Aquinas does not depict him as entering a sphere of experience of reality from which non-philosophers are debarred. Nor does he depict the philosopher as going on a voyage of exploration and coming back with the startling news that there is a God 'out there'. He starts where everyone else starts, and he reflects on the normal data of experience. But he has a power of reflective analysis which, when stimulated by the necessary interest, enables him to be a philosopher. And he raises to the level of conscious and explicit reflection truths which many people perhaps never consciously apprehend, though the truths, once apprehended, throw a flood of light on the content of their experience.

When therefore Aquinas depicts the philosopher as arriving at the affirmation of God's existence, he does not mean to imply that the philosopher can transcend human experience and the limitations of the human mind. For him the human mind, as mind, is open to the amplitude of reality or being, in the sense that it is the faculty of apprehending the intelligible and that every being is, as such, intelligible. At the same time, considered precisely as a human mind, that is as an embodied mind, it is dependent on sense-perception for the acquisition of knowledge. This dependence does not take away or destroy its openness to reality in a wider sense than material reality; but it means that in its present life the human mind can know spiritual or supersensible reality only in so far as it is manifested in the material world, that is, in so far as the mind's active reflection discerns the relatedness of the finite object of direct experience to what transcends our direct natural experience. 'Our natural knowledge takes its beginning from sense. Therefore it can extend only so far as it can be brought by (reflection on) the things of sense' (*S.T.*, Ia, 12, 12). Again, 'those things which do not fall under the senses cannot be apprehended by the human mind except in so far as knowledge of them can be gathered from the senses' (*C.G.*, 1, 3). Thus we can have a natural knowledge of God only in so far as finite things point beyond themselves and manifest the existence of that on which they depend. Hence the proofs of the existence of God say something primarily about things, the things which fall within the field of experience. They say that these things depend on something which transcends them. They cannot give the philosopher or anyone else an intuition of God. Any more immediate experience of God must be supernatural in character and the work of God Himself within the soul; it cannot be obtained by philosophical analysis and reflection.

To make Aquinas' position clearer it should be added that it is not only in the initial acquisition of knowledge that the mind depends on sense-experience. For he held that we cannot use the knowledge which we have already acquired without the employment of images or 'phantasms'; and images are the result of sense-perception. 'For the mind actually to understand something there is required an act of the imagination and of other (sensitive) faculties not only in receiving fresh knowledge but also in using knowledge already acquired.... Anyone can experience in himself that when he tries to understand something he forms for himself some images by way of examples in which he can see, as it were, what he is trying to understand. Hence also when we wish to make anyone understand something we set before him examples from which he can form for himself images with a view to understanding' (*S.T.*, Ia, 84, 7). Aquinas did not believe in imageless thinking, and he regarded the necessity of recourse to images as an illustration of the factual dependence of mental activity on the sensitive faculties or powers. Whether or not thinking is always accompanied by images is a controversial matter, and in any case to make Aquinas' view tenable the term 'image' would have to be understood as covering 'word' and 'symbol'. Otherwise it would be very difficult to show that symbolic logic and pure mathematics require the use of images. But Aquinas regarded the truth of the general proposition that mental activity requires as a matter of fact the use of the imagination as being confirmed by experience. He remarks, for instance, that 'if the use of the imagination is hindered by an organic lesion, a man's power to use knowledge already acquired is thereby impaired' (*ibid.*, and cf. *De fotentia*, 3, 9 *ad* 22).

The point of adding these remarks is that Aquinas applied his theory of the necessity of what he calls the 'recourse to the phantasm' to our thinking about spiritual things. 'Incorporeal things, of which there are no images, are known by us by means of their relation to sensible bodies of which there are images. . . . And so when we understand something about incorporeal things, we have to have recourse to the images of bodies, although there are no images of incorporeal things themselves' (*S.T.*, Ia, 84, 7, *ad* 3). For example, when we conceive the divine immensity we cannot help imagining God as extending everywhere, as though He were spread out in space. We cannot avoid using some image or symbol, even though we know that God is not a material thing which is capable of being extended or spread out. Not even the philosopher can free himself from the mind's dependence on sense-perception.

Any pretended disclosure of the divine essence, any unveiling of the inner nature of God, by the power of the speculative reason would thus be for Aquinas no more than pseudo-knowledge. He was convinced that there is a natural desire to know the supreme being, a desire which shows itself on the conscious level in, for example, metaphysical reflection. But he would add that it is rational to want to do this in so far as the means are available. And philosophic reflection is not a means for satisfying this desire, not simply because theologians say that it is not or because they erect a barrier with the notice 'trespassers will be prosecuted', but because our natural dependence on sense-experience and the imagination renders it impossible for us to penetrate the divine essence. If we attempt to do so with Hegel, the result will be a progressive elimination of the divine transcendence and the creation of a caricature of the unfathomable mystery of God. As we shall see in the chapter on God, Aquinas thought that philosophic reflection gives us knowledge of what He is not rather than of what He is. The metaphysician cannot transcend the limitations of the human mind which are common to himself and others. We cannot therefore expect startling discoveries in metaphysics comparable to the startling discoveries which are made in the particular sciences or by explorers.

*

Even though Aquinas did not make extravagant claims on behalf of metaphysics, he none the less thought that the metaphysician can attain certainty within a limited sphere. And it may appear that he simply assumed the mind's ability to know. Indeed, it has been suggested that the medieval philosophers in general were naïve dogmatists in that they did not preface their philosophies with theories of knowledge. But though this point of view is understandable, and though it is true that Aquinas did not preface his philosophy with an explicit theory of knowledge, there is little reason to think that he would have had much sympathy with an attempt to 'justify' knowledge, if this is taken to mean a justification from outside, as it were. For how could knowledge ever be justified from outside? None the less, Aquinas did take steps to justify our spontaneous conviction that knowledge of truth is attainable by analysing the grounds of this conviction and by drawing attention to indubitable acts of knowing. We can call this, if we like, a justification from inside. And though Aquinas may not have said very much on the matter, he at any rate said enough to make his general position clear and to show the general line which he would adopt against scepticism.

According to Aquinas it is in the act of knowing truth that the mind is aware of its ability to attain truth. Truth is predicated primarily of propositions; or, as he puts it, truth is found primarily in the judgement. Now, there are indubitable propositions, the truth of which cannot really be doubted, though they can, of course, be verbally denied. 'The whole is greater than any one of its parts' would be a case in point. And in recognizing the truth of such indubitable propositions the mind recognizes both the fact that it knows their truth and that it is its own nature to be conformed to reality and so to know. In a rather cryptic passage Aquinas states that truth is 'a resultant of the activity of the mind, when the mind's judgement is about the thing as it is. Truth is known by the mind according as the mind reflects on its act, not only as knowing its act but also as knowing the relation of conformity between the act and the thing (*proportionem eius ad rem*). This indeed cannot be known unless the nature of the act itself is known; and this in turn cannot be known unless the nature of the active principle, that is, of the mind itself, is known, to whose nature it pertains to be conformed to reality (to things, *rebus*). Therefore the mind knows truth according as it reflects on itself' (*De veritate*, 1, 9). Thus the mind knows its own power of attaining truth by reflecting on itself in the act of knowing truth. Aquinas' point of view was that sometimes at least we know something with certainty, that we know that we know it and that in knowing it we know that the object is knowable. It may be objected that this point of view is uncritical and naïve on the ground that it amounts to accepting the ordinary man's spontaneous conviction that he can attain truth and often does so. But the point is that for Aquinas the ordinary man's conviction on this matter is not simply 'naïve'. It is in the act of knowing that the mind's ability to know is recognized; and it is recognized by the ordinary man. The philosopher can reflect on this recognition and make explicit what for the ordinary man is implicit. And this procedure can be called 'second reflection'. The passage quoted above is an instance of second reflection.

But the 'reflection' about which the passage speaks is not itself philosophic reflection: it is what we may call 'first reflection', the awareness of knowing truth which at least sometimes accompanies the ordinary man's mental activity. In other words, the philosopher can reflect on the ordinary man's awareness of attaining truth, but he has not at his disposal some extraordinary and special means of proving that we can know truth or that 'knowledge' is knowledge. If a philosopher were to comment that in this case we can never prove that we can attain truth and that if we cannot prove it we can never know it, Aquinas might reply that the sort of proof which the philosopher is looking for is inherently useless and indeed impossible, but that it does not follow that we cannot both attain truth and also know that we can attain it. We do not need any further guarantee of our ability to attain truth than our awareness or recognition of the fact that we do in fact attain it.

In the *De veritate* (10, 12, *ad* 7) we read that though one can think about the statement that one does not exist, no one can give his assent to it: that is, no one can affirm with a real interior assent that he does not exist. 'For by the fact that he perceives something, he perceives that he exists.' In enunciating the proposition 'I exist' I know that I am enunciating a true proposition, and I cannot be sceptical about its truth, though I can, of course, say in words 'I do not exist'. But it is to be noted that Aquinas does not say that a man perceives that he has a spiritual soul or that he affirms his existence as a thinking subject, if by this we mean simply a mind. The awareness of one's own existence of which Aquinas is speaking is an awareness enjoyed also by those who are innocent of all philosophy; it is anterior to any metaphysical theory of the self. The ordinary man, of whom Aquinas is speaking, would certainly affirm that he exists, if he were questioned on the matter, but he would not mean by this that he exists simply as a mind. Indeed, Aquinas did not use, and could not have used, the proposition 'I exist' in the way that Descartes used his *Cogito: ergo sum*. For example, the idea of starting with the affirmation of one's own existence as a thinking substance or mind and then trying to prove the existence of the external world, including one's own body, would have been quite foreign to his point of view. For, as we have seen, he was convinced that the human being's knowledge and awareness of himself pre-supposes sense-perception. Our initial awareness of self starts with the awareness of outwardly-directed acts as our acts. Hence to start with a kind of detached ego or mind and then to try to prove the existence of things other than this ego or mind would necessarily have seemed to Aquinas a highly artificial and paradoxical proceeding. He uses the proposition 'I exist' as an example of a proposition which I know to be true if I enunciate it. And in knowing it to be true I know that I can attain truth. And in knowing that I attain truth I know that it is the nature of the mind to attain truth. For Aquinas everyone really knows this. But the fact that Aquinas takes the proposition 'I exist' as an example of a proposition which I know to be true if I enunciate it should not lead us to imagine that the proposition occupies or could occupy the same position in his philosophy that the *Cogito: ergo sum* occupies in the philosophy of Descartes.

It would, however, be a mistake to interpret Aquinas' appeal to the ordinary man's awareness of attaining truth as equivalent to saying that whenever anyone thinks that he knows the truth he does in fact know it. In the case of some propositions there can be no error, but this does not mean that we cannot enunciate false propositions while believing them to be true. If I say 'That object in the distance is a tree', my statement may turn out to be false, even though I now believe it to be true. But though error is possible, Aquinas did not regard this possibility as any valid reason for unlimited scepticism. In cases where there is a possibility of error or where there is reason to suspect error Aquinas speaks of a 'resolution to first principles'. But we must not interpret 'first principles' as meaning exclusively the first principles of logic and mathematics. True, if we have reason to suspect that there is an error in our mathematical reasoning, we have to go back and retrace our steps. But under 'first principles' in the present connexion Aquinas includes actual sense-perception. 'Because the first principle of our knowledge is sense, it is necessary to reduce in some way to sense all things about which we judge' (*De veritate*, 12, 3, *ad* 2). If my statement that the object in the field is a tree is open to doubt, the way to resolve the doubt or to correct the error is to look more closely. It may be said that this does not touch the problem whether all sense-perception may not be illusory. But I do not think that Aquinas would have had much patience with a problem of this kind. The term 'illusion' has meaning for us only in contrast with what is not illusion and is known not to be illusion, and the word 'false' has meaning for us only in contrast with the word 'true'. And we know the meaning of the word 'true' because we enunciate and know that we enunciate true propositions. Again, the word 'knowledge' is meaningful for us because we actually know. And to ask whether the knowledge we have is 'really' knowledge is to pursue a profitless inquiry. Of course, if when we ask whether what we think to be knowledge is 'really' knowledge, we mean to ask whether knowing that there is a cat under the table is 'mathematical knowledge', the answer is that it is not. And if we insist that only the conclusions of mathematical demonstrations can properly be said to be 'known', it follows that knowledge of non-mathematical truths is not knowledge. But all we are doing is to propose a peculiar use of the words 'know' and 'knowledge' which is different from the normal use and which has little, if anything, to recommend it. In other words, I suggest that Aquinas would have considerable sympathy with those modern philosophers who examine with the aid of linguistic analysis what precisely is being asked when it is asked whether all that we take to be knowledge may not be something other than knowledge, whether all sense-perception may not be illusory, whether all experience may not be a dream, and so on.

For Aquinas, therefore, it is in actually knowing something that we know that we know and that the object is knowable. And he was convinced that further reflection shows that the object is knowable or intelligible because and in so far as it has being. The truth that being is intelligible is revealed in the concrete act of knowing anything, though its expression in the form of an abstract proposition is the work of reflection. And this is for Aquinas the reason why the mind goes forward confidently to investigate reality, whether in the sciences or in philosophy. And if his philosophical interpretation of the world forms in some sense a system, the reason why it does so is not for him that reality is forced into a preconceived and presupposed mould but that the world is in itself an intelligible system and that this intelligible system discloses itself to the reflective mind. It is rather that the system is imposed on the mind by reality than that the mind reads a system into phenomena.

*

Mention has just been made of 'system' in connexion with Aquinas' philosophy. And it will, I hope, become clear in the course of the following chapters that his cosmological, metaphysical, psychological, and ethical discussions form together a unified interpretation of the world, which permits one to speak of a system, provided that one does not understand the word in the sense which it would have if applied to the philosophy of Spinoza. At the same time it is clear that Aquinas never worked out a philosophical system in a treatise or series of treaties devoted exclusively to philosophy. He was neither simply a philosopher nor simply a theologian; and the fact that he was a theologian-philosopher, as one might put it, is reflected in his writings. But he had quite definite ideas about the relation of philosophy to theology; and it is necessary to outline these ideas if his thought is to be understood.

The word 'theology' is often used to cover all discourse about God, and this is a quite natural and proper use. And if one understands 'theology' in this wide sense, it may appear that the problem of the relation between theology and philosophy can be settled by saying that the former is composed mainly of discourse about God whereas the latter is not concerned with God. But this was not at all Aquinas' view of philosophy. It is true that the philosopher performs analyses in which no mention of God is made or need be made. The logical analysis of universal terms is a case in point. But Aquinas was convinced, as we have seen, that reflection on material things can disclose to the philosopher their relation of existential dependence on a transcendent being possessing attributes which make it proper to speak of this being as 'God'. If therefore we use the word 'theology' to cover all discourse about God, it follows that there is a part of philosophy which can be called 'theology'. And it is obvious that when Aquinas draws a distinction between philosophy and theology he is not drawing a distinction between philosophy considered as a whole and one of its parts. What he is thinking of is the distinction between philosophy, including what is now called 'natural theology', and Christian theology proper, that is to say, theology based on the Christian revelation. We cannot understand Aquinas' distinction between theology and philosophy unless we bear in mind the concept of a Christian revelation. For the problem which he considered is one which arises for a man who believes in a Christian revelation on the one hand and on the other in the metaphysician's power of attaining some knowledge of God by the power of his reflective reason.

According to Aquinas, therefore, the distinction between philosophy and theology is not primarily a distinction between truths considered with regard to their content. In many cases there is indeed a difference of content between theological and philosophical propositions. The philosopher can arrive at conclusions about, for example, the right analysis of universal terms, which form no part of Christian revelation. The theologian, on the other hand, concerns himself with revealed truths like the doctrine of the Trinity, which could not be known without revelation. But there can be a certain overlapping as regards content. For instance, both the theologian and the philosopher assert that the world depends existentially on God. But whereas the former asserts it because it is the teaching of the Scriptures, the latter asserts it as the conclusion of a process of rational reflection, and not as a proposition accepted on authority and believed by faith. Hence the distinction between philosophy and theology is a distinction between different ways of arriving at and viewing truths rather than primarily a distinction between propositions considered with regard to their content. 'There is no reason why another science should not treat of the very same objects, as known by the light of divine revelation, which the philosophical sciences treat of according as they are knowable by the light of natural reason. Hence the theology which belongs to sacred doctrine differs in kind from that theology which is a part of philosophy' (S.T., Ia, 1, 1, ad 2). Similarly, both the theologian and the moral philosopher consider the ultimate good or end of man. But 'the philosopher considers as the ultimate good that which is proportionate to human power', while 'the theologian considers as the ultimate good that which exceeds the power of nature, namely eternal life' (De veritate, 14, 3).

The matter can be elucidated in this way. The theologian, who bases his reflection on revelation, naturally starts with God and only afterwards proceeds to a consideration of God's creation. But the philosopher proceeds the other way round. He starts with the immediate data of experience, and it is only by reflection on these data that he comes to some knowledge of what, considered in its essence, transcends natural experience. Hence the part of metaphysics which treats of God comes last in order from the philosophical point of view. The philosopher cannot start with God and deduce finite things; he starts with the finite things given in experience and comes to know spiritual reality only by reflection on these things. But this distinction refers, of course, to the theologian acting as a theologian and to the philosopher acting as a philosopher. Aquinas does not mean to imply either that the theologian as a man is exempt from the human being's dependence on sense-perception or that individual man may not have received his first idea of God from his parents or from the teaching of the Church.[1]

It is occasionally said that this way of looking at things is due rather to the 'Thomists' than to Aquinas himself. But this suggestion is erroneous. Aquinas not only made a distinction in explicit terms between philosophy and what would now be called 'dogmatic theology', but he also observed the distinction and took it seriously. This can be seen from the fact that though as a Christian theologian he was convinced that the world was not created from eternity he stoutly maintained that philosophers had never succeeded in showing that creation from eternity is impossible. He did not state dogmatically that reason alone cannot prove the impossibility of creation from eternity; what he said was that in his opinion no philosopher had ever succeeded in showing its impossibility by philosophical or mathematical arguments. That is to say, no philosopher had ever succeeded in showing the impossibility of a series of events without a first assignable member. And if philosophy cannot show that such a series is impossible it cannot answer the question whether the world was created from eternity or not. We thus have a question to which the answer has never been given by philosophy, though it is provided by theology. And it is therefore clear that Aquinas took seriously his own distinction between theology and philosophy. Furthermore, one can draw attention in passing to a point to which I shall return in the chapter on God. If Aquinas believed that no philosopher had ever succeeded in showing the impossibility of an infinite series stretching back into the past, it is clear that when in his proofs of God's existence he rules out an infinite regress he is not talking about this sort of series, as some critics have mistakenly supposed.

It is perfectly true, of course, that Aquinas did not

1. It is perhaps worth adding that according to Aquinas one cannot at the same moment believe in the truth of a proposition by faith, accepting it on authority, and know its truth as the conclusion of a philosophic argument. One can do so at different times, but one cannot do both simultaneously.

elaborate a philosophical system in accordance with his own canons of philosophical method. After all, he was a professor of theology. And some historians have argued that because he begins with God in both *Summas* the exposition of his philosophy should proceed in the same way. But this is to my mind a mistaken view, at least if it is interpreted in a narrow and literal manner. It seems to me out of place to feel bound by the order of treatment which Aquinas adopted in works written for specific and not primarily philosophical purposes. He says explicitly that before coming to the part of metaphysics which concerns God it is necessary to know many other things first. 'For the knowledge of those things which reason can find out about God it is necessary to know many (other) things first, since the mind in almost the whole of philosophy is directed towards the knowledge of God. Hence metaphysics, which treats of the divine, is the last part of philosophy to be learned' (*S.G.*, 1, 4). I feel, therefore, no hesitation in including a chapter on 'The World and Metaphysics' before the chapter on God.

Now, in view of this distinction between philosophy and theology many Thomists have said that Aquinas affirmed the autonomy of philosophy and that it is therefore a mistake to speak of his philosophy as a 'Christian philosophy' in any other sense than that it is compatible with Christianity. The fact that a philosophy is compatible with Christianity no more makes it a specifically Christian philosophy than the fact that a mathematical system is compatible with Christianity makes it a Christian mathematical system. On Aquinas' premisses there can be true and false philosophical propositions just as there can be true and false propositions in biology; but there can no more be a specifically Christian philosophy than there can be a specifically Christian biology.

That this point of view brings out important points seems to me undeniable. For it brings out the fact that Christianity is essentially a revealed way of salvation and not an academic philosophical system. It also brings out the fact that there is no revealed philosophy. One philosophy may be more compatible than another with Christianity. A purely materialistic philosophy is obviously incompatible with Christianity in a sense in which Cartesianism, for example, is not. But in the long run a philosophical system stands or falls on its own intrinsic merits or demerits. And to realize this fact prevents one from treating Thomism or any other philosophy as being part of the Christian faith. On the other hand, if one overstresses this legitimate point of view when talking about Aquinas himself, one may tend to give an impression of artificiality and even of a certain disingenuousness. For it is obvious that Aquinas was not a split personality. He remained a Christian whether he was pursuing theological or philosophical themes; and there is certainly a sense in which it is true to say that he was a believing Christian who tried to give a unified interpretation of the world and of human life and experience, using the methods of both theology (in his sense) and of philosophy. He was a Christian, and his interpretation of reality was a Christian's interpretation. In saying this, however, I do not mean to take back what I have said about the seriousness with which he understood his own distinction between philosophy and theology. And I think that I can indicate briefly how the two points of view come together in his conception of the function of philosophy in human life.

It is true to say, I think, that Aquinas sees the function of philosophy in the light of man's supernatural vocation; that is, he interprets it in the light of the Christian doctrine of man's vocation to a supernatural destiny, the vision of God in heaven. Through knowledge the potentialities of the human mind, which for Aquinas is man's highest power, are actualized, and through knowledge man is enriched. Knowledge of the material world in the sciences and natural philosophy is itself an enrichment of the human personality, a partial fulfilment of man's striving after truth. But by reflection on the finite things of the empirical world the human mind is able to know something of the infinite being on which all finite things depend, and philosophy culminates in the metaphysical knowledge of God which is the highest perfecting and development of the mind on the purely natural level. But because of our dependence on sense-perception our minds are not at home, as it were, in the sphere of spiritual reality, and the glimpse of infinite being which is possible for the philosopher is difficult to attain and difficult to preserve. 'Instruction by divine revelation was necessary even about truths concerning God which are accessible to the human reason. For otherwise they would have been found only by a few men and after a long time and, even then, mixed with many errors. And the whole salvation of man, which is to be found in God, depends on the knowledge of this truth' (S.T., Ia, 1, 1). Revelation confirms the truth about God which the metaphysician can attain without it, though only with difficulty; and it also sheds on man's way to his final goal a light which is unattainable by philosophy alone. In this sense, therefore, philosophy, though not resting on specifically Christian foundations, is directed towards Christian theology. But faith is not vision, and man's knowledge of God through revelation still remains analogical knowledge. Grace enables the will to outrun the intellect in the sense that it enables men to love God immediately though they cannot in this life know Him immediately. But it is only in the vision of God in heaven that man's quest achieves its goal. 'The natural desire to know cannot be stilled until we know the first cause, not in any sort of way but in its essence. Now, the first cause is God. Therefore the final end of the rational creature is the vision of the divine essence' (Compendium theologiae, 104). This vision is the actualization of man's highest potentialities. Supernatural in character it yet involves the fullest perfecting of the human personality both in its cognitive and affective aspects.

This is not a fashionable view of the function of philosophy, so far as this country is concerned. But it should be remembered that philosophers have not infrequently emphasized the connexion between philosophy and human life and destiny. We have only to think of Plato and Plotinus in the ancient world, of Spinoza in the seventeenth century, and of a thinker such as Karl Jaspers in the modern world. Even those who recommend a different use of the word 'philosophy' can recognize that there are various possible conceptions of the nature and function of philosophy. And in the case of Aquinas it is important to have mentioned at least this aspect of his thought. For in the Middle Ages people looked to Christianity itself for a message of salvation: once Christianity had been born those who accepted it could no longer look on philosophy in the same light that the non-Christian Neo-platonist had regarded his philosophy. And thus medieval philosophy very naturally tended to become something purely academic, a thing for holders of university chairs and their students, an abstract analysis divorced from man's constant striving to understand himself and his destiny. But whatever it may have tended to become, it was not only this in the eyes of the great theologian-philosophers of the thirteenth century. As a Christian theologian, a preacher, and a saint, Aquinas was primarily interested, of course, in man's attainment of his supernatural destiny. And he certainly did not think that it is necessary to be a philosopher in order to attain it. At the same time he thought that philosophy can throw some light, even if not a very strong light, on the significance of man's desire for truth and clarity and of his restless search after happiness. He was not the type of theologian who considers it his business to represent the sphere of the natural as being no more than the sphere of alienation from God and the work of philosophic reflection, analysis, and synthesis as being simply a sign of the pride of the human intellect. Just as for him grace perfects nature but does not destroy it, so for him revelation, while shedding further light on the significance of human existence and of the natural tendencies of the human mind and will, no more renders philosophic reflection otiose and superfluous than the foundation of the Church did away with man's need for the State or annulled the latter's positive function. In the understanding of reality faith and reason go hand in hand. And in expounding this ideal harmony and balance Aquinas was the representative thinker, theologian, and philosopher combined, of the high Middle Ages. In the course of time the factors which he combined in his intellectual synthesis became estranged, a process which began within the medieval period itself. And the latent tensions and centrifugal forces have worked themselves out in history. Whether at some future period a culture will arise in which the factors which Aquinas synthesized will again be harmoniously combined, it is obviously impossible to say. But if it comes it will clearly not be a literal repetition of the medieval culture; nor indeed is it desirable that it should be. And if a philosophy of the type represented by Aquinas ever wins general acceptance, it will not be a mere reproduction of what he wrote. But unless men in general ever become entirely absorbed in practical materialism, there will always be some who will be alive to the questions about man's destiny which the particular sciences can hardly answer, not because we can set any *a priori* limits to scientific advance but because they are not the sort of questions which any of the particular sciences asks. And for any Christian who stands in the tradition of Aquinas, we cannot, when considering these problems, reject all philosophy in the name of revelation or the idea of revelation in the name of philosophic autonomy. In this respect Aquinas remains as the great example of a balanced Christian thinker. And whether we agree with him or not, he deserves our respect.

It would, however, be a great mistake to think that for Aquinas the function of philosophy is to 'edify' in the sense of uttering pious sentiments or earnest exhortations. He did not consider the function of the philosopher to be that of the preacher or of the popular moralist. On the contrary, he was convinced that philosophy is a form of intellectual activity which demands patient, open-minded and unremitting mental effort. Living when he did, he naturally took for granted some things which can hardly be taken for granted in a very different intellectual climate. But he would be the first to admit the need for an examination and analysis of the very foundations of his philosophy. If he saw in philosophy the striving of the human mind after truth, a striving which for him can be completely satisfied only in the vision of God, the infinite being, this does not mean that he wished to substitute mystical elevations or affective attitudes for philosophical analysis and reflection. I hope that this will become apparent in the course of the book.

*

In developing his philosophy Aquinas made considerable use of Aristotle. When he speaks, as he so often does, of 'the Philosopher', he means Aristotle. This was indeed a common way of referring to the Greek thinker in the thirteenth and fourteenth centuries; and it indicates the peculiar position which he occupied in the estimation of the medievals. And since the significance of the rôle played by Aristotle in medieval thought is liable to be misunderstood, and indeed has often been misinterpreted, it is advisable to say something about the matter here for the benefit of any readers who know little of medieval philosophy.

Aristotle had always been known by medieval thinkers, but for a considerable time he was thought of primarily as a logician. The reason for this was that though the early medievals possessed at any rate some of the logical works of Aristotle in Latin translations, they did not possess the *Corpus Aristotelicum* as a whole.[1] But in the second half of the twelfth and the first part of the thirteenth centuries the physical and metaphysical works of Aristotle were made available in Latin translations, some of which were made from the Arabic while others were made from the Greek. Thus by the time that Aquinas began his teaching career at Paris the Aristotelian philosophy had become known to the medieval Christian world.[2] But it met with a very mixed

1. In speaking of the *Corpus Aristotelicum* I prescind altogether from the difficult question, what contributions and additions and changes by other hands (by Theophrastus, for example) form part of the *Corpus* as we have it. This problem is important for the study of Aristotle, but it is irrelevant to the present theme.

2. By saying this I do not mean to imply that Aquinas acquired no knowledge of Aristotle while he was a student at Naples. And he learned a great deal more about Aristotelianism when studying under Albert the Great at Paris and Cologne.

reception. On the one hand it was received with enthusiasm by considerable numbers of professors and students. On the other hand, when the statutes of the university of Paris were sanctioned by the papal legate in 1215 Aristotle's works on metaphysics and natural philosophy were prohibited, though the study of the *Ethics* was not forbidden and that of the logical works was ordered. In 1229 the professors of Toulouse, in order to attract students, issued a notice saying that lectures could be heard there on the works of Aristotle which had been prohibited at Paris in 1210 and again in 1215. An attempt was made in 1245 to extend the prohibition to Toulouse also, though by that date it had become impossible to check the spread of Aristotelianism. Generally speaking, the prohibitions had little effect, and in the course of time the official policy was reversed. But what must appear strange in the eyes of those who think of medieval philosophy as synonymous with a somewhat arid and petrified Aristotelianism is that the prohibitions ever took place. We find an enthusiastic interest in Aristotle in the universities coupled with an initial hostility on the part of the ecclesiastical authorities and of a number of theologians; and both these facts need some explanation for the modern student who may find it difficult to understand how Aristotle aroused either enthusiasm or fear and hostility. Moreover, an understanding of the facts is required in order to be able to appreciate the attitude adopted by Aquinas.

In the early Middle Ages philosophy, if one excepts the system of John Scotus Eriugena (d. *c*. 877), was to all intents and purposes synonymous with dialectic or logic. This is one reason why philosophy was commonly regarded as the 'hand-maid of theology'. For logic was looked on as an instrument, and the theologians naturally saw in it an instrument for the development of theology from the data supplied by the Scriptures and the writings of the Fathers. In the course of time the scope of philosophy was broadened, and Abelard (1079–1142) in particular raised the whole standard of philosophical thinking and analysis. But, in comparison with later conceptions of its scope, philosophy was still confined within rather narrow channels. When, however, the *Corpus Aristotelicum* was made known to medieval Christendom, a new world was opened to men's minds. For here was a wealth of observation, reflection and theory which was new to the medieval. It came with the charm of novelty and it was impressed with the stamp of an outstanding thinker: it offered an interpretation of reality which far exceeded in its richness and comprehensiveness anything which the medieval philosophers had yet provided. Thus if one tries to put oneself in the place of a university student in the early part of the thirteenth century, it is not difficult to understand the interest and enthusiasm which Aristotle aroused. For many people today Aristotelianism is something old and obsolete; but for the student of whom I am speaking it was like a new revelation, throwing a fresh light on the world. Moreover, since it was obvious that Aristotelianism stood, as it were, on its own feet and owed nothing to Christianity, men's ideas of the nature and scope of philosophy were necessarily enlarged.

At the same time it should also be easy to understand that the philosophy of Aristotle appeared to a number of theologians to be a dangerous and seductive influence. In the first place, in the name of reason it contradicted Christian doctrine on several points. For example, Aristotle taught that the world is and must be eternal, and he rejected what he took to be the Platonic idea of creation. God is mover but not creator. Whereas for the Christian all finite things are existentially dependent on God, for Aristotle the world is independent of God so far as existence is concerned. But more important than any isolated points on which the philosophy of Aristotle clashed with Christian doctrine was the general impression it made of being a naturalistic rival to supernatural religion. It appeared to some to be a closed system, in which God was little more than a physical hypothesis to explain 'motion' or change and in which the human person was incapable of having a supernatural destiny. Plato, so far as the medievals were acquainted with him, was

regarded as having developed ideas which looked forward
to Christian revelation for adequate completion and statement. And this was indeed the way in which many early
Christian writers and Fathers had interpreted Plato. But
Aristotle seemed to some at first sight to have elaborated a
naturalistic system in which no room was left for Christianity. It must be remembered that the medievals thought
of Aristotle as being much more of a dogmatizing systema-
tizer than he appears to a modern commentator. And the
sympathy of the ecclesiastical authorities for the 'pagan'
system was not increased by those professors and lecturers
of the faculty of arts at Paris who in their enthusiasm for
Aristotle chose to regard him as having said the last word
on every matter which he treated.

If we bear in mind the intense interest aroused by the
writings of Aristotle and also the initial reserve and hostility
of the ecclesiastical authorities, we can understand how it
was that in adopting and utilizing so much of his ideas
Aquinas was regarded in his day as an innovator, as a modern
and advanced thinker. For though Aquinas was convinced
of the great value and of the potentialities of Aristotelianism
as an intellectual instrument, the weight of conservative
opinion was against him. I do not mean to imply that other
thinkers did not utilize Aristotle's ideas to a greater or less
extent; for they did. But the more conservative thinkers
tended to stress a division between the Christian theologian-
philosophers like St Augustine (d. 430) and St Anselm (d.
1109) and the pagan philosophers. For St Bonaventure, a
contemporary of Aquinas who died in the same year (1274),
Aristotle was a great scientist and natural philosopher but
he did not merit the name of metaphysician. At a later date
we find Roger Marston (d. 1303), an English Franciscan,
speaking of the pagan philosophers, in comparison with St
Augustine and St Anselm, as those 'infernal men'. And even
Duns Scotus, who was one of the greatest thinkers of the
Middle Ages and who himself made copious use of Aristotle
and of the Islamic philosophers, evidently regarded Aquinas
as having compromised himself with the 'philosophers' and

as having maintained points of view under the influence of Aristotle which a Christian theologian should not have maintained.

It is, however, a great mistake to interpret Aquinas' very sympathetic attitude towards Aristotle as being simply that of an 'apologist'. I mean, it is a mistake to think that Aquinas set out to diminish the danger attending on the renaissance of pagan philosophy by seeing if he could 'baptize' Aristotle and bring him safely into the fold as a Christianized sheep. He was not concerned with patching together Aristotle as Aristotle with Christian theology. If he adopted and adapted a number of Aristotelian theories, this was not because they were Aristotle's, nor yet because he thought them 'useful', but because he believed them to be true. Given the state of historical scholarship at the time, Aquinas' commentaries on Aristotle show a remarkable penetration into the thought of the Greek philosopher, and to a great extent he thought that the latter's theories were valid. Aquinas' attitude throughout was one of serene confidence. There is no need to be alarmed by Aristotle or by any other non-Christian thinker. Let us examine what he has said with an open mind. Where he supports a position with valid reasons, let us adopt it. When he asserts conclusions which are in fact incompatible with Christian doctrine, the proper procedure is to examine whether these conclusions follow validly from true premises: it will be found that they do not. Aristotle was not infallible, and the fact that he taught or appeared to teach doctrines which are incompatible with Christianity is no good reason for bluntly rejecting Aristotelianism and turning a blind eye on the new learning.

Inasmuch as Aquinas adopted from Aristotle what he thought was true and made it his own, it is unnecessary to cumber the following chapters with constant reminders that this or that statement or theory was based on the writings of Aristotle; for the book is about the former's and not the latter's philosophy. It may, however, be appropriate at times to draw attention to similarities and divergences in order to illustrate how Aquinas, while utilizing Aristotelianism, rethought it critically in the process of building up his own synthesis and of showing the harmony between theology and philosophy. But it may be as well to remark here that the divergences between the views of the two men are sometimes concealed or obscured by Aquinas' 'charitable' interpretations. That is to say, on those occasions when Aristotle's thought conflicts with Christian doctrines or seems to lead to conclusions which are incompatible with Christianity Aquinas tends to interpret him in the most favourable light from the Christian point of view or to argue that the conclusions drawn by Aristotle do not necessarily follow from the latter's premisses. But of greater importance is the fact that Aquinas made of the philosophy of Aristotle something rather different from historic Aristotelianism. The Greek philosopher was concerned with the problem of 'motion', in the wide sense of becoming, whereas Aquinas made the problem of existence the primary metaphysical problem. The former asked what things are and how they come to be what they are, but he did not raise the question why they exist at all or why there is something rather than nothing. And there is a very great difference between these questions. In his *Tractatus logicophilosophicus* (No. 644) Wittgenstein stated that 'Not *how* the world is, is the mystical, but *that* it is'. If the word 'metaphysical' is substituted for the word 'mystical', this statement, though it would not be entirely acceptable to Aquinas, can serve as an illustration of the difference between the philosophy of the historic Aristotle and that of Thomas Aquinas. The change in emphasis doubtless owed a lot to the Judaeo-Christian tradition, as Étienne Gilson showed in his Gifford lectures on the spirit of medieval philosophy; but that there was a change can hardly be denied. And this is one reason why some writers like to speak of Aquinas' philosophy as 'existential'. The use of the term can be misleading, since the word 'existence' means something different in modern existentialism from what it meant for Aquinas. But the use of the term may be justified if it is accompanied by an explanation of one's purpose in using it, namely to exhibit the change in emphasis between historic Aristotelianism and Aquinas' philosophy.

*

This long introductory chapter can perhaps be fittingly brought to a close with some remarks on Aquinas' use of language. He wrote, of course, in Latin, the common language of the learned world in the Middle Ages. This Latin was not indeed the Latin of Cicero's orations, as the scholars and humanists of the Renaissance were not slow to note. Moreover, the Latin of the medieval Scholastics contained a large number of terms which are not to be found in the classical writers. But it does not at all follow that these terms were all unnecessary accretions. The deficiencies of Latin from a philosophical point of view had been noticed centuries before : Seneca, for example, complained that the meaning of Latin words had to be forced or changed in order to express the concepts of Greek philosophy. And it was only natural that the medieval theologians and philosophers found themselves compelled not only to invent new terms to render Greek terms and phrases, which were themselves often technical terms coined by Greek writers, but also to invent entirely new terms. And these were designed to express or refer to aspects of reality and to distinctions which were not catered for by ordinary language. From the point of view of the classicist some of these terms are certainly strange or barbarous. The word *quidditas* (whatness) is a case in point. Aristotle had coined a phrase (τὸ τί ἦν εἶναι) to mean essence or the 'whatness' of a thing, and the medievals translated this term by the word *quidditas*. It is certainly a neologism, and from the purely classical point of view a barbarous one, but it does not follow that it was a purely gratuitous addition which bore no relation to common experience or to ordinary language. For we are accustomed to ask what a thing is, and ordinary language implies a distinction between saying *what* a thing is and *that* it is. Often enough the somewhat strange terms used by the medieval philosophers were due to the need of expressing in technical and abstract language, for purposes of economy and clarity, concepts and distinctions which were present implicitly, though in an imprecise, confused and blurred way, in ordinary language. It is a mistake to dismiss the medieval theologians and philosophers on the ground that they employ 'jargon'.

It is also a mistake to assume that the medievals, because they lived centuries ago, must all have been linguistically naïve. They were aware, for example, that the same word may have different senses in common usage, that the meaning of a word when used as a technical term in philosophy may not be exactly the same as the meaning or meanings which it bears in non-philosophical language, and that the meaning of a word in its philosophical use needs to be precisely stated. Again, they were well aware of the distinction between the etymological origin of a term and its meaning in use. Thus Aquinas says that 'The etymology of a name is one thing, and the meaning of the name is another. For etymology is determined by that from which the name is taken to signify something, while the meaning of the term is determined by that which it is used to signify' (S.T., IIa, IIae, 92, 1, ad 2). Aquinas' views on etymology are indeed frequently naïve; like his contemporaries he often adopted the views expressed by Isidore of Seville (d. c. 636) in his famous *Etymologies*. Nobody would be prepared to maintain that philology was highly developed in the Middle Ages. But Aquinas was perfectly capable of distinguishing between the etymological origin of a term and its meaning in use.

It may also be worth pointing out that the distinction between the grammatical form of a sentence and its logical form, a distinction which has been given considerable prominence by contemporary philosophers, was not unknown to the medievals. For example, when Aquinas talks about 'creation out of nothing' he is careful to explain, as St Anselm had done before him, that 'out of nothing' means 'not out of anything', 'as if it were said, he is speaking of nothing because he is not speaking of anything' (S.T., Ia, 45, 1, ad 3). Aquinas was not so silly as to suppose that because the sentence 'God created the world out of nothing' is grammatically similar to the sentence 'Michelangelo made this statue out of marble' the word 'nothing' must signify a peculiar kind of something. I am certainly not prepared to state dogmatically that Aquinas was never 'misled by language'; but he certainly recognized that there is such a thing as being misled by language. The example of analysis just quoted shows that. Again, though there had been ultra-realists in the early Middle Ages, Aquinas did not imagine that because we can say *Joannes est homo* (John is a man) and *Petrus est homo* (Peter is a man) there must be a universal essence of man existing outside the mind.

Aquinas' concern with language cannot be called in question. He certainly used analogy and metaphor. And when speaking of the Scriptural use of metaphor he defended it on the ground that our knowledge begins with sense-experience and that spiritual realities are more easily understood if they are represented in the form of metaphors taken from material things (*S.T.*, Ia, 1, 9). But the bent of his mind was opposed to any unnecessary use of pictorial language. He much preferred to state his meaning in exact and precise terms rather than to multiply metaphors and illustrations suggesting meaning in an allusive and, as it were, cumulative way. The style of a Bergson, with its use of pictorial imagery, may be pleasanter and more attractive to read than the somewhat bald and apparently arid style of Aquinas; but the latter would have wanted to know precisely what the imagery and metaphors of the former were meant to convey. He fully sympathized with Aristotle's condemnation of the use of poetical and metaphorical language in philosophy. He remarks, for example, that Plato had a bad way of expressing himself. 'For he teaches all things figuratively and by symbols, meaning by the words something else than the words themselves mean, as when he said that the soul is a circle' (*In De anima*, 3, c. 1, *lectio* 8). Whether this is altogether just to Plato is another question; but it at any rate shows Aquinas' concern with language. There is perhaps a natural tendency to associate this concern with those philosophers of the fourteenth century who were in varying degrees critical of the speculative metaphysics of the preceding century. But it is important to remember that the leading metaphysicians of the thirteenth century had themselves given an example in this respect. In recent times in this country some attention has been paid to the meaning of terms when used analogically in metaphysics. And the fact that some analysts have cast doubt on the meaningfulness of terms predicated analogically of God has sometimes created the impression that inquiries of this sort are a prerogative of anti-metaphysicians. Yet the analysts are simply reviving a line of inquiry which occupied a prominent position in the thought of men like Aquinas in the thirteenth century and which was practically neglected in post-medieval times. Indeed, a concern for language belonged to the general climate of thought in the thirteenth and fourteenth centuries. One can certainly find in the writings of the philosophers of the period much that is difficult to understand for a reader who belongs to a very different historic epoch, and one finds too a preoccupation with some problems which cannot be expected to arouse a very lively interest today. But these features of their writings should not blind us to their passion for clear and accurate thinking and expression. Aquinas was a saint and a mystic, he was also a theologian and a metaphysician; but he was careless neither of logic nor of terminological exactitude. His opinions, like those of any other philosopher, are open to criticism; but he was far from being a woolly-minded individual who based his philosophy on 'hunches' and had recourse to rhetoric to support their validity.

CHAPTER TWO

The World and Metaphysics

IT would not be true to say that there is one universally-held opinion among contemporary philosophers about the precise relation between philosophy and the particular sciences. But all recognize that there is a distinction and that the precise nature of this distinction constitutes a problem. This recognition presupposes, however, the development of the particular sciences. For it is only because they have developed as branches of study distinct from philosophy that the problem of the precise relation between them and philosophy forces itself on our attention. One would not expect, therefore, to find this problem being stated and treated in any very explicit form in the Middle Ages. Research has indeed shown that more attention was given to scientific inquiry in the thirteenth and fourteenth centuries than used to be supposed. It has also been shown that the medieval physicists were by no means all slavish copiers of Aristotle and of the Islamic scientists. But when all is said it remains true that the sciences were in a rudimentary state of development in the Middle Ages in comparison with the post-Renaissance era. It is therefore useless to look to the writings of Aquinas for any explicit and thorough discussion of the relation between philosophy and sciences which were still in an embryonic condition. But he does say enough to indicate his general line of thought and to suggest what his point of view would be, were he alive today.

A reader of Aquinas' writings would, however, find it difficult to understand his line of thought unless he was aware of certain important points of terminology. For example, he would go hopelessly astray if he understood the word *scientia* in Aquinas as meaning what the word 'science' is usually taken to mean today. For Aquinas the word 'science' meant certain knowledge possessed in virtue of the application of principles which are either self-evident or known as true in the light of a higher science. Dogmatic theology was considered to be the primary science, in the sense of a branch of study with absolutely certain first principles, revealed by God and yielding certain knowledge. Metaphysics was also a science for him, possessing its own self-evident principles. It is therefore evident that Aquinas' use of the word 'science' was not the modern use. Whatever one may think about the cognitive value of theology and metaphysics, one would not normally call them 'sciences' today, not at least without explanation of the sense in which one was employing the terms. Again, one cannot legitimately take it that when Aquinas employs terms like 'natural science' and 'physics' he is using these words in the senses which we should normally attribute to them today. 'Natural science' meant for him the body of certain propositions about nature; and 'natural science' or physics was for Aquinas part of philosophy, namely the part of philosophy which treats of things as capable of motion. He could discuss, therefore, the relation between physics and metaphysics. But the question what is the precise relation between physics and philosophy would not be a natural question for him to ask, since he regarded physics as part of philosophy.

Aquinas does indeed talk about 'special' sciences or 'particular' sciences. But here also there is room for misunderstanding. Mathematics, for example, is said to be a 'special' science, because it has its own principles; but it is none the less classed under the general heading of philosophy. It is true that Aquinas makes a distinction between physics and, say, medical science in terms of the general Aristotelian distinction between theoretical science, which is pursued primarily for the sake of knowledge, and practical science, which is pursued primarily for a practical purpose. Thus medical science, though it possesses, of course, a theoretical aspect, is developed for a practical purpose. And it is therefore declared by Aquinas (cf. *In Boethium de Trinitate*, 5, 1, *ad* 5) not to be a part of physics, which is a speculative or theoretical science. Medical science is indirectly related to physics inasmuch as it presupposes a knowledge of the properties of natural things, but it does not fall directly under physics as part of physics. But we are not thereby entitled to regard this distinction between physics and medicine as a distinction between philosophy and science in our sense of the terms. For though 'physics' included for Aquinas much that would later be called cosmology or philosophy of nature or philosophy of science, it also included much that we would regard as belonging to science. It included, for instance, the general principles of astronomy.

Given this use of terms and the outlook which it implies, the problem, as we understand it, of the relation between philosophy and the sciences can hardly arise. For it to arise it was first necessary that the particular sciences should develop to such an extent as to compel the recognition of their distinction from philosophy. But if we prescind from the terminology and read Aquinas carefully, we can find more than a hint of a distinction between the philosophical propositions which he regarded as certain and empirical hypotheses which are only probable. He remarks, for example, that the Ptolemaic theory of epicycles may 'save the appearances' but that this is not sufficient proof that the theory is true, 'for the appearances might perhaps also be saved on another hypothesis' (S.T., Ia, 32, 1, ad 2). Thus although the astronomer may presuppose some very general principles about motion which are regarded by Aquinas as belonging to natural philosophy or physics, it does not follow that the hypotheses which he offers to explain the actual phenomena can be deduced from these general and certain principles. What the astronomer does is to offer a hypothesis which, even if it does in fact account for the phenomena in question (in the sense that if the hypothesis were true, the phenomena would follow), is not thereby proved to be true, since the phenomena might be explained as well or better on another hypothesis.

It has been said by some writers that Aquinas regarded Aristotle's astronomical hypotheses as philosophically true.

And they have interpreted his statement that the Ptolemaic theory is a hypothesis which may be superseded as an expression of his hope that a hypothesis might some day be produced which would account for the phenomena and yet not contradict Aristotle. But there seems to be no adequate reason for attributing to Aquinas this exceptional preference for Aristotle's hypotheses. In his commentary on Aristotle's *De caelo et mundo* (2, c. 12, *lectio* 17) he remarks that though a hypothesis offered in explanation of the movements of the planets seems to explain the facts it does not necessarily follow that the explanation is true, 'for the facts might be explained in another way as yet unknown to men'. And he is speaking here of Aristotle's theory of homocentric spheres. Hence he seems to put Aristotle's theory of homocentric spheres and the Ptolemaic theory of epicycles and excentrics on exactly the same level. They are both empirical hypotheses which are subject to revision. We cannot, therefore, legitimately attribute to Aquinas the view that contemporary science was irreformable or that it enjoyed the certainty attaching to what he regarded as certainly true propositions of natural philosophy. We cannot deduce from any general definition of motion, for example, the physical explanations of particular motions or sets of motions; and the explanations which are offered are hypothetical in character and not irreformable.

Although therefore we cannot find in Aquinas a clear-cut distinction between philosophy and science in a later sense of the word 'science', we can certainly say that the germ of such a distinction is implicitly contained in the distinction which he draws between philosophical propositions and the empirical hypotheses of contemporary physics and astronomy. And it is clear that if he were alive today he would have no difficulty in recognizing the distinction between philosophy and the particular sciences. And this shows us that we have to beware of taking too seriously the examples which he sometimes borrows from contemporary science to illustrate metaphysical arguments. They are illustrations in terms of ideas familiar to himself and to other thinkers of the time; but they are illustrations and not proofs, and we should not attach too much weight to them or imagine that his metaphysics rested simply on contemporary science in our sense of the word 'science'.

We can, however, ask whether Aquinas supposed that the philosopher should first have studied what we would call science. Logic being presupposed, the order, he says, in which the branches of theoretical philosophy should be studied is this: mathematics, physics, metaphysics. A knowledge of mathematics is required, for example, in astronomy. We cannot study the heavenly bodies 'without astronomy, for which the whole of mathematics is pre-required' (*In Boethium de Trinitate*, 5, 1, *ad* 9). And because of its formal character mathematics is best studied before physics, which demands empirical knowledge and a greater maturity of judgement. Finally comes metaphysics, 'that is, trans-physics, which is so called because it is to be learned by us after physics' (*ibid., in corpore*). This does not mean that Aquinas thought that the conclusions of 'physics', which included for him, as for Aristotle, psychology, can be derived from mathematical premisses or that metaphysics is dependent on particular astronomical hypotheses. That physics or natural philosophy should be studied before metaphysics follows from his general principle that the material for reflection is provided by the senses. It is natural to start with what is nearer to us from the cognitive point of view and to consider the physical world as consisting of mobile things before considering things precisely as beings in a science, metaphysics, which culminates in the knowledge of what is most removed from sense-perception, namely God. Metaphysics has its own principles which are of wider application than those of physics, but it is natural for us to come to a knowledge of the more general and abstract through a knowledge of the less general and abstract. And this point of view may well suggest that Aquinas expected of the philosopher a knowledge of the science of his time.

He certainly did not demand of the student of philosophy a knowledge of all the sciences which he recognized as such.

He did not expect the metaphysician to have studied, for example, medical science. And when he said that physics should be studied before metaphysics he was doubtless thinking primarily of the general principles and concepts of natural philosophy. At the same time he obviously thought of the natural philosopher as acquainting himself with the relevant empirical data. Without some knowledge of the empirical data the psychologist, for example, could not discuss in an intelligent manner the relation between soul and body. This is simply a matter of common sense. But it would be extremely rash to make the dogmatic and unverifiable statement that because Aquinas said that 'physics' should be studied before metaphysics he would therefore say, were he alive now, that the metaphysician should first have studied science, if we mean by this that he should be a specialist in some particular science. After all, it is a life's work to become a specialist in any science. And the demand for a universal knowledge of science would be simply fantastic. He would doubtless say that if we wish to philosophize about science or about the relation of soul to body, we must have a good knowledge of the relevant empirical data. This would be demanded not only by common sense but also by Aquinas' general conceptions of the way in which we acquire knowledge. But if we consider his idea of metaphysics, to which I shall turn presently, we can hardly avoid the conclusion that he would be particularly concerned with vindicating the independence of metaphysics from the empirical hypotheses of the sciences. For example, he would doubtless point out that the advance of science in no way alters the facts on which he bases his arguments for the existence of God. Whether we think of things in terms of the four elements or whether we think of them in terms of the atomic and electronic hypotheses makes no difference to the fact that there are things which change or to the fact that there are things which come into being and pass away. If the existence of finite things implies the existence of infinite being, the relation of existential dependence of the former on the latter is unaffected by the varying stages of our scientific knowledge about finite things. Of course, the retort might be made that if Aquinas were alive today he would change his conception of metaphysics. But if in asking what Aquinas would hold today about the relation between metaphysics and science one intends to ask a sensible question and not to give free play to the construction of unverifiable hypotheses, the question must, I think, be equivalent to asking what view of the relation between metaphysics and science, in the modern use of this word, would be demanded by the idea which he actually had of metaphysics. And the answer can hardly be anything else but that he would have to emphasize rather than minimize the distinction between metaphysics and science. The view that metaphysical theories are nothing but themselves empirical hypotheses, depending on the empirical hypotheses of the sciences, is a possible view of metaphysics, but it was not that of Aquinas.

There is one further point which can be alluded to briefly. The fact that many themes which we would classify as belonging to science were classified by Aquinas under the general heading of 'philosophy' gives rise to the question whether the whole content of what he called 'physics' has been absorbed in what we would call 'science'. Does there remain any room at all for 'natural philosophy'? Possibly an answer can be suggested on these lines. In his discussions of motion, time, and space, which are to be found principally in the commentaries on Aristotle, Aquinas accepted the latter's definitions. In the *Summa theologica* we read that 'since in any sort of motion there is succession, and one part after another, by the very fact that we number before and after in motion we apprehend time, which is nothing else but the number of before and after in motion' (*S.T.*, Ia, 10, 1). But whatever we may think of the Aristotelian definitions the point is that in discussing time, space, and motion Aquinas did not think that he was discussing subsistent things. Space, for example, is not a thing. Hence it is reasonable to say that he was engaged in analysing or clarifying the concepts of time, space, and motion or the meanings of these terms. And if we are prepared to call this sort of analysis 'philosophical', we can say that it is not the whole content of what Aquinas called 'physics' and classed under the general heading of 'philosophy' that has been absorbed in what we call 'science'.

*

The different particular sciences are concerned, Aquinas would say, either with different kinds of beings or with the same things considered under different aspects and from different points of view. Astronomy and psychology, for example, though they may both belong to 'natural philosophy', do not treat of the same objects. Both the anatomist and the psychologist, however, are concerned with the human being. But they do not consider the human being from the same point of view, and their sciences are different, even though there may be points of connexion between them. Again, biology is concerned with organic being or with corporeal living being. Certainly, a more natural way of expressing this might be to say that the biologist studies living bodies or that he studies the life of animals and plants. But though he obviously has to study individual specimens he is not concerned with definite individual organisms in the way in which an amateur gardener is concerned with the individual flowers and shrubs which he plants and tends. The biologist is concerned with type and species rather than with the individual as such. We can therefore say that he is concerned with organic being or with being considered precisely as organic, provided that we do not take this to imply that there is a subsistent organic being separate from concrete individual organisms.

It is possible, however, to abstract from differences like organic and inorganic and to consider things simply as beings. And Aquinas follows Aristotle in defining metaphysics as the science of being as being. But it would be a great mistake to interpret this as meaning that there is something called 'being', apart from individual beings or things. Aquinas certainly speaks of God as Being; but when he says that metaphysics is the science of being as being, he is not making it synonymous with what is called 'natural theology'. He means, in part at least, that metaphysics is concerned with the analysis of what exists or can exist, considered as such. And that of which we say primarily that it exists or can exist is, according to him, substance (a concept to which I shall return presently). If we say that Peter exists we assert that a definite substance or thing exists. If we assert that Peter is white, we predicate a quality of Peter. We say that it exists, but as a quality of Peter and not in its own right, so to speak. And if we assert that whiteness exists as a quality of Peter, we assert by implication that Peter exists. For it would be absurd to say both that Peter does not exist and that he is white. It is therefore substances of which we primarily affirm existence. Accordingly, if 'being' is taken in the sense of that which exists or can exist, metaphysics is primarily concerned with the analysis of substance and its modifications. Thus it is an analysis of the fundamental categories of being; of substance, that is to say, and of the various types of accident, such as quality and relation.

Metaphysics is also, for Aquinas as for Aristotle, an analysis of the causes of substance. It includes, for example, an analysis of efficient causality. In the course of ordinary life we often ask for or look for the particular cause of a particular event. We ask, for example, what caused the door to bang, and we receive the answer perhaps that the banging of the door was caused by a gust of wind coming in through a window which had just been opened. But it is also possible to inquire into the nature of efficient causality as such, in abstraction from this or that particular efficient cause or particular type of efficient cause. So, too, it is possible to inquire into the nature of final causality. Thus the metaphysician concerns himself with the analysis of the different kinds of causality as well as of the categories of substance and accident.

Now, if this aspect of metaphysics is taken to be the whole of metaphysics, it is obvious that the activity of the metaphysician is one of analysis. The metaphysician's business would be to clarify the concepts of causality, of substance, of relation, and so on. Indeed, we could say that he is concerned with analysing the meanings of certain terms, provided, of course, that we allowed for the fact that he seeks to exhibit the real or true meanings of the terms in the light of experiential data and is not acting as a grammarian. Some may prefer to say that he is concerned with 'essences'; but we can just as well say that he is concerned with 'meanings'. There is, for example, no causality-in-itself subsisting apart from particular causal relations; nor did Aquinas ever think that there is. When, therefore, the metaphysician analyses causality, we can legitimately say that he is analysing the meaning of the term 'causality', provided that this is understood as implying that he is concerned with exhibiting what people ought to mean by the term and not with saying simply what Smith or Brown imagines that it means or may mean.

This aspect of metaphysics is a real aspect of it as conceived by Aquinas; but it is certainly not the only aspect. The word 'being' can be understood in the verbal sense of 'to be' or 'to exist' (*esse*). And then to say that metaphysics is concerned with being is to say that it is concerned with existence. And existence here means the concrete act of existing. Looked at under this aspect metaphysics is concerned above all, for Aquinas, with accounting for or explaining the existence of things which change and which come into being and pass away. As we have seen earlier, Aquinas asserts that the whole of metaphysics is directed towards the knowledge of God. And since God lies beyond our natural experience and we can know Him only in so far as we can understand the relation of the objects of experience to the ground of their existence, an assertion of the theocentric character of metaphysics necessarily implies that it centres round the analysis of the existential dependence of finite existence.

The two aspects of metaphysics cannot, indeed, be dissociated from one another. But if we like to call the first aspect the 'essentialist' aspect and the second the 'existentialist' aspect, as some writers like to do, we can say that it is in emphasizing the existentialist aspect that Aquinas goes beyond Aristotle. For the latter did not raise the problem of the existence of finite things; and this means, of course, that he did not see that there is any problem. And he did not see that there is any problem because he concentrated on what a thing is, on the ways in which something is or can be, and not on the act of existing itself. Aquinas, however, while retaining the Aristotelian analyses of substance and accident, form and matter, act and potency, placed the emphasis in his metaphysics, not on 'essence', on *what* a thing is, but on existence, considered as the act of existing. This notion of the act of existing is indeed very difficult, and I shall return to it; but it is worth while pointing out here that this change of emphasis had its repercussions on the metaphysical analyses which Aquinas inherited from Aristotle. For example, though for Aristotle substances exist, in the sense that there are substances, he is concerned as a metaphysician with the analysis of concepts, with the concepts, in this case, of substance and accident, and he says nothing about the existential dependence of finite substances. The world is a world of substances or things, but the world is eternal and uncreated, and it is against the background of this eternal and uncreated world that Aristotle analyses the concept of substance. Aquinas took over the Aristotelian analysis of substance, but at the same time the world for him consisted of finite substances, each of which is totally dependent on God. It is true that this does not intrinsically alter the analysis of the nature of substance; but it sets substances in a new light. And it sets them in a new light because emphasis is placed on the act by which substances exist, an act of existing received from an external cause. Thus in general, while it is perfectly true that Aquinas took over the Aristotelian metaphysical analyses of substance and accident, act and potency, causality and so on, it is also true that his concentration on being considered as existence (as *esse*) set in a new light the world which Aristotle described in his metaphysics.

*

We may talk about a tree as a thing, but we would hardly describe the colour of its leaves as a thing. And if we examine ordinary language we find many instances of a distinction being made or implied between a thing and its attributes or between a thing and the relations in which it stands to other things. We may say at one time, for example, that John is pale and at another time that he is sunburnt, or at one time that he is well and at another time that he is ill. We say of a traveller that he is in one city on Monday, in another city on Tuesday. We all make statements in which we successively attribute to ourselves different states. The ordinary man does not indeed reflect on this fact about the language he uses; but the statements which he makes imply a recognition in practice of a distinction between things and their modifications, between 'substance' and accidents, between that of which we predicate qualities, quantity, and relations and qualities and relations which exist only as qualities and relations of that of which they are predicated. We can say that Peter is sitting on a chair, but nobody would expect to encounter the relation of 'sitting on' existing as an entity apart from any sitter.

There cannot be any doubt, therefore, that the ordinary man makes a distinction between things and their modifications. We have only to examine what we are accustomed to say about the changing size of a tree or the changing colour of its leaves to see that this is the case. Nor can there be any doubt that the ordinary man would regard this linguistic distinction as objectively justified. And it is this spontaneous conviction of the ordinary man which lies at the basis of the substance-accident metaphysic. For the philosopher like Aquinas who accepts this metaphysic, ordinary language reflects the common experience of men, and in common experience a distinction between substance and accident is implicitly recognized. What the philosopher does is not to invent a gratuitous theory or even to make a discovery of which the ordinary man has no inkling, but rather to express explicitly and in abstract terms a distinction which is implicitly recognized by the ordinary man in concrete instances. A substance is that of which we say primarily that it exists and which is not predicated of something else in the way in which we predicate pallor of John or redness of a rose, while an accident is that which exists only as a modification of a substance or thing and which is predicated of a substance. The theory of substance and accidents as maintained by Aquinas has, of course, several refinements. It is necessary, for example, to distinguish between accidents like quantity and quality on the one hand and relations on the other. But so long as the theory is expressed in a very general way, with reference to the distinctions which we make in ordinary language between things and their modifications, it can be grasped by practically anyone. The difficulties begin at the point when exact analysis is undertaken.

These difficulties are only increased if the theory is taken to mean that there is an unknowable substratum called 'substance' which serves to hold together a collection of phenomena or accidents. This may represent the theory of Locke, but it does not represent the theory of Aquinas. For the latter the distinction between substance and accident is a distinction not between an unknowable substratum and knowable modifications but between that which exists, if it does exist, as subject and that which exists only as a modification of a subject. In Aquinas' own terminology the word 'substance' signifies 'an essence to which it pertains to exist by itself' (*per se*; *S.T.*, Ia, 3, 5, *ad* 1). This phrase *per se* has to be carefully understood. It does not mean that a substance exists 'by itself' in the sense that it has no cause : it has to be taken in opposition to existing by another, that is, as a modification of something else. A substance does not exist *per se* in the sense in which God can be said to exist *per se*. Indeed, God does not fall under the category of substance, and He can be called 'substance' only in an analogical sense. A human being, for example, does not exist *per se*, if by this we mean that he or she has no cause and is completely independent. But at the same time a human being does not exist as the modification of another thing, in the sense in which John's anger has no existence apart from John. And in this sense a human being exists *per se*. But this is not to say that John's substance is an unknowable substratum hidden away under John's accidents: it is not an unknowable and completely unchanging X, entirely inaccessible to the human mind. In knowing John's accidents or modifications we know John's substance in so far as it reveals itself in and through these modifications. Considered in itself a substance is not a phenomenon, that is to say, apart from its modifications it is not the direct object either of any sense or of introspection. When I look at a tree, I do not and cannot see the substance of the tree apart from the tree's colours and so on. But inasmuch as the colours of the tree manifest the substance, I can properly be said to perceive the substance. What I perceive is neither an unattached accident or set of accidents nor an unmodified substance: I perceive a modified thing. Similarly, through introspection I can perceive desires, emotions, and thoughts, but in perceiving them I perceive the substance. We can say that the accidents of a thing change. The colour of the leaves of many trees changes, and the size of a human being changes as he or she grows up. But strictly speaking, it is the substance which changes; it changes 'accidentally'. That is to say, a human being, for example, changes in many ways during the course of his or her life, while it remains the same definite human being. The changes do not take place round an unchanging core called 'substance': it is the latter itself which changes. Hence in knowing the changing states or modifications or accidents we know, to that extent at least, the substance itself. Aquinas does indeed say that the name 'substance' is derived from standing under (*nomen enim substantiae imponitur a substando*; *In I Sent.*, 8, 4, 2) and that substance is that whose act is to stand under (*substantia (dicitur) cuius actus est substare*; *In I Sent.*, 23, 1, 1). And we see here how the use of the word *substantia* tends to emphasize an aspect of substance which is not so emphasized by the use of the Greek word *ousia*. But all the same Aquinas is not talking about an unchanging and unknowable substratum but about a subject which is not itself a determination of another thing but which has determinations or modifications through which it is known. It is true that according to Aquinas we do not ordinarily have direct intuitions of the essences or substances of things. He says, for example, that 'substantial differences, because they are unknown, are manifested by accidental differences' (In De generatione et corruptione, I, c. 3, lectio 8). But the last words of this quotation show the impropriety of ascribing to him the doctrine that there is an unknowable substrate called 'substance'. As we have seen, Aquinas did not admit that we have a direct intuition of our souls, but he did not mean that they are unknowable ghosts hidden away in our bodies.[1] They are knowable in and through their activities.

The point can be expressed in this way. Considered as a centre of activity, substance is called by Aquinas 'nature', just as it is called 'essence' when considered as definable. And one of his principles was that activity or operation 'follows', and so manifests, being: operatio sequitur esse. Hence we can say that for him we distinguish different substances as different individual centres of characteristic activity. And in knowing these activities we know the substances from which they proceed. I come to know another person by listening to his words and observing his actions; for his words and activities reveal him in different ways.

The connexion between the substance-accident metaphysic and ordinary language has been noted above. But it should also be mentioned that this metaphysical theory is not infrequently interpreted as being no more than a reflection of the linguistic distinction between subject and predicate or a projection into reality of the subject-predicate form of proposition. In other words, it is maintained that the theory was the result of linguistic practice. If Aristotle had spoken a language in which this form of proposition did not occur, he would not have developed the substance-

1. I do not mean to imply that for Aquinas the soul is the whole essence or substance of the human being. Peter is a unity of soul and body, not a soul in a body.

accident theory.[1] The fact that he did develop it shows that he was misled by language. And medieval Scholastics who proposed this theory were misled in the same way.

Aquinas would doubtless regard this interpretation of the substance-accident theory as an instance of putting the cart before the horse. We are aware in experience of our own changing states as ours and of the changing states and activities of other things as belonging to those things. And it is this experience which lies at the basis of the substance-accident metaphysic rather than a mistaken conviction that the structure of reality must correspond to the structure of language. Aquinas could point out that a distinction between a thing and its states or modifications can be made and is made even in languages in which the subject-copula-predicate form of proposition is not normally used. It may be urged, of course, that though Semitic languages like Hebrew and Arabic can give expression without the normal use of the copula to the fact that a person or a thing is in this or that state or possesses this or that quality, the substance-accident metaphysic was actually developed by a philosopher, Aristotle, who spoke a language in which this form of proposition is used, and that the medieval philosophers who adopted this metaphysic also used languages in which the same form appears. This can, indeed, hardly be said of the medieval Islamic philosophers. Avicenna, for example, generally wrote in Arabic. It might perhaps be maintained that the Islamic Aristotelians adopted the substance-accident theory simply because it was Aristotle's. But they also thought that it was true. If Aquinas were alive today he would certainly be compelled to meet objections against the substance-accident metaphysic which were not raised in his own time, when this theory was common property. But as far as the purely linguistic interpretation is concerned I think that he would argue on the lines indicated above,

1. It is sometimes said that Aristotle had no doctrine of substance, and that *ousia* should not be translated as substance. This is true if by 'substance' is meant Locke's unknowable substratum. But Locke's theory was held neither by Aristotle nor by Aquinas.

trying at the same time to avoid falling into Locke's theory of an unknowable substratum.

*

The world therefore consists of a multiplicity of substances: it is not itself a substance. There is a multiplicity of individual things which stand in different relations to one another and each of which undergoes accidental changes, that is, changes which do not alter the specific character of the substance. A man undergoes many changes while remaining a man. But it is possible to pursue further the analysis of material things. An oak tree grows, and the colour of its leaves changes, but we still speak of it as though it were the same oak tree. But if the tree is burned and reduced to ashes, we do not speak of the ashes as an oak tree. When bread has been digested we no longer speak of it as bread. Yet neither in the case of the oak tree which has been reduced to ashes nor in the case of the bread which has been digested is the matter of the oak tree or of the bread annihilated. There is permanence, and yet at the same time there is a change which is more than 'accidental'. And the combination of these two factors gave rise to a problem for Aquinas as for Aristotle. What does change of this kind, substantial change, imply with regard to material things?

It implies, Aquinas answered, that in every material thing or substance there are two distinguishable constitutive principles.[1] One of these he called 'substantial form'. In the case of an oak tree, for example, the substantial form, corresponding to Aristotle's 'entelechy', is the determining principle which makes the oak tree what it is. This form must not, of course, be confused with the outward shape or figure of the tree: it is an immanent constitutive principle of

1. The word 'element' might suggest chemical element and so be misleading. By calling matter and form 'principles', Aquinas means that they are the primary co-constituents of a material thing. The word is obviously not being used in the sense of a logical principle; nor does it refer to observable chemical elements. Matter and form are 'principles of being' (*principia entis*); they are not themselves physical entities.

activity which makes the oak tree an oak tree, stamping it, as it were, as this particular kind of organism and determining it to act as a totality in certain specified ways. But what is it that the substantial form of the oak tree 'informs' or determines? We might be inclined to answer that it is the matter of the tree, meaning by this the visible material which can be chemically analysed. But ultimately, Aquinas thought, we must arrive at the concept of a purely indeterminate potential element which has no definite form of its own and no definite characteristics. This he called 'first matter' (*materia prima*). Visible matter, secondary matter, is already informed and possesses determinate characteristics; but if we think away all forms and all determinate characteristics we arrive at the notion of a purely indeterminate constitutive principle which is capable of existing successively in union with an indefinite multiplicity of forms. When the oak tree perishes, its substantial form disappears, relapsing into the potentiality of matter, but the first matter of the tree does not disappear. It does not, and indeed cannot, exist by itself; for any existent material substance is something definite and determinate. When the oak tree perishes, the matter immediately exists under another form or forms. When a human being dies and his body disintegrates, the matter is at once informed by other forms. But there is continuity, and it is first matter which is the element of continuity.

According to Aquinas, therefore, every material thing or substance is composed of a substantial form and first matter. Neither principle is itself a thing or substance; the two together are the component principles of a substance. And it is only of the substance that we can properly say that it exists. 'Matter cannot be said to be; it is the substance itself which exists' (*C.G.*, 2, 54).

This theory of matter and form[1] was not new. Derived from Aristotle it was common property in the Middle Ages,

1. It is commonly known as the 'hylomorphic' theory, this name being derived from the combination of the Greek words ὕλη and μορφή.

though different thinkers propounded it in different ways. But I do not want to discuss its origins or the different versions of it: for our present purpose it is more appropriate to note the following points. In the first place there is at least some connexion between the theory and ordinary experience and language. We are accustomed to speak of one thing becoming another thing or of one kind of thing becoming another kind of thing. And this way of speaking seems to imply that change involves both continuity and discontinuity. There is continuity because that which changes is not annihilated, and there is discontinuity because there is first one kind of thing and then another kind of thing. In the second place, however, the theory seems to be clearly a metaphysical theory. First matter is not, and cannot be, the direct object of experience: it is postulated as the result of an analysis of experience. And this analysis is obviously not physical or chemical analysis. Aquinas knew nothing, of course, of modern chemistry or of the atomic-electronic hypothesis; but he regarded the hylomorphic theory as being independent of contemporary ideas about, for example, physical elements like fire and water. For him it was the result of metaphysical analysis, not of physical or chemical analysis. The language of the theory of form and matter belongs to the language of metaphysics.

This does not mean that for Aquinas form and matter are occult entities in the sense that nothing at all can be known about them. True, first matter does not and cannot exist by itself; it cannot as such be seen; but its presence as a component metaphysical factor in corporeal substances is manifested by substantial change. Again, we may not be able to know the form of a given corporeal substance to the extent of being able to define it in terms of genus and specific difference: in practice we may have to be content with a definition in terms of properties. But the form is the principle or source of the characteristic qualities, activity and behaviour of a substance, and it is known to the extent in which it is manifested in these qualities and activities. For example, the presence and nature of a vital form in an organism is revealed through the characteristic activities of the organism.

There is a further point to be noted. If the theory of matter and form is interpreted as a metaphysical theory and as being independent of the results of empirical scientific research, it follows that no new empirically verifiable scientific propositions can be derived from it. One could certainly deduce from the theory the conclusion that changes of a certain type are possible. But observation of these changes is one of the main grounds for asserting the theory in the first place. The statement therefore that such changes are possible would not be a new empirically verifiable proposition. Hence the theory cannot be used as an instrument in the progress of natural science. And those Aristotelians of a later date, namely of the time of the Renaissance, who talked as though the theory had a place in natural science misconceived its nature. For the purposes of natural science the theory is 'useless', if by a theory's being 'useful' in natural science one means that new empirically verifiable, or rather testable, propositions can be derived from it.

It does not follow, however, that the theory may not have proved useful to science in another sense. For the theory of forms presents us with a world which is not simply and solely a Heraclitean flux but a world shot through, as it were, with intelligibility. Through reflection on the activity and behaviour of things we can come to some knowledge at least of their intelligible structure. And it is arguable that this picture of the world as intelligible and of material substances as proportionate to the human mind and as relatively transparent in their formal structure acted as a preparatory condition for, and stimulus to, empirical scientific research.

This consideration gives rise in turn to the question whether the metaphysical theory of form and matter, in its application to inorganic substances at least, has not been rendered otiose by scientific research, in the sense that scientific research gives body and concrete shape to the vague idea of form presented in the metaphysical theory. This question is connected with the general question of the relation between scientific hypotheses and metaphysical theories about visible things; and this general question is too far-reaching to discuss here. But it is worth while mentioning it at any rate. As regards the particular question about the relation of the hylomorphic theory to scientific theories of atomic and electronic structure it should be noted that those followers of Aquinas who maintain the truth of the theory, even in its application to the inorganic world, insist on its metaphysical character and on its independence of the changing hypotheses of science. Form and matter are the metaphysical constitutive elements of bodies, in the sense that reflective analysis of bodies or of corporeal substance as such, rather than as this or that kind of corporeal substance, reveals their presence. The theory may be 'useless' in the sense indicated above; but to say this is simply to say that the theory is not a theory of empirical science. There are, however, other followers of Aquinas who consider that the theory was the result of a speculative attempt to cope with a problem which is solved, so far as it can ever be finally solved, by scientific research. I do not feel inclined to hazard any opinion as to what Aquinas himself would say on this matter, were he alive today. Questions of this sort obviously cannot be answered in a definitive manner. It is sufficient to say that Aquinas regarded the theory as being independent of contemporary 'scientific' ideas.

*

Though corporeal things or substances are alike in that each is composed of form and matter, not all corporeal forms are alike. Dogs and cats are both corporeal things, but they differ specifically from one another; in the language of the form-matter theory the canine form differs specifically from the feline form. The form of salt differs from that of water. We have therefore groups of corporeal things, the members of each group possessing similar substantial forms. The members of a species do not, of course, possess numerically the same substantial form. Aquinas rejected altogether the ultra-realist theory which supposes that because we can use the same word of a number of individuals there must therefore be one thing corresponding to that word. It is fallacious to argue that because we say *Petrus est homo* (Peter is a man) and *Joannes est homo* (John is a man) there is therefore one universal entity present in both Peter and John. Universality as such is only 'in the mind' (cf. *S.T.*, Ia, 85, 2, *ad* 2). But at the same time Aquinas was convinced that there are real species, and that the members of a species possess similar substantial forms. And it is this objective similarity of form which enables us to have universal specific concepts, and so to apply the same universal term to all the members of a specific class. The members of a class possess similar natures. And so when the mind forms universal concepts it does not construct a false picture of reality. For that which is conceived, say human nature, exists extra-mentally, though it does not exist outside the mind in the way in which it is conceived, that is, as a universal (cf. *S.T.*, Ia, 85, 1, *ad* 1). Ordinary people are, of course, implicitly aware of this; for they use universal terms quite correctly in the concrete propositions of everyday language without ever looking for universal entities corresponding to the terms they use. It is when philosophical analysis starts that the trouble begins. And we can say that one of the services of Aquinas and his forerunners in the matter of universals was to expose the falsity of ultra-realism.

Perhaps it might be as well to remark at this point that when Aquinas talks about groups of corporeal things possessing similar 'natures' or 'essences' he does not refer simply to the form. 'The word *essence* in regard to composite substances signifies that which is composed of matter and form' (*De ente et essentia*, II). The universal idea of man, for instance, abstracts from the individual characteristics of Peter and John, but it does not abstract from the possession of matter. That is to say, the universal idea of 'human being' is the idea of a substance composed of matter and rational soul, which for Aquinas is the form in the case of man; it is not the idea of the soul alone. It is, however, the form which determines a substance to be a substance of a particular kind, to fall, that is to say, into a particular class. And so it is the similarity of form in members of a species which is the objective foundation of the universal specific concept.

But this view gives rise to a problem. If the substantial forms of the members of any given species are radically alike, it follows, argued Aquinas, that the difference between the members cannot be ascribed primarily to the form as such. That which makes two pieces of flint two pieces and not one is not the fact that both are flint; for in this respect they do not differ. To what factor, then, must individuation be primarily ascribed? It must be due primarily to matter, not to matter considered as purely indeterminate, but to matter as quantified. In the case of the two pieces of flint their flintness brings them together, as it were, and, considered in itself, does not distinguish them. They are distinguished by the fact that the flintness of the one is present in this matter and the flintness of the other in another matter. It is matter which is the principle of individuation and which marks off one corporeal thing from other members of the same species.[1] This must not be taken to mean that the form of an oak tree, for example, existed with some kind of universal status before the tree came into existence. As we have seen, there are no extra-mental universal entities. But if one supposes that the oak is composed of form and matter, it makes sense to ask which component element is primarily responsible for the oak being this particular oak. And in Aquinas' opinion it is matter which is primarily responsible. For the oak-ness of one oak does not differ from that of another save through the fact that it informs different matter.

There are various rather obscure refinements of the theory of matter as the principle of individuation which might be added. But I prefer to omit them and to draw attention to

1. Aquinas drew the logical conclusion that in the case of immaterial beings there can be no multiplication within a species. Each angel is the sole member of its species.

one important application of the theory. The latter was by
no means acceptable to all the contemporaries of Aquinas;
and one of the reasons why it was attacked was that it
seemed to a number of theologians to be incompatible with
the Christian view of the soul. It seemed at least to be de-
rogatory to the dignity of the human soul to say that it is
individuated by matter. But Aquinas did not hesitate to
grasp the bull by the horns. He certainly maintained, as will
be seen in a later chapter, that the human soul is spiritual
and that it survives bodily death; but he also held, as we saw
in the last chapter, that the mind is originally like a wax
tablet on which nothing has been written. What makes
human souls different from one another is their union with
different bodies. 'For this soul is commensurate with this
body and not with that, that soul with that body, and so
with all of them' (C.G., 2, 81). And Aquinas draws the logical
conclusion. 'It is clear that the better disposed a body is the
better is the soul which falls to its lot.'[1] This is obvious in the
case of those things which are specifically different. And the
reason is that act and form are received in matter according
to the capacity of the matter. Therefore since some human
beings have better disposed bodies, they possess souls with
a greater power of understanding. Hence it is said (by Aristotle in the De anima, 2, 9; 421a, 25–6) that we see that
those with soft flesh are mentally more alert' (S.T., Ia, 85, 7).
Some of this is rather crude, of course, but it is obvious that
Aquinas' theory of matter as the principle of individuation
would lead him to welcome, as confirmation of the theory,
rather than to fear the results of modern research into the
dependence of psychical on physical differences.

*

The distinction between form and matter was for Aquinas a
subdivision of the wider distinction between act and poten-

1. These words must not be understood as implying that Aquinas
thought of human souls as existing before their union with bodies.
He believed that each human soul is created by God but not that
it is created previous to the body's formation.

tiality. First matter, considered in abstraction, is pure potentiality for successive actualization by substantial forms, each of which stands to its matter as act to potentiality, actualizing the matter's potentiality. But the distinction between matter and form is applicable only to corporeal things, whereas the distinction between act and potentiality is found in all finite things.

The general idea of a distinction between act and potentiality can be illustrated easily enough from ordinary language. I might say of myself, 'I am writing, but I can go for a walk if you wish.' Or we might say of someone, 'He is perfectly capable of lifting that weight if he chooses to do so.' Or it might be said of a wooden plank, 'Yes, it is a fine plank, but it can be split up into small bits for firewood, if necessary.' Or it might be said of water that it is water but that it can become or be turned into steam. I am actually writing, but I am capable of or have the potentiality for going for a walk. The man is not actually lifting the heavy weight, but he is capable of doing so; he has the capacity or potentiality for it. The plank is actually a plank, but it is capable of being divided. The water is actually water, but it possesses the power or potentiality of becoming steam. Of course, it might be maintained that the distinctions which I have appealed to in propositions of ordinary language are linguistic distinctions simply, and that all that I have done is to draw attention to distinctions we make when speaking about things. But Aquinas was convinced that the linguistic distinctions exhibit objective distinctions in things. 'That which can be and is not is said to exist in potency, while that which already is is said to exist in act' (De principiis naturae, in first sentence).

This distinction between act and potentiality is found, according to Aquinas, in every finite thing, though not necessarily in the same way. An oak tree can undergo substantial change, but a spiritual being cannot. Yet an angel has the potentiality of making acts of love of God. Wherever there is finitude, there is, so to speak, a mixture of act and potentiality. No finite being can exist without being actually something definite, but it never exhausts its potentialities all at once. Development of some sort, further actualization of some sort, is always possible.

Possibility of development is thus a manifestation of finiteness. For example, it makes sense to talk of mental development through the acquisition of knowledge only in the case of a finite intelligent being. It would be a contradiction to speak of an infinite omniscient mind acquiring knowledge. For knowledge can be acquired only by a mind which does not already possess that knowledge. But it does not follow that a finite mind's capacity for acquiring knowledge is an imperfection in the sense that it is something which it would be better to be without. The human mind, which begins in a state of total ignorance, has a capacity for developing itself by acquiring knowledge; and Aquinas certainly never imagined that it would be better for the human mind if it lacked that capacity and was doomed to remain completely ignorant. The mind's capacity for acquiring knowledge cannot therefore be called an imperfection, though it manifests the mind's finiteness. Thus Aquinas did not deny or belittle a 'dynamic' conception of the universe. On the contrary, he saw in all things a natural tendency to realize or develop their several potentialities, and he regarded this tendency as something good. There is nothing in the idea of self-development and self-perfection through activity which is incompatible with Aquinas' philosophy. At the same time the capacity of acquiring knowledge, for example, exists for the actual acquisition of knowledge, and the habitual possession of it exists for its exercise. 'The end (that is, purpose) of a potentiality is act' (S.T., Ia, IIae, 55, 1). 'Each thing is perfect in so far as it is in act, for potentiality without act is imperfect' (S.T., Ia, IIae, 3, 2). A capacity for self-development is not an imperfection in the sense that it is something which it would better to be without; but it is imperfect when compared with the actual development. Aquinas was not the man to exalt striving at the expense of possession, to say, for example, that it is better to search endlessly for truth than to know what is true or that the striving for moral virtue is superior to its possession. Yet the habitual knowledge exists for its exercise, and moral virtues are acquired with a view to moral action.

These points of view come together in Aquinas' hierarchic conception of reality. At the bottom of the scale, so to speak, is 'first matter', which cannot exist by itself because it is sheer potentiality for the successive reception of substantial forms capable of informing matter.[1] At the top of the scale (though this is an inexact way of speaking, since God, as infinite transcendent being, cannot be placed in a common class with finite things) is God, who is pure act without any unrealized potentialities. If therefore we compare the levels of the hierarchy of being, we shall have to say that the possession of potentiality as such – I mean unrealized capacity – is an imperfection in the sense that it indicates a lack of possible perfection, a need to be fulfilled. Finite beings are less perfect than God. But at the same time any finite being would be less perfect than it actually is, if it lacked all capacity for self-development. The development which we find in the universe is a sign of the finitude of the things which compose it, but any finite being is necessarily a mixture of potentiality and act, and development is a movement towards the full realization of form. A static universe, were such a thing possible, would not be better than a dynamic universe. God is the measure of all things, to quote Plato's retort to Protagoras; but it is only through self-development that finite things can imitate, as it were, the fullness of the divine actuality.

*

For Aquinas, therefore, the distinction between potentiality and act is found in all finite things. But to say that these factors are found in every finite thing does not by itself tell us very much. A human being, for instance, certainly possesses potentiality or capacity, but we want to know what precise capacities he possesses. However, we are keeping at

1. Nor can substantial forms, apart from the human soul, exist by themselves.

present to the most general principles of Aquinas' philosophy and to his assertions about finite things in general rather than about one kind of finite being. We first considered a particular exemplification of the distinction between potentiality and act that is found in all corporeal things, namely the distinction between matter and form, of which the latter stands to the former as act to potentiality. And we used this particular distinction as an introduction to the more general distinction. We must now consider an example of the potentiality–act relation which is found, according to Aquinas, in all finite things, whether corporeal or incorporeal, namely the relation between essence and existence.

Aquinas' distinction between essence and existence is somewhat difficult to understand. It is true that a preliminary notion of it can be given in terms of ordinary language. For in ordinary language we are accustomed to distinguish between the *whatness* or nature or essence of a thing and the fact *that* it exists. If a child comes across the words 'elephant' and 'dinosaur' in a book and does not know what the words mean, the meanings could be explained to him without its being added that there are elephants but no dinosaurs. In this case the child would have some notion of the *whatness* of an elephant without knowing that there are things to which the description applies. But though a preliminary idea of Aquinas' distinction between essence and existence can be given in some such way, difficulties arise directly we try to go beyond this preliminary idea (which can itself be misleading). However, as Aquinas attached a very considerable importance to the distinction it cannot possibly be passed over in a book on his philosophy.

First of all, what does Aquinas mean by 'essence'? Essence is that which answers the question what a thing is; it is substance considered as definable. 'It is clear that essence is that which is signified by the definition of a thing' (*De ente et essentia*, 2). In the case of material things 'the word *essence* signifies that which is composed of matter and form' (*ibid.*).

Existence, on the other hand, is the act by which an essence or substance is or has being. 'Existence denotes a certain act; for a thing is not said to exist by the fact that it is in potentiality but by the fact that it is in act' (*C.G.*, I, 22, 4). Essence is the potential metaphysical component in a thing (it is that which is or has being, the *quod est*), while existence is the act by which essence has being (it is the *quo est*). This distinction is not, be it noted, a physical distinction between two separable things; it is a metaphysical distinction within a thing. Essence and existence are not two things. There is no objective essence without existence, and there is no existence which is not the existence of something. When Aquinas talks about existence being 'received' or 'limited' by essence (cf. *De ente et essentia*, 6), he does not mean that there is a kind of general existence which is divided up, as it were, among individual things. Inasmuch as existence is always, as far as our experience goes, the existence of some essence, of some particular kind of thing, it can be said to be 'limited' by essence; for it is always the existence of a man or of a horse or of a dog or of some other substance. And inasmuch as the substance, considered as essence, is that which has being, that of which we say that it exists, it can be said to 'receive' existence. But these ways of speaking are not meant to imply either that existence is something apart from an essence or that an essence has objective reality apart from existence. The distinction between them is a distinction within a concrete finite being.

Aquinas does not, as far as I know, make explicit use of the term 'real distinction' in this connexion. But he speaks of a 'real composition' of essence and existence in finite things (*De veritate*, 27, 1, *ad* 8), and he says that the distinction between essence and existence in God is only mental (*In Boethium de Hebdomadibus*, 2), a statement which clearly implies that in finite things the distinction is not only mental. Moreover, he habitually speaks of existence as being other than essence. In my opinion, then, there can be no doubt that Aquinas asserted an objective distinction between essence and existence in finite things, a distinction, that is to say, which is not dependent simply on our way of thinking and speaking about things. He distinguished the use of the verb 'to be' in existential propositions like 'Peter Brown exists' and its use in descriptive or predicative propositions like 'Man is rational'; but the distinction between essence and existence was certainly not in his view a purely linguistic distinction. It is manifested in linguistic distinctions, but what is manifested is, he thought, an objective distinction in things and not itself a linguistic distinction. At the same time, if this objective distinction is called a 'real' distinction, this must not be taken to mean a distinction between two physically separable things like two parts of a watch. Before the union of essence and existence to form a concrete and actual thing there was no objective essence and no existence. And their 'separation' simply means the destruction of that thing.

Aquinas' distinction between essence and existence is thus a distinction between the essence and existence of an actual finite being. It is not a distinction between our idea of the essence of a thing and the thing itself; this distinction is taken for granted. Nor does it mean, for example, that before a given man existed the essence of the man subsisted in some peculiar realm of essences awaiting existence. For Aquinas did not believe in any such ghostly realm of subsistent essences. In a sense the essence pre-existed in God as a divine 'idea'. But Aquinas was well aware that to speak of 'ideas' in God is to speak anthropomorphically and that there is no objective distinction between the divine ideas and the divine being. The existence of the 'divine ideas' and the divine existence are one and the same. And the distinction between essence and existence is not a distinction between God and creatures; it is a distinction within the actual finite being itself. When Aquinas says that existence 'comes from outside and together with the essence forms a composite being' (*De ente et essentia*, 5) he does not mean that a previously 'existing' existence is given to a previously 'existing' essence, which would be sheer absurdity: he means that the act by which an essence has being is caused, the cause being external to the thing itself. That which comes into being is an existent substance; but it does not exist simply because it is the sort of thing which it is, for example a man.

Aquinas' way of approaching the matter, however, is sometimes apt to mislead. The *De ente et essentia* was an early work, and in it Aquinas' way of approaching the distinction between essence and existence was influenced by Alfarabi and Avicenna. 'Whatever does not belong to the concept of an essence or quiddity comes from outside and with the essence forms a composite being. For no essence can be understood without the parts of that essence. Now, every essence or quiddity can be understood without its actual existence being understood. For I can understand what a man or a phoenix is and yet not know whether they exist in nature. It is clear, therefore, that existence is different from quiddity, unless perhaps there is something whose essence is existence' (*De ente et essentia*, 5). This passage may suggest that Aquinas founded his distinction between essence and existence simply on our ability to learn the meaning of a word by description without knowing whether there is anything to which this description actually applies. For instance, as we have already seen, if a small boy comes across the words 'elephant' and 'dinosaur' in a book and does not understand them, he may ask his father to explain. And though his father would in practice probably refer to the facts that there are elephants and that there are now, so far as we know, no dinosaurs, this would not be necessary. The meanings of the words could be explained by description without any reference being made to the existence of elephants and the non-existence of dinosaurs. The conclusion might thus be drawn that all that Aquinas is really doing is to draw our attention to our ability to learn the meaning of a word by description without adverting to the question whether anything exists to which the description applies. But Aquinas did not think that this ability is an infallible sign of an objective distinction between essence and existence in the thing named. For he expressly says that a man can know the meaning of the word 'God' without knowing that God exists. 'It is not necessary that immediately the meaning of the word *God* is known it should be known that God exists' (*C.G.*, 1, 11). As Aquinas was convinced that there is no objective distinction between essence and existence in God, he cannot have considered that our ability to learn the meaning of a word by description without knowing whether there is anything to which the description applies is an infallible proof of an objective distinction between essence and existence in the thing named.

If there is no objective distinction between essence and existence in God, then presumably to learn the meaning of the word 'God' involves learning that it means a Being whose essence involves existence. But it does not follow that to learn the meaning of the word 'God' is necessarily to learn that God exists. This would follow only if learning the meaning of the word God involved an intuition or direct apprehension of the divine essence. And Aquinas did not believe that we have anything of the kind. It would seem, therefore, that we are entitled to interpret the statement that our ability to understand the essence of, say, man without adverting to the existence of men postulates an apprehension of the essence of man, existence not being included in this apprehension.[1] Or, better, the mind apprehends the concrete essence or nature as that which has being, that is, as existing. The distinction between essence and existence is explicitly understood only by philosophic reflection; but it is implicitly present in our direct apprehension of things and implicitly manifested in ordinary language.

Aquinas would therefore presumably justify the essence-existence language, which doubtless seems so strange to many of us, as being necessary in order to render explicit the implications of ordinary knowledge and ordinary language. It is not that the metaphysician discovers a new fact, namely that essence is distinct from existence, in the way

1. Aquinas did not hold that we ordinarily have direct intuitions of the essences of things.

that an explorer may discover a hitherto unknown island or flower : it is rather that he makes explicit what is implicitly contained in our apprehension of actual things.

Certain modern Thomists postulate as the foundation of metaphysics an initial metaphysical intuition of 'being' which some philosophers apparently have while others do not, the former being the metaphysicians. But if there is such an intuition, it cannot be equivalent to a privileged mystical experience on the part of metaphysicians, a conception which Aquinas certainly did not admit. Nor can it be equivalent to the communication of a piece of factual information to a select few. It would presumably be more akin to seeing something familiar 'for the first time' or 'in a new light', in this case to seeing the existential aspect of finite things in a clear light. As Aquinas already believed in God and in divine creation, he was obviously predisposed to see a finite substance as not involving its own existence. Or, in other terms, he was predisposed to view every existential proposition about a finite thing as a contingent proposition. But he clearly thought that the distinction between essence and existence in finite things can be apprehended apart from knowledge of God's existence. In a passage already quoted (*De ente et essentia, 5*) he asserts that 'it is clear therefore that existence is different from essence (*quidditas*); unless perhaps there is some thing whose essence is existence'. The phrasing of the last part of this statement makes it clear that he did not look on the recognition of the essence-existence distinction as dependent on a previous knowledge of God's existence. Nevertheless as belief in God predisposed him to recognize this distinction, it is easily understandable that he makes no explicit statement about any 'metaphysical intuition', and it may well be that those are right who think that an intuition of this kind is implicitly presupposed. As I have indicated, however, it would be quite foreign to Aquinas' mind to accept the idea of a quasi-mystical 'intuition of being', enjoyed by a select company of metaphysicians. In his view 'that which the intellect first conceives . . . is being' (*De veritate, 1, 1*). Whatsoever

I apprehend, I apprehend as some thing, as a being. But this implicit apprehension of being which accompanies all our mental contact with things is not the 'intuition of being' of which Thomists like Étienne Gilson and Jacques Maritain speak, though it is its foundation and condition. They are talking rather of a conscious advertence to the existential aspect of things, of seeing this aspect in a sharp light, as it were. And it may well be that the prominence attributed in Aquinas' philosophy to the problem of existence presupposes some such conscious 'experience' of what is there for all but of which not all are as vividly conscious as was Aquinas.

I do not pretend that the foregoing considerations eliminate all difficulties which arise in the use of the essence-existence language; far from it. One can scarcely avoid using this language if one is to see the distinction between essence and existence on the plane on which Aquinas placed it, namely on the metaphysical plane. And it can be pointed out that the structure of our language makes it very difficult to speak about the subject without using terms and phrases which appear to 'thingify' essence and existence. None the less, a thorough analysis of the essence-existence language by those who wish to retain it is certainly required. To speak simply of an 'intuition' is scarcely satisfactory. For even if the intuition, interpreted on the lines suggested above, is granted, the language used to render it explicit is still open to critical analysis. Aquinas himself was obviously not called upon to justify the use of a language familiar to his contemporaries, but a term like 'essence' cannot be taken for granted today. It is one thing to say what Aquinas meant by it; it is another thing to make it acceptable to one's own contemporaries. However, considerations of space do not permit further development of this theme; and I want to conclude the section with some brief remarks on the question whether Aquinas' doctrine implies that he thought that existence is a predicate.

The assertion of a distinction between essence and existence was not new. Islamic philosophers like Alfarabi (d. *c.*

950), Avicenna (d. 1037), and Algazel (d. 1111) had already made this distinction. But they spoke of existence as an 'accident', though Avicenna saw that it cannot be an accident like other accidents. Aquinas saw this clearly, and for him existence was not an accident at all but that which rendered the possession of accidents possible. It would be absurd to say, for example, that Peter is white, tall, existing, and amusing. For if Peter did not exist he could be neither white nor tall nor amusing. Existence was for Aquinas the act by which substance has being; and unless it has being it cannot have accidental modifications. He speaks of it as being that which is most intimate and most profound in a thing, being like a form in relation to all that is in the thing (S.T., Ia, 8, 1, ad 4). He does indeed speak of it as a 'perfection', but it is 'the actuality of all acts and thus the perfection of all perfections' (De potentia, 7, 2, ad 9). In other words, existence cannot be numbered among a list of attributes, since it is the foundation of all attributes. Aquinas' language may suggest that it is an attribute of essence; but it is in a real sense the foundation of the essence itself, because without the act of existing the essence would not have being. It may indeed appear to constitute a contradiction in terms if it is said on the one hand that existence is the act by which essence has being and on the other that essence receives existence. But Aquinas did not look on essence as an existent something which can receive 'existence' as a kind of accident. A thing's coming into being involves the simultaneous production of two inseparable metaphysical constituents, of an essence as determining its act of existence to be the existence of this or that kind of thing, and of existence as actualizing the essence. There is no question of the one principle being temporally prior to the other. As I have said, there are difficulties enough about this conception, but one cannot begin to understand Aquinas' theory if one persists in interpreting him as thinking of essence and existence as two things or as two physical components of a thing. One thing is produced and exists; but in that one thing we must, according to Aquinas, distinguish essence and existence, which are objectively distinct though they are not distinct as separate or separable things. Aquinas would be the first to acknowledge that though one may predicate existence of essence as far as grammar goes, existence is not and cannot be an attribute in the sense in which other attributes are attributes.

*

The foregoing outlines of the distinctions between substance and accident, matter and form, essence and existence, all of which illustrate in their several ways the general distinction which runs through all finite being, namely the distinction between act and potentiality, may give the impression that Aquinas' metaphysic consists simply of arid and tortuous discussions, couched in unfamiliar language and without much relevance to the world as we know it. As a conclusion to this chapter, therefore, I want to bring out some implications of his metaphysics, which may perhaps help to render the latter more easily intelligible.

The distinctions between substance and accident and between matter and form draw attention to two features of the world, namely permanence and change. We all speak of things as though they were in some degree permanent. Although a human being is born and dies and although a tree has a certain span of life, we all speak of the human being and of the tree, which each is alive, as an individual entity. Even in the abnormal and pathological case of 'split personality' or dual personality we think of the relevant phenomena as happening to a definite human being and as taking place within that human being. We may say, for example, 'he is suffering from schizophrenia', attributing the phenomena to a definite and individual being. At the same time we all think and speak of things both as capable of undergoing change and as actually undergoing change. We ourselves change within certain limits, while retaining our identities. The tree changes, though the changes are predicated of the tree considered as a relatively permanent thing. Objects with certain names are changed into objects with other names by chemical action for example. Permanence and change are both features of the world as presented in common experience and described in the ordinary language which reflects and expresses this experience. And these features find abstract expression in Aquinas' distinctions between act and potency, substance and accident, form and matter. He may speak in an unfamiliar way, but he speaks about the familiar. He does not construct a static world like that of Parmenides, nor does he present us with a Heraclitean flux; fundamentally he describes the world as it is known by us in daily experience. He presents us with a world which is shot through, as it were, by form, by intelligible structure, and which is therefore to that extent intelligible. On the other hand he presents us with a changing and a developing world. And in emphasizing these aspects of the world he lays too the theoretical foundations for the particular sciences. If the world were in no way intelligible, science would not be possible, except as a purely mental and unverifiable construct. On the other hand, emphasis on change and development are characteristic of the sciences. One cannot, of course, deduce the conclusions of the empirical sciences from abstract metaphysical principles; nor did Aquinas think that one could. But there is not that cleavage between the world as presented in Aquinas' metaphysics, when distinguished from the contemporary scientific ideas that he accepted, and modern science which there would be, for example, between the philosophy of Parmenides and modern science. Both Aquinas' metaphysics and modern science presuppose the familiar world of common experience, though Aquinas' metaphysics moves on a more abstract plane than the empirical sciences.

This aspect of Aquinas' metaphysics, namely the presentation of a world combining permanence and change, can be called perhaps the construction of the world. That is to say, it presents an abstract theoretical picture of a developing universe which has at the same time sufficient permanence and intelligibility to make knowledge possible. But there is another aspect, which can perhaps be termed the destruction of the world, if by 'world' one here means a self-sufficient Absolute. This aspect is represented by the distinction between essence and existence. There is a natural inclination to imagine all individual things as existing and acting 'in the world', as though the world were a kind of containing entity, in which other things are situated. For Aquinas, however, the world is the system of interrelated finite substances and not something different from them; and in each finite substance he finds what may be called a radical existential instability, expressed abstractly in the essence-existence distinction. Under this aspect his metaphysic goes in a sense beyond the familiar workaday world, even though he thought of the distinction as reflected in ordinary language. It also forms a transition to his metaphysical theory about God, to the knowledge of whom metaphysics is, he insists, essentially orientated. This aspect of his metaphysics can be linked, of course, with the systems of other metaphysicians who have concerned themselves with the reduction of multiplicity to unity, of the dependent to the independent or absolute. But it is to be noted that in making the transition from the world to God Aquinas does not, as it were, annul the world of finite substances or turn them into accidents or modes of the Absolute: he relates the finite substances of experience to God, and it is in these concrete things that he finds a relation to a ground of their existence. His 'destruction' of the world is a critique of the idea of the world as a quasi-entity, as a pseudo-Absolute, and not of the things which in their inter-relatedness form the world. How he makes the transition from finite beings to God will be considered in the following chapter.

CHAPTER THREE

God and Creation

AQUINAS was a Christian before he became a metaphysician. And he did not come to believe in God simply as a result of his own metaphysical arguments. He already believed in an ultimate reality conceived as possessing the attributes ascribed by Christians to God. Why then, it may be asked, did he offer any proofs of God's existence at all? Various reasons can be suggested. For example, in a systematic treatise on theology like the *Summa theologica*, devoted as it is to expounding the content of the Christian faith, it was only natural to start with what Aquinas called the 'preambles' of faith. But much more important than any purely methodological consideration is his conviction that the existence of God is not self-evident. What we know of his life suggests a serene and profound faith, flowering in mystical experience; but this does not mean that he was unaware of the possibility of agnosticism and of atheism. And they are possible because God's existence is not self-evident. 'No one can think the opposite of that which is self-evident. ... But the opposite of the proposition "God exists" can be thought. ... Therefore the proposition that God exists is not self-evident' (*S.T.*, Ia, 2, 1, *sed contra*). Aquinas mentions an argument which was not infrequently adduced (by St Bonaventure, for example) to show that knowledge of God's existence is naturally implanted in all men. The argument runs more or less as follows. All men have a natural innate desire for happiness. Now, it is the possession of God which constitutes happiness. Therefore all men have a natural desire for God. But in this case they must have an innate knowledge of God, since desire for something presupposes knowledge of that thing. Aquinas does not deny all force to this line of argument. For he admits that man's natural desire for happiness implies a kind of implicit knowledge of God, in the sense that when we once know that God exists and that the possession of Him constitutes human happiness we can interpret the desire for happiness as the desire for God. But this does not show that anyone has a natural innate knowledge of the truth of the proposition that God exists. 'To know that someone is coming is not to know that Peter is coming, although the person coming is in fact Peter. And many have thought that man's perfect good, which is happiness, consists in riches; others that it consists in pleasure; others that it consists in some other thing' (*S.T.*, I*a*, 2, 1, *ad* 1). Nor is one entitled to argue that it is self-evident that there is truth, on the ground that anyone who denies that there is truth affirms it implicitly, and then to conclude that God's existence is self-evident because He is truth. For the fact that there is truth 'in general' does not make God's existence self-evident.

Aquinas also denied that once the meaning of the word 'God' is understood it is immediately evident that God exists. When he treats of this theory in the two *Summas* he does not mention St Anselm by name, but it is the latter's so-called 'ontological argument' which he has in mind. St Anselm assumed that the idea of God is the idea of the being 'than which no greater can be thought', that is, of the supremely perfect being. He then argued that if the being than which no greater can be thought existed only mentally or in our idea, it would not be that than which no greater can be thought. For a greater (that is, more perfect) being could be thought, namely one which existed apart from our idea of it. And he concluded that no one can have the idea of God and understand it and yet at the same time deny that God exists. Aquinas commented, however, that it is not everyone who understands by God 'that than which no greater can be thought', since 'many of the ancients said that the world is God' (*C.G.*, 1, 11). In any case, even if we grant that the meaning of 'God' is 'supremely perfect being', it does not follow without more ado that God exists. To think that it does is to be guilty of an illicit transition from the conceptual to the existential order. It is not infrequently said that Aquinas did not do justice to Anselm's argument and, in particular, that he did not consider the argument in the context and light in which its author regarded it. This contention may be true. But it is unnecessary to discuss this exegetic question here: the point is that Aquinas refused to allow that we can start with an idea of God or with a definition of the term 'God', and conclude immediately that God exists. If we enjoyed an intuition of the divine essence we could not deny God's existence: for there is, Aquinas maintained, no real distinction between them. And in this sense the proposition 'God exists' is self-evident 'in itself'. But we do not enjoy any such intuition, and the proposition 'God exists' is not self-evident or analytic for the human mind.

This refusal to allow that God's existence is a self-evident truth for the human mind is closely bound up with what I have called the 'empiricist' side of Aquinas' philosophy. Our knowledge begins with sense-experience, and on account of man's psychophysical constitution material things constitute the primary natural object of the human mind. Any natural knowledge which we have of a being or beings transcending the visible world is attained by reflection on the data of experience. And it is this process of reflection, when carried through systematically, that constitutes the proofs of the proposition that God exists. It is doubtless understandable that some writers have accused Aquinas of 'wishful thinking' on the ground that he produced proofs of the truth of a proposition which he already accepted on other grounds. But one should bear in mind his general philosophical position. The mind must start with the data of sense-experience; but reflection on these data, he was convinced, discloses the existential relation of dependence of empirical realities on a being which transcends them. Aquinas was not an empiricist in the modern sense, but it was the 'empiricist' elements of his philosophy which in large measure dictated his approach to the problem of ultimate reality, the approach, that is to say, by reflection on the data of experience. He believed that the mind of the agnostic, if it gives unprejudiced attention to rational argument setting out the implications of these data, can be led to see how the existence of realities which nobody really doubts involves the existence of God. As for Christians, a full understanding of their faith demands a realization of the ways in which the world of finite things discloses to the reflective mind the God in whom they already believe with a faith sustained by prayer.

*

Aquinas did not, of course, deny that people can come to know that God exists by other ways than by philosophic reflection. Nor did he ever assert that the belief of most people who accept the proposition that God exists is the result of their having elaborated metaphysical arguments for themselves or of their having thought through the metaphysical arguments developed by others. Nor did he confuse a purely intellectual assent to the conclusion of such a metaphysical argument with a living Christian faith in and love of God. But he did think that reflection on quite familiar features of the world affords ample evidence of God's existence. The reflection itself, sustained and developed at the metaphysical level, is difficult, and he explicitly recognized and acknowledged its difficulty: he certainly did not consider that everyone is capable of sustained metaphysical reflection. At the same time the empirical facts on which this reflection is based were for him quite familiar facts. In order to see the relation of finite things to the being on which they depend we are not required to pursue scientific research, discovering hitherto unknown empirical facts. Nor does the metaphysician discover God in a manner analogous to the explorer who suddenly comes upon a hitherto unknown island or flower. It is attention and reflection which are required rather than research or exploration.

What, then, are the familiar facts which for Aquinas imply the existence of God? Mention of them can be found in the famous 'five ways' of proving God's existence, which are outlined in the *Summa theologica* (Ia, 2, 3). In the first way Aquinas begins by saying that 'it is certain, and it is clear from sense-experience, that some things in this world are moved'. It must be remembered that he, like Aristotle, understands the term 'motion' in the broad sense of change, reduction from a state of potentiality to one of act; he does not refer exclusively to local motion. In the second way he starts with the remark that 'we find in material things an order of efficient causes'. In other words, in our experience of things and of their relations to one another we are aware of efficient causality. Thus while in the first way he begins with the fact that some things are in motion or in a state of change, the second way is based upon the fact that some things act upon other things, as efficient causes. In the third way he starts by stating that 'we find among things some which are capable of existing or not existing, since we find that some things come into being and pass away'. In other words, we perceive that some things are corruptible or perishable. In the fourth proof he observes that 'we find in things that some are more or less good and true and noble and so on (than others)'. Finally in the fifth way he says: 'we see that some things which lack knowledge, namely natural bodies, act for an end, which is clear from the fact that they always or in most cases act in the same way, in order to attain what is best.'

There is, I think, little difficulty in accepting as empirical facts the starting-points of the first three ways. For nobody really doubts that some things are acted upon and changed or 'moved', that some things act on others, and that some things are perishable. Each of us is aware, for example, that he is acted upon and changed, that he sometimes acts as an efficient cause, and that he is perishable. Even if anyone were to cavil at the assertion that he is aware that he himself was born and will die, he knows very well that some other people were born and have died. But the starting-points of the two final arguments may cause some difficulty. The proposition that there are different grades of perfections in things stands in need of a much more thorough analysis than Aquinas accords it in his brief outline of the fourth way. For the schematic outlining of the five proofs was designed, not to satisfy the critical minds of mature philosophers, but as introductory material for 'novices' in the study of theology. And in any case Aquinas could naturally take for granted in the thirteenth century ideas which were familiar to his contemporaries and which had not yet been subjected to the radical criticism to which they were later subjected. At the same time there is not very much difficulty in understanding the sort of thing which was meant. We are all accustomed to think and speak as though, for example, there were different degrees of intelligence and intellectual capacity. In order to estimate the different degrees we need, it is true, standards or fixed points of reference; but, given these points of reference, we are all accustomed to make statements which imply different grades of perfections. And though these statements stand in need of close analysis, they refer to something which falls within ordinary experience and finds expression in ordinary language. As for the fifth way, the modern reader may find great difficulty in seeing what is meant if he confines his attention to the relevant passage in the *Summa theologica*. But if he looks at the *Summa contra Gentiles* (1, 13) he will find Aquinas saying that we see things of different natures cooperating in the production and maintenance of a relatively stable order or system. When Aquinas says that we see purely material things acting for an end, he does not mean to say that they act in a manner analogous to that in which human beings consciously act for definite purposes. Indeed, the point of the argument is that they do not do so. He means that different kinds of things, like fire and water, the behaviour of which is determined by their several 'forms', cooperate, not consciously but as a matter of fact, in such a way that there is a relatively stable order or system. And here again, though much more would need to be said in a full discussion of the matter, the basic idea is nothing particularly extraordinary nor is it contrary to our ordinary experience and expectations.

It is to be noted also that Aquinas speaks with considerable restraint: he avoids sweeping generalizations. Thus in the first argument he does not say that all material things are 'moved' but that we see that some things in this world are moved or changed. In the third argument he does not state that all finite things are contingent but that we are aware that some things come into being and pass away. And in the fifth argument he does not say that there is invariable world-order or system but that we see natural bodies acting always or in most cases in the same ways. The difficulty, therefore, which may be experienced in regard to Aquinas' proofs of God's existence concerns not so much the empirical facts or alleged empirical facts with which he starts as in seeing that these facts imply God's existence.

Perhaps a word should be said at once about this idea of 'implication'. As a matter of fact Aquinas does not use the word when talking about the five ways: he speaks of 'proof' and of 'demonstration'. And by 'demonstration' he means in this context what he calls *demonstratio quia* (*S.T.*, Ia, 2, 2), namely a causal proof of God's existence, proceeding from the affirmation of some empirical fact, for example that there are things which change, to the affirmation of a transcendent cause. It is, indeed, his second proof which is strictly the causal argument, in the sense that it deals explicitly with the order of efficient causality; but in every proof the idea of ontological dependence on a transcendent cause appears in some form or other. Aquinas' conviction was that a full understanding of the empirical facts which are selected for consideration in the five ways involves seeing the dependence of these facts on a transcendent cause. The existence of things which change, for instance, is, in his opinion, not self-explanatory: it can be rendered intelligible only if seen as dependent on a transcendent cause, a cause, that is to say, which does not itself belong to the order of changing things.

This may suggest to the modern reader that Aquinas was concerned with causal explanation in the sense that he was concerned with framing an empirical hypothesis to explain certain facts. But he did not regard the proposition affirming

God's existence as a causal hypothesis in the sense of being in principle revisable, as a hypothesis, that is to say, which might conceivably have to be revised in the light of fresh empirical data or which might be supplanted by a more economical hypothesis. This point can perhaps be seen most clearly in the case of his third argument, which is based on the fact that there are things which come into being and pass away. In Aquinas' opinion no fresh scientific knowledge about the physical constitution of such things could affect the validity of the argument. He did not look on a 'demonstration' of God's existence as an empirical hypothesis in the sense in which the electronic theory, for example, is said to be an empirical hypothesis. It is, of course, open to anyone to say that in his own opinion cosmological arguments in favour of God's existence are in fact analogous to the empirical hypotheses of the sciences and that they have a predictive function; but it does not follow that this interpretation can legitimately be ascribed to Aquinas. We should not be misled by the illustrations which he sometimes offers from contemporary scientific theory. For these are mere illustrations to elucidate a point in terms easily understandable by his readers: they are not meant to indicate that the proofs of God's existence were for him empirical hypotheses in the modern sense of the term.

Does this mean, therefore, that Aquinas regarded the existence of God as being logically entailed by facts such as change or coming into being and passing away? He did not, of course, regard the proposition 'there are things which come into being and pass away' as logically entailing the proposition 'there is an absolutely necessary or independent being' in the sense that affirmation of the one proposition and denial of the other involves one in a verbal or formal linguistic contradiction. But he thought that metaphysical analysis of what it objectively means to be a thing which comes into being and passes away shows that such a thing must depend existentially on an absolutely necessary being. And he thought that metaphysical analysis of what it objectively means to be a changing thing shows that such a thing depends on a supreme unmoved mover. It follows that for Aquinas one is involved in a contradiction if one affirms the propositions 'there are things which come into being and pass away' and 'there are things which change' and at the same time denies the propositions 'there is an absolutely necessary being' and 'there is a supreme unmoved mover'. But the contradiction can be made apparent only by means of metaphysical analysis. And the entailment in question is fundamentally an ontological or causal entailment.

Not a few philosophers (certainly all 'empiricists') would presumably comment that if this represents Aquinas' real mind it is clear that he confused the causal relation with logical entailment. But it should be remembered that though Aquinas was convinced that the proposition stating that everything which begins to exist has *a* cause is absolutely certain he did not think that the existence of any finite thing entails the existence of any other finite thing in the sense that the existence of any finite thing can be said to entail the existence of God. In theological language, if we once admit that there is an omnipotent Creator, we can say that he could create and maintain in existence any finite thing without the existence of any other finite thing. But it does not follow that there can be any finite thing without God. In other words, Aquinas is not bound to produce other instances of the ontological entailment which he asserts between the existence of finite things and God. Though the relation of creatures to God is analogous in some way to the relation of causal dependence of one finite thing on another, the former relation is, if we consider it as such, unique. Aquinas was not confusing causal relations in general with logical entailments: he was asserting a unique relation between finite things and the transfinite transcendent cause on which they depend.

It is worth emphasizing perhaps that it does not necessarily follow from Aquinas' view that a metaphysical approach to God's existence is an easy matter. It is true that he was confident of the power of the human reason to attain knowledge of God's existence; and he did not regard his arguments as standing in need of support from rhetoric or emotional appeal. And in the *Summa theologica*, where he is writing for 'novices' in theology, he states the argument in a bald and perhaps disconcertingly impersonal manner. But we cannot legitimately conclude that he thought it easy for a man to come to the knowledge of God's existence by philosophic reflection alone. Indeed, he makes an explicit statement to the opposite effect. He was well aware that in human life other factors besides metaphysical reflection exercise a great influence. Moreover, he would obviously agree that it is always possible to stop the process of reflection at a particular point. For Aquinas every being, in so far as it is or has being, is intelligible. But we can consider things from different points of view or under different aspects. For example, I might consider coming-into-being and passing-away simply in regard to definite instances and from a subjective point of view. It grieves me to think that someone I love will probably die before me and leave, as we say, a gap in my life. Or it grieves me to think that I shall die and be unable to complete the work which I have undertaken. Or I might consider coming-into-being and passing-away from some scientific point of view. What are the finite phenomenal causes of organic decay or of the generation of an organism? But I can also consider coming-into-being and passing-away purely as such and objectively, adopting a metaphysical point of view and directing my attention to the sort of being, considered as such, which is capable of coming into being and passing away. Nobody can compel me to adopt this point of view. If I am determined to remain on the level of, say, some particular science, I remain there; and that is that. Metaphysical reflections will have no meaning for me. But the metaphysical point of view is a possible point of view, and metaphysical reflection belongs to a full understanding of things so far as this is possible for a finite mind. And if I do adopt this point of view and maintain it in sustained reflection, an existential relation of dependence, Aquinas was convinced, should become clear to me which will not become clear to me if I remain on a different level of reflection. But just as extraneous factors (such as the influence of the general outlook promoted by a technical civilization) may help to produce my decision to remain on a non-metaphysical level of reflection, so also can extraneous factors influence my reflections on the metaphysical level. It seems to me quite wrong to suggest that Aquinas did not regard metaphysical reflection as a possible way of becoming aware of God's existence and that he looked on it, as some writers have suggested, as being simply a rational justification of an assurance which is necessarily attained in some other way. For if it constitutes a rational justification at all, it must, I think, be a possible way of becoming aware of God's existence. But it does not necessarily follow, of course, that it is an easy way or a common way.

After these general remarks I turn to Aquinas' five proofs of the existence of God. In the first proof he argues that 'motion' or change means the reduction of a thing from a state of potentiality to one of act, and that a thing cannot be reduced from potentiality to act except under the influence of an agent already in act. In this sense 'everything which is moved must be moved by another'. He argues finally that in order to avoid an infinite regress in the chain of movers, the existence of a first unmoved mover must be admitted. 'And all understand that this is God.'

A statement like 'all understand that this is God' or 'all call this (being) God' occurs at the end of each proof, and I postpone consideration of it for the moment. As for the ruling out of an infinite regress, I shall explain what Aquinas means to reject after outlining the second proof, which is similar in structure to the first.

Whereas in the first proof Aquinas considers things as being acted upon, as being changed or 'moved', in the second he considers them as active agents, as efficient causes. He argues that there is a hierarchy of efficient causes, a subordinate cause being dependent on the cause above it in the hierarchy. He then proceeds, after excluding the hypothesis of an infinite regress, to draw the conclusion that there must be a first efficient cause, 'which all call God'.

Now, it is obviously impossible to discuss these arguments profitably unless they are first understood. And misunderstanding of them is only too easy, since the terms and phrases used are either unfamiliar or liable to be taken in a sense other than the sense intended. In the first place it is essential to understand that in the first argument Aquinas supposes that movement or change is dependent on a 'mover' acting here and now, and that in the second argument he supposes that there are efficient causes in the world which even in their causal activity are here and now dependent on the causal activity of other causes. That is why I have spoken of a 'hierarchy' rather than of a 'series'. What he is thinking of can be illustrated in this way. A son is dependent on his father, in the sense that he would not have existed except for the causal activity of his father. But when the son acts for himself, he is not dependent here and now on his father. But he is dependent here and now on other factors. Without the activity of the air, for instance, he could not himself act, and the life-preserving activity of the air is itself dependent here and now on other factors, and they in turn on other factors. I do not say that this illustration is in all respects adequate for the purpose; but it at least illustrates the fact that when Aquinas talks about an 'order' of efficient causes he is not thinking of a series stretching back into the past, but of a hierarchy of causes, in which a subordinate member is here and now dependent on the causal activity of a higher member. If I wind up my watch at night, it then proceeds to work without further interference on my part. But the activity of the pen tracing these words on the page is here and now dependent on the activity of my hand, which in turn is here and now dependent on other factors.

The meaning of the rejection of an infinite regress should now be clear. Aquinas is not rejecting the possibility of an infinite series as such. We have already seen that he did not think that anyone had ever succeeded in showing the impossibility of an infinite series of events stretching back into the past. Therefore he does not mean to rule out the possibility of an infinite series of causes and effects, in which a given member depended on the preceding member, say X on Y, but does not, once it exists, depend here and now on the present causal activity of the preceding member. We have to imagine, not a lineal or horizontal series, so to speak, but a vertical hierarchy, in which a lower member depends here and now on the present causal activity of the member above it. It is the latter type of series, if prolonged to infinity, which Aquinas rejects. And he rejects it on the ground that unless there is a 'first' member, a mover which is not itself moved or a cause which does not itself depend on the causal activity of a higher cause, it is not possible to explain the 'motion' or the causal activity of the lowest member. His point of view is this. Suppress the first unmoved mover and there is no motion or change here and now. Suppress the first efficient cause and there is no causal activity here and now. If therefore we find that some things in the world are changed, there must be a first unmoved mover. And if there are efficient causes in the world, there must be a first efficient, and completely non-dependent cause. The word 'first' does not mean first in the temporal order, but supreme or first in the ontological order.

A remark on the word 'cause' is here in place. What precisely Aquinas would have said to the David Humes either of the fourteenth century or of the modern era it is obviously impossible to say. But it is clear that he believed in real causal efficacy and real causal relations. He was aware, of course, that causal efficacy is not the object of vision in the sense in which patches of colours are objects of vision; but the human being, he considered, is aware of real causal relations and if we understand 'perception' as involving the cooperation of sense and intellect, we can be said to 'perceive' causality. And presumably he would have said that the sufficiency of a phenomenalistic interpretation of causality for purposes of physical science proves nothing against the validity of a metaphysical notion of causality. It is obviously possible to dispute whether his analyses of change or 'motion' and of efficient causality are valid or invalid and whether there is such a thing as a hierarchy of causes. And our opinion about the validity or invalidity of his arguments for the existence of God will depend very largely on our answers to these questions. But mention of the mathematical infinite series is irrelevant to a discussion of his arguments. And it is this point which I have been trying to make clear.

In the third proof Aquinas starts from the fact that some things come into being and perish, and he concludes from this that it is possible for them to exist or not to exist: they do not exist 'necessarily'. He then argues that it is impossible for things which are of this kind to exist always; for 'that which is capable of not existing, at some time does not exist'. If all things were of this kind, at some time there would be nothing. Aquinas is clearly supposing for the sake of argument the hypothesis of infinite time, and his proof is designed to cover this hypothesis. He does not say that infinite time is impossible: what he says is that if time is infinite and if all things are capable of not existing, this potentiality would inevitably be fulfilled in infinite time. There would then be nothing. And if there had ever been nothing, nothing would now exist. For no thing can bring itself into existence. But it is clear as a matter of fact that there are things. Therefore it can never have been true to say that there was literally no thing. Therefore it is impossible that all things should be capable of existing or not existing. There must, then, be some necessary being. But perhaps it is necessary in the sense that it must exist if something else exists; that is to say, its necessity may be hypothetical. We cannot, however, proceed to infinity in the series or hierarchy of necessary beings. If we do so, we do not explain the presence here and now of beings capable of existing or not existing. Therefore we must affirm the existence of a being which is absolutely necessary (*per se necessarium*) and completely independent. 'And all call this being *God*.'

This argument may appear to be quite unnecessarily complicated and obscure. But it has to be seen in its historical context. As already mentioned, Aquinas designed his argument in such a way as to be independent of the question whether or not the world existed from eternity. He wanted to show that on either hypothesis there must be a necessary being. As for the introduction of hypothetical necessary beings, he wanted to show that even if there are such beings, perhaps within the universe, which are not corruptible in the sense in which a flower is corruptible, there must still be an absolutely independent being. Finally, in regard to terminology, Aquinas uses the common medieval expression 'necessary being'. He does not actually use the term 'contingent being' in the argument and talks instead about 'possible' beings; but it comes to the same thing. And though the words 'contingent' and 'necessary' are now applied to propositions rather than to beings, I have retained Aquinas' mode of speaking. Whether one accepts the argument or not, I do not think that there is any insuperable difficulty in understanding the line of thought.

The fourth argument is admittedly difficult to grasp. Aquinas argues that there are degrees of perfections in things. Different kinds of finite things possess different perfections in diverse limited degrees. He then argues not only that if there are different degrees of a perfection like goodness there is a supreme good to which other good things approximate but also that all limited degrees of goodness are caused by the supreme good. And since goodness is a convertible term with being, a thing being good in so far as it has being, the supreme good is the supreme being and the cause of being in all other things. 'Therefore there is something which is the cause of the being and goodness and of every perfection in all other things; and this we call *God*.'

Aquinas refers to some remarks of Aristotle in the *Metaphysics*; but this argument puts one in mind at once of Plato's *Symposium* and *Republic*. And the Platonic doctrine of participation seems to be involved. Aquinas was not immediately acquainted with either work, but the Platonic line of thought was familiar to him from other writers. And it has not disappeared from philosophy. Indeed, some of those theists who reject or doubt the validity of the 'cosmological' arguments seem to feel a marked attraction for some variety of the fourth way, arguing that in the recognition of objective values we implicitly recognize God as the supreme value. But if the line of thought represented by the fourth way is to mean anything to the average modern reader, it has to be presented in a rather different manner from that in which it is expressed by Aquinas, who was able to assume in his readers ideas and points of view which can no longer be presupposed.

Finally, the fifth proof, if we take its statement in the *Summa theologica* together with that in the *Summa contra Gentiles*, can be expressed more or less as follows. The activity and behaviour of each thing is determined by its form. But we observe material things of very different types cooperating in such a way as to produce and maintain a relatively stable world-order or system. They achieve an 'end', the production and maintenance of a cosmic order. But non-intelligent material things certainly do not cooperate consciously in view of a purpose. If it is said that they cooperate in the realization of an end or purpose, this does not mean that they intend the realization of this order in a manner analogous to that in which a man can act consciously with a view to the achievement of a purpose. Nor, when Aquinas talks about operating 'for an end' in this connexion, is he thinking of the utility of certain things to the human race. He is not saying, for example, that grass grows to feed the sheep and that sheep exist in order that human beings should have food and clothing. It is of the unconscious cooperation of different kinds of material things in the production and maintenance of a relatively stable cosmic system that he is thinking, not of the benefits accruing to us from our use of certain objects. And his argument is that this cooperation on the part of heterogeneous material things clearly points to the existence of an extrinsic intelligent author of this cooperation, who operates with an end in view. If Aquinas had lived in the days of the evolutionary hypothesis, he would doubtless have argued that this hypothesis supports rather than invalidates the conclusion of the argument.

No one of these arguments was entirely new, as Aquinas himself was very well aware. But he developed them and arranged them to form a coherent whole. I do not mean that he regarded the validity of one particular argument as necessarily depending on the validity of the other four. He doubtless thought that each argument was valid in its own right. But, as I have already remarked, they conform to a certain pattern, and they are mutually complementary in the sense that in each argument things are considered from a different point of view or under a different aspect. There are so many different approaches to God.

Does any particular argument possess a special or pre-eminent importance? Modern Thomists often assert that the third proof, bearing explicitly on the existence of things, is fundamental. But if we look at the two *Summas*, we do not find Aquinas saying this. So far as he gives explicit preference to any particular proof it is to the first, which he declares, somewhat surprisingly, to be the clearest. Presumably he means that 'motion' or change is so obvious and familiar that it forms a natural starting-point, though he may also have been influenced by the use which Aristotle made of the argument from motion. In any case it is this argument which he selects for a more elaborate discussion in the *Summa contra Gentiles*, while he does not treat at all of the third way in this work. So it cannot be said that Aquinas gives any special prominence to the third argument. At the same time I must confess that my sympathies are with those Thomists who regard this argument as fundamental and who restate it in other forms. And if it is true to say that Aquinas brought into prominence the existential aspect of metaphysics, it can hardly be said that this procedure is alien to his spirit. All the arguments, indeed, treat of dependence in some form or other. And I think that this idea will be found to be involved in all arguments for the existence of God which are in any real sense *a posteriori*. It seems to me to be involved even in those forms of the moral argument which some theists, who accept the Kantian criticism of the cosmological proofs, substitute for the traditional arguments. But it is the idea of existential dependence which most clearly introduces us to the metaphysical level. And it is the problem arising from the existence of finite and contingent things at all which most clearly points to the existence of a transfinite being. What I mean is this. Some people argue that mystical experience, for example, gives rise to a problem, in the sense that it calls for explanation, and that it is best explained on the hypothesis that this experience involves contact with an existent being, God. But there are others who admit the reality of the problem, namely that mystical experience calls for explanation, but who think that it can be satisfactorily explained without postulating God's existence. Thus whatever one may think of the right solution to the problem it is clear, as a matter of empirical fact, that it is possible to admit the reality of the problem and yet not admit that the solution involves affirming the existence of a transcendent being. But one can hardly admit that the existence of finite being at all constitutes a serious problem and at the same time maintain that the solution can be found anywhere else than in affirming the existence of the transfinite. If one does not wish to embark on the path which leads to the affirmation of transcendent being, however the latter may be described (if it is described at all), one has to deny the reality of the problem, assert that things 'just are' and that the existential problem in question is a pseudo-problem. And if one refuses even to sit down at the chess-board and make a move, one cannot, of course, be checkmated.

Since the time of Kant, Aquinas' arguments have been widely regarded as patently invalid,[1] and many people tend to dismiss them out of hand. Others regard the validity of all or at least of some of them as evident to anyone who con-

1. As a matter of fact they were criticized in the fourteenth century, by Ockham, for example.

siders them dispassionately and without prejudice. But a thorough discussion of the various points of view would take us too far afield. There are several important relevant points which Aquinas seems to me to have left obscure. Sometimes, for instance, he gives the impression of thinking that to prove the existence of God is simply a matter of applying certain general principles. And some Thomists appear to have interpreted him in this sense. Other Thomists have pointed out the difficulties involved in this proceeding. If the causal proof, for example, is simply a case of applying a general causal principle, how do we know in advance that the principle can be used in this particular way? If we do know it, do we not already know God's existence? And a like remark may be made about the following argument. 'If there are things which come into being and pass away, there is an absolutely necessary being. But there are things which come into being and pass away. Therefore there is an absolutely necessary being.' No doubt, if we admit the major premiss, the conclusion can scarcely be avoided. The argument follows the type: if p, then q; but p; therefore q. But can we *in fact* admit the major premiss in question without admitting the existence of God? Surely the whole difficulty lies in proving the major premiss. And in this case we can hardly say that to prove the existence of God is simply to apply to a particular case a general principle, the validity of which is known independently of any reference to God. And it is noticeable that Aquinas does not start from general principles but from existential propositions, such as 'we find among things some which are capable of existing or not existing, since we find that some things come into being and pass away'. It is doubtless possible to take Aquinas' arguments exactly as they stand and examine each successive proposition in turn, to determine the validity or invalidity of the whole argument. But for a fruitful discussion it would be desirable, I think, to come first to some conclusion concerning his real mind about points such as these which I have just raised. And as this is a controversial matter, it can hardly be embarked upon here without devoting a disproportionate amount of space to one particular subject.

It is, however, worth raising the question with what justification Aquinas ends each proof with a remark such as, 'And all call this being *God*'. For it might be argued that even if it is granted that there is a first or supreme unmoved mover, a first efficient cause and an absolutely necessary being, it does not immediately follow that this being can with propriety be called 'God'.

It can be pointed out, of course, that the fifth argument concludes with affirming the existence of an intelligent supra-mundane being and that the fourth argument implies that the supremely perfect being possesses, for example, the perfection of intelligence. If, therefore, the five ways are taken together, it is the existence of a personal supreme being which is affirmed. It can also be pointed out that, once given Aquinas' analysis of motion or change and of efficient causality, the first unmoved mover and first efficient cause must transcend the level of empirical causes precisely because it is unmoved, uncaused and independent. And it is true to say that 'all men' call this being 'God', in the sense that all who acknowledge the existence of a transcendent, supreme and uncaused cause do in fact recognize this being as divine. At the same time Aquinas is well aware that the notion of a first cause or of a first unmoved mover or of an absolutely necessary being is not, taken by itself, all that is generally meant by the word 'God'. And he proceeds in the following sections of the *Summa theologica* to argue that this being must possess certain attributes. If therefore we are looking for Aquinas' establishment of theism, we have to take his five ways in conjunction with the succeeding sections on the divine attributes.

*

In the five ways Aquinas argued *a posteriori*, that is, from the things which fall within the sphere of our natural experience to the being on which they depend. But when he comes to discuss the attributes of this being, he has to proceed in a largely *a priori* manner, asking what attributes the first unmoved mover, first efficient cause, absolutely necessary and supremely perfect being must possess. For we obviously cannot describe God in the same way in which we can describe a visible object like a tree or an animal: we have no direct vision or intuition of God. And the fact that we have no direct vision or intuition of God means that our approach to the divine nature must be largely negative in character. 'The existence of a thing having been ascertained, the way in which it exists remains to be examined if we would know its nature. Because we cannot know what God is, but rather what God is not, our method has to be mainly negative. . . . What kind of being God is not can be known by eliminating characteristics which cannot apply to Him, like composition, change, and so forth' (*S.T.*, Ia, ʒ, prologue). Aquinas argues, for example, that God cannot be a corporeal or material being. Every material thing is capable of change, of reduction from potentiality to act: it is capable of 'motion'. But God, as the unmoved mover, cannot undergo any such transition from potentiality to act: He is necessarily all that He can be. Therefore God cannot be material.

Here we have the application of the so-called 'negative way', the approach to the nature of God by successively denying of Him certain characteristics either of all or of some finite things: God is neither this nor that. This negative way was by no means Aquinas' invention: it had a long history behind it. It was present in the Platonic tradition. If we look, for example, at the celebrated description of absolute Beauty in Plato's *Symposium* we find it described as 'unproduced, indestructible, subject neither to increase nor decay, . . . not at one time beautiful and at another time not beautiful', and so on. And this way of speaking about God was present in Christian philosophy from a very early date, being explicitly insisted on by the Pseudo-Dionysius, who wrote at the end of the fifth century A.D. and whose writings exercised a profound influence on medieval thinkers. It is summed up in the famous saying of Aquinas that we know of God rather what He is not than what He is. By successively denying of God certain characteristics we increase in a sense our knowledge of the divine nature : we know, for example, that God is neither material nor composite. But we cannot, of course, obtain any adequate positive insight into the divine nature through the application of this method.

A point to be noticed is that the application of this method can result in predicating of God attributes which are expressed by apparently positive words. In the case of a word like 'immutable' it is obvious that it is equivalent to not-mutable. Similarly, 'infinite' is equivalent to 'not-finite'. But this negation-aspect is not immediately obvious in the case of words like 'simple' and 'eternal', though analysis shows that they signify 'not-composite' and 'not subject to temporal succession'. Aquinas was careful about his analysis of terms. He points out, for instance, that the word 'infinite' can be used in two senses. It can be used 'first in a privative sense; and a thing is called infinite in this sense when it should naturally have limits but lacks them; and this applies only to quantities. In another sense a thing is called infinite negatively, that is, when it has (absolutely) no limit. If infinitude is understood in the first sense, it cannot belong to God . . . but infinitude in the second and negative sense does belong to God . . .' (*De potentia*, 1, 2). But when Aquinas insists on the negative aspects of some of the words predicated of God, he does not mean to imply that nothing positive corresponds to the word or is connoted by it. The divine simplicity, for example, or the divine infinitude is not a negation. But we can approach the positive reality, so to speak, only by way of negation. The things of which we have experience are composite and finite and temporal, and our concepts of absolute simplicity, infinity and eternity are arrived at by a process of negation. 'Just as we have come to knowledge of simple things through composite things, so we have to approach the knowledge of eternity through time' (*S.T.*, Ia, 10, 1). That there is a positive reality denoted by the word 'simplicity' is known to us by reflection on the attributes which must be possessed by the divine being, the existence of which has been proved. But a positive and adequate knowledge of that reality remains an unattainable ideal, so far as our natural knowledge is concerned. For psychological reasons, that is, because of the empirical basis of our concepts, we can know it only to the extent permitted by the use of the way of negation.[1]

Aquinas points out (S.T., Ia, 13, 2) that when we predicate of God negative terms like 'immutable' or 'incorporeal' we remove, as it were, something from God, mutability or corporeity; that is, we deny the applicability to God of terms like 'mutable' or 'corporeal'. We are concerned primarily with denying something of God rather than with affirming something positively of the divine substance. But there are other terms, like 'wise' and 'good', which are predicated of God positively and affirmatively; and it is in regard to the meaning of these terms that a special difficulty arises. Exclusive adherence to the negative way would lead to agnosticism about the divine nature; for a mere addition of negations would not result in positive knowledge. On the other hand, the use of the affirmative way, that is, affirming of God positive predicates, gives rise to a difficult problem. Some terms are predicated of God only metaphorically, as when God is called a 'rock'. But we are not concerned now with metaphor. When it is said that God is 'wise' or 'good', the terms are not used merely metaphorically: it is said that God is 'really', and not merely metaphorically, wise and good. But at once we seem to be faced with a dilemma. If we mean that God is wise in precisely the same sense that a human being is or can be wise, we make God a kind of superman, and we are involved in anthropomorphism. If on

1. If we are going to say that 'infinite' and 'simple' are negative terms, this statement must be understood in the light of the particular context. For example, every object of natural experience is, according to Aquinas, composite, at least metaphysically. Composition is then denied of God, who is said to be 'simple'. But as God is not an object of natural experience we conceive the divine simplicity as absence of composition. And in this sense the term 'simple' is, in the context, a 'negative' term. At the same time it connotes a positive reality, and looked at from this point of view it is a positive term.

the other hand the term is used purely equivocally, if, that is, its meaning when predicated of God is entirely different from its meaning when predicated of a human being, it would have no significance for us in the first context. The reason of this is clear. 'Terms signify God to the extent that our intellect knows Him. And since our intellect knows God from creatures it knows Him to the extent that creatures represent Him' (S.T., Ia, 13, 2). If, then, we take a term, the primary meaning of which is determined by the content of our experience, and apply it in an entirely different sense to a being which transcends our experience, its meaning is evacuated, without any other meaning being substituted. And Aquinas points out that the difficulty cannot be evaded by saying that a statement like 'God is wise' means simply that God is the cause of wisdom. For if this were the meaning of affirmative statements about the divine nature 'it would be impossible to explain why certain terms, and not others, are predicated of God. For He is the cause of bodies, just as He is the cause of goods' (S.T., Ia, 13, 2). If God is called 'good' because He is the cause of goodness, He might with equal reason be called a body, since He is the ultimate cause of bodies.

Aquinas' answer to the problem is that when terms like 'wise' or 'good' are predicated of God they are predicated neither univocally nor equivocally but in an analogical sense. Some terms denote characteristics or modes of being or 'perfections' which can be found only in finite things. Nothing, for example, which is not finite and material can be a stone. And terms of this sort can be predicated of God only metaphorically. But 'pure perfections', like goodness, which are not inextricably bound up, as it were, with a particular level of being, can be predicated of God; and it is these terms which are predicated in an analogical sense. This is possible because creatures have a real relation to God; they depend on God and derive their perfections from Him. In the case of 'pure perfections', like goodness or wisdom, these pre-exist in God in a super-eminent and infinite degree. It is not merely that God causes these perfections in creatures: the perfections really exist in God and can be properly predicated of Him, though in an analogical sense. To say that certain terms are predicated analogically of God does not mean, of course, that we have an adequate positive idea of what is objectively signified by the term when it is predicated of God. Our knowledge of perfections is derived from creatures, and this origin necessarily colours our concepts of those perfections. We necessarily think and speak of God in terms which, from the linguistic point of view, refer primarily to creatures, and we can only approximate towards, while never reaching, an adequate understanding of what is meant by saying that God is 'wise' or 'good' or 'intelligent' or 'living'. Aquinas therefore distinguishes between what he calls the perfection signified by a term and the mode of signification. 'In the terms which we predicate of God there are two things to consider, namely, the actual perfections signified, like goodness, life and so forth, and the mode of signification. As regards the former, these belong properly to God, indeed more properly than to creatures; and the terms are predicated primarily of God. But as regards the mode of signification, they are not properly predicated of God. For they have a mode of signification which belongs to creatures' (S.T., Ia, 13, 3). From the psychological and linguistic point of view a word like 'intelligence' denotes primarily human intelligence, the intelligence of which we have experience. When it is predicated of God, it is affirmed that there is in God a perfection to which human intelligence is at the same time like and unlike; and inasmuch as this perfection in God is the supreme origin and standard of all created intelligence the word is predicated primarily of God, from a metaphysical point of view. But it does not follow that we can give any adequate positive account of what this perfection actually is in God. We can only attempt to purify our creaturely concept of intelligence, and this means combining the negative with the affirmative way. 'The manner of super-eminence (or super-excellence) in which the aforesaid perfections are found in God cannot be signified by the names which we impose unless (they are qualified) by a negation, as when we say that God is eternal or infinite, or by a relation, as when we say that God is first cause or supreme good. For we cannot understand of God what He is: but (we understand of Him) what He is not and how other things are related to Him' (*S.G.*, 1, 30).

In Aquinas' account of our natural knowledge of the divine nature there is, then, a certain agnosticism. When we say that God is wise we affirm of God a positive attribute; but we are not able to give any adequate description of what is objectively signified by the term when it is predicated of God. If we are asked what we mean when we say that God is wise, we may answer that we mean that God possesses wisdom in an infinitely higher degree than human beings. But we cannot provide any adequate description of the content, so to speak, of this infinitely higher degree; we can only approximate towards it by employing the way of negation. What is affirmed is positive, but the positive content of the concept in our minds is determined by our experience of creaturely wisdom, and we can only attempt to purify it or correct its inadequacies by means of negations. Obviously enough, this process will never lead to an adequate positive understanding of the objective meaning of (that is, of what is objectively signified by) the terms predicated of God. But Aquinas never claimed that it would. On the contrary, he did not hesitate to draw the logical conclusion. 'The first cause surpasses human understanding and speech. He knows God best who acknowledges that whatever he thinks and says falls short of what God really is' (*In librum De Causis, lectio* 6). Aquinas would have been quite unmoved by the accusation that he could not give the exact significance of the terms predicated of God; for he never pretended to be able to give it.

Now, it is clear that predicating intelligence of God is not exactly like predicating intelligence of a dog. If I call a dog 'intelligent', I use the word analogically; but if I am asked what I mean by it I can point to some of the dog's activities. Human beings and their intelligent activities, dogs and their activities, all the terms of the analogy fall within the range of experience. But we cannot observe God or point to God. The question therefore arises whether there is any objective justification for predicating certain terms of God rather than other terms. Or the question can be put in this way. Although no sensible man would demand an adequate account of the positive meaning of the word 'intelligent' as used of God, how do we know that the word denotes a reality when it is predicated of God? Aquinas would answer that the possession of certain attributes and not of others can be deduced by means of reflection on the nature of the first unmoved mover, first cause and necessary being. In other words, descriptive statements about the divine nature are not made arbitrarily; they are made for certain reasons. If, for example, God has created intellectual beings, we cannot suppose that He is Himself less than intelligent. Moreover, the ultimate cause and necessary being cannot be corporeal, and an incorporeal being is an intelligent being. We can know therefore that that which is signified by a term predicated analogically of God exists in Him, even though we cannot understand adequately what it is. The objective foundation of analogical predication in natural theology is the dependence of creatures on God as their efficient and exemplary cause. And unless we had some positive knowledge of God we should not be able even to deny of Him any characteristic. 'Unless the human intellect knew something positively about God, it could not deny anything of Him' (De potentia, 7, 5). Talk about analogy in natural theology would be pointless unless there were good reasons for affirming the existence of God.

It may be said, of course, that there is in fact some resemblance between the case of calling a dog 'intelligent' and that of calling God 'intelligent'. For though I cannot point to God acting in the same way that I point to the dog acting, I can draw attention to effects of God's activity which fall within the field of our experience. Does not Aquinas himself do this in his fifth proof of God's existence? And does he not make it clear that in his opinion the objective ontological foundation for predicating terms analogically of God is the creature's participation in or reflection of the divine perfections? 'And thus whatever is predicated of God and creatures is predicated in virtue of the latter's relation to God as principle and cause in which all the perfections of things pre-exist in a more excellent manner' (*S.T.*, Ia, 13, 5). Can I not therefore by pointing to the perfections of creatures indicate the meaning of the terms which I predicate of God?

This is true. But the meaning which I indicate in this way is, as Aquinas was well aware, the meaning which the term has for me in my own mind, and it by no means follows that this is adequate to the objective reality connoted by the term when predicated of God. This can be shown by an example. Suppose that my one and only reason for calling God 'intelligent' is that I consider that there is an intelligible world-system and that this is the creation of a transcendent being whom I name 'God'. In this case when I think of God as intelligent I think of Him as the sort of being capable of creating this world-system. And if I am asked to explain what I mean by calling God 'intelligent', I mention the world-system. But it does not follow that I can give an adequate positive explanation of what the divine intelligence is in itself. The divine intelligence is identical with the divine being, and God transcends all His effects. There must, of course, be some control of analogical predication in the context. That is to say, if analogical predication about God is not to be wild talk, there must be some assignable reason for using one term rather than another. And these reasons will colour the meaning of the terms in my mind. But the explanation of the meaning of the terms which I can give is not adequate, and cannot be adequate, to the objective reality connoted by the terms. As Aquinas saw clearly, a certain measure of 'agnosticism' is inevitable. It could be avoided only by relapsing into anthropomorphism on the one hand or on the other by holding that all statements about God are so many myths which may have some useful function, perhaps as a stimulus to moral conduct and certain affective attitudes, but which are not put forward as being true. And Aquinas was not prepared to accept either an anthropomorphic view of God or an interpretation of theological propositions as so many myths.

Aquinas' 'agnosticism', then, is not agnosticism in the modern sense. He has no doubt about the existence of God, and he is far from saying that we can know nothing about the divine nature or that we can make only negative statements about it. At the same time he is acutely conscious of the empirical foundation of all human knowledge and of the consequences of this in natural theology. We cannot help thinking and speaking of God in terms which, linguistically speaking, refer primarily to the finite objects of our experience, and we move always within the sphere of analogy. This means that our knowledge of God is necessarily imperfect and inadequate. We can indeed try to correct the anthropomorphic conceptions which come naturally to us. For example, though we cannot help speaking as though God 'foresees' future events, we can correct the erroneous conception implied by such language by reflecting that God transcends time and that the future is not future to Him.[1] But this does not mean that we can attain any adequate positive understanding of the divine intellect and knowledge.

The idea may occur to the reader that in all this talk about the divine attributes Aquinas is the victim of the structure of our language. For it may appear at first sight as though Aquinas argues from our way of talking about God to the presence in Him of distinct attributes. But as a matter of fact Aquinas is careful to distinguish between linguistic forms and the reality referred to by those forms or modes of speech. We say, for example, that God is merciful and that God is just, and if we went simply by these propositions considered in themselves we might be led to think that

1. If God literally foresees events which are future to us, He is involved in temporal succession. And Aquinas was convinced that involvement in temporal succession is incompatible with the divine nature, which is infinite and immutable.

there is something in the divine nature which is called 'mercy' and something else which is called 'justice', the two attributes being objectively distinct. But in the infinite being there cannot be really distinct attributes. The divine justice and the divine mercy are ontologically identical. 'All divine perfections are in reality identical' (*Compendium theologiae*, 22); they·are identical with one another and with the divine nature. The divine nature, however, can be known by us only piecemeal, as it were. Our ideas are derived from creatures, and we conceive God under different aspects according to His different representations in finite things. We naturally introduce distinctions where there are no real distinctions. The infinity of the divine perfection, which cannot be comprehended by our minds, forces us to do this. For the infinite richness of the divine nature cannot be apprehended by us in one concept. As our concepts are based on experience of creatures and connote the different attributes of creatures, the terms predicated of God are not for us synonymous; they do not all mean the same thing if we are talking about the meaning which they have for our minds and which we can state. Ontologically, however, they all refer to the same being, in which there is no real distinction of attributes. If in predicating different attributes of God we really thought that these attributes were distinct modifications of the divine substance, we should think what is false. But if we enunciate different descriptive propositions about God while at the same time we realize the lack of proportion between our (inevitable) way of speaking and the reality spoken of, we do not affirm what is false. 'Although the names attributed to God signify one thing, they signify it under many different aspects, and they are not synonymous' (*S.T.*, Ia, 13, 4). 'But although our intellect conceives God under different concepts, it knows that to all its concepts there corresponds one and the same simple being' (*S.T.*, Ia, 13, 12).

According to Aquinas the most appropriate name for God is the name disclosed to Moses (*Exodus*, 3, 19), *Qui est*, He Who is. 'First, it does not signify any form, but being itself

... secondly, on account of its universality.... For it names the infinite ocean of substance.... Thirdly, because of its connotation. For it signifies being entirely present. And this is most properly affirmed of God, whose being knows neither past nor future' (*S.T.*, Ia, 13, 11). God does not receive His existence: there is in Him no distinction between essence and existence. He is infinite existence or being itself. We cannot form any clear concept of what this is; for we inevitably distinguish between essence and existence, between what a thing is and the fact that it exists. But the total absence of this distinction in God means that the most appropriate name for Him is a name taken from being considered as existence. The very uttering of the name which is not and cannot be clear to us reminds us of the divine mystery and of the divine transcendence beyond all finite things, each of which is shot through, as it were, by existential dependence.

*

If one speaks of the existential dependence of finite things on God, one means, of course, that they depend for their existence on God. They stand to God in the relation of creature to creator. But the meaning of terms like 'create' and 'creation' is not self-evident. That God created the world was the orthodox Judaeo-Christian belief; but as theologian and philosopher combined Aquinas was concerned to analyse what this means, so far as the human mind is capable of analysing its meaning.

In the first place, to say that the world was created by God means that it was made 'out of nothing'. But the meaning of this phrase is itself ambiguous, as Aquinas points out (*S.T.*, Ia, 45, 1, *ad* 3; *De potentia*, 3, 1, *ad* 7). If we say of something that it was created out of nothing, we might mean that it was not created at all, the negation implied in the word 'nothing' covering, as it were, the verb in the proposition. 'And in this sense we can say of God that He is made from nothing, because He is not made at all; though this way of speaking is not customary' (*De potentia, loc. cit.*). But this is obviously not what is meant when it is said that the world was created out of nothing; for we intend to affirm creation or making, and not to deny it. However, an ambiguity still remains. For we can speak of a statue being made from or out of marble; and someone might suppose that to speak of the world being created out of nothing is to say that the world was made out of nothing as out of a kind of pre-existent material. But this is not the meaning of the phrase. The true meaning of 'out of nothing' is 'not out of anything'. Creation in the sense here intended is not any kind of transmutation, implying a pre-existent material. We can, indeed, speak of a 'creative' artist; but creation in this context implies a pre-existing material and has not got the same meaning as it bears in the proposition affirming the creation of the world by God.

In the second place, it is important to realize that Aquinas' conception of creation is not deistic. If he speaks of God having created the world, he does not mean that God brought the world into existence and that it thereafter exists independently. Every finite thing depends existentially on God at every moment of its existence, and if the divine conserving or sustaining activity were withdrawn, it would at once cease to exist. Making his own some statements of St Augustine he remarks (S.G., 3, 65) that it is not as though God were like someone who builds a house and can then go away and attend to something else, leaving the house standing. Finite things have a constant relation of existential dependence on the creator.

Thirdly, that things depend on God can be shown by philosophic reasoning, according to Aquinas. The metaphysician can show that the relation of finite things to God is that of creature to creator. And we are accustomed to say that the world 'was created' by God, using a manner of speaking which implies that there is an ideally first assignable moment of time. Now, Aquinas believed that this is in fact the case, namely that the world had a beginning; but he did not think that the fact that it had a beginning is known with certainty from any other source than revelation. On his view, as we have already seen elsewhere, no philosopher had ever succeeded in proving that the world must have had a beginning, in the sense that there was an ideally first assignable moment of time. 'That the world did not always exist is known only by faith, and it cannot be proved demonstratively. It can be demonstrated neither from the side of the world (i.e. by analysis of the concept of 'world') . . . nor from the side of an active cause acting voluntarily (i.e. by analysis of the idea of creation)' (S.T., Ia, 46, 2). As God exists eternally, He could, so far as we can see, have created the world from eternity, and no argument based on the supposed impossibility of an infinite series of successive events has shown that God could not have acted in this way. Whereas some of his contemporaries, notably St Bonaventure, thought that the notion of creation from eternity was self-contradictory, Aquinas considered that the idea of creation is independent of the idea of a temporal beginning. 'It belongs to the idea of eternity to have no beginning of duration; but it does not belong to the idea of creation to have a beginning of duration, but only a principle of origin – unless we understand "creation" as it is understood by faith' (De potentia, 3, 14, 8, ad 8). Again, 'there is no contradiction in affirming that a thing was created and also that it was never non-existent' (De aeternitate mundi contra murmurantes).

In the first quotation cited in the last paragraph mention is made of an 'active cause acting voluntarily'. Plotinus and the Neo-platonists had depicted the world as proceeding by stages from the One as the result of a necessary overflowing or self-diffusion of the divine goodness. But though Aquinas held that God's purpose in creating was 'solely to communicate His perfection, which is His goodness' (S.T., Ia, 44, 4), he maintained that the world did not proceed or emanate from God of necessity. God created for a purpose, and that the world exists at all and that this particular world exists is the result of divine choice.

This insistence that the world was not the result of a necessity in God to create leads Aquinas into very deep waters. Given the conception of God as simple and unchangeable, the creative act, as existing in God, must be identical with the divine nature or substance. And this could not be otherwise than it is. Aquinas explicitly recognizes that the creative act, as it is in God, is identical with the necessary and immutable divine nature (cf. *De potentia*, 3, 15, *ad* 8, 18 and *ad* 20). But he argues that it does not follow that the world proceeded necessarily from God. And this holds good even on the hypothesis that the world existed from eternity. If the world had been created from eternity, it would have been freely created from eternity. In actual fact, however, it was not created from eternity. We have to say, therefore, that though the creative act, as it exists in God, is eternal and identical with the divine nature, the external effect of that act, namely the world, is not eternal but that it came into existence in such a way that there is an ideally first moment of time. God eternally willed that out of all possible worlds this particular world should begin to exist in such a way that the temporal order is what it is.

Obviously, we are here in the region of mystery; in the region of contradiction, some would say. On the one hand Aquinas was convinced that as a personal and perfectly self-luminous being God must have chosen intelligently out of the infinite realm of possibility the finite things which He has created. He was not compelled by His nature either to create or to create this or that possible world. On the other hand Aquinas was also convinced that the creative act, as it exists in God, is identical with the divine nature which is essentially immutable. Again, he was also convinced on the one hand that the creative act, as it is in God, is necessarily eternal and on the other hand that the external effect of this act is not eternal. The truth of this last point has not been proved by philosophers, but they have not proved the contrary; and we know the truth from theology. He therefore considered that we must assert all these propositions, and he believed that they are not incompatible. At the same time we reach a point in our analysis of creation where we are forced to admit that a full understanding of God's creative activity exceeds the competence of the human reason. And if we are left with mystery, this is nothing to be surprised at in such a connexion. After all, experience provides us only with analogies of creative activity in the proper sense. It is not the business of the Christian thinker to eliminate all mystery but rather to point out where the mystery lies.[1]

It is, however, easy to understand the possible comment that the root of the whole trouble lies in Aquinas' attempt to reconcile the demands of theological orthodoxy with the demands of the philosophic reason. He was determined, it may be said, to preserve the Judaeo-Christian belief that God is distinct from the created world. And this itself involves him in an antinomy. For if God is infinite, He cannot be distinct from creatures, there can be nothing 'outside' Him; and if creatures are distinct from Him, God cannot be infinite. Moreover, if God and finite things are distinct, the relation between them must be one of creator to creatures, and if creation is free Aquinas is at once involved in another antinomy: the creative act is eternal and identical with the divine nature which is necessary, whereas the world is not eternal and, whether eternal or not, does not proceed from God by a necessity of nature. Would not Aquinas have solved his problems more satisfactorily if he had adopted some form of pantheism? If he had made creatures internal to God, as modifications of the divine substance, he would not have had to say that there can be something ontologically distinct from the infinite and he would have avoided the difficulties involved in the notion of free creation.

One cannot, of course, expect from Aquinas a discussion of Spinoza's philosophy. At the same time he says enough to indicate the line of answer he would give to the sort of

1. Obviously, if the word 'contradiction' is substituted for the word 'mystery', this statement is not true. For the Christian thinker is committed to showing that the propositions which he asserts do not contradict one another. But though Aquinas considered, very reasonably, that we cannot fully understand a creative activity which transcends our experience, he did not think that one is involved in a contradiction by asserting that God freely chose from eternity to create a world such that there would be a beginning of time.

criticism just mentioned. For example, when talking about the monism of Parmenides (*In Metaph.*, I, c. 5, *lectio* 9), he says that the latter's mistake lay in treating the term 'being' as though it had one meaning and drawing the conclusion that apart from one single reality nothing can exist. For Aquinas there are different levels of being or different kinds of beings, which do not belong to one genus and cannot be added together. To speak as though the infinite being, God, and finite beings can be added together to make more than infinite being, with the result that one ends in self-contradiction, is to speak as though God and creatures were members of a genus. In reality they are incommensurable.[1] As for the idea of finite things being internal modifications of the divine nature, this idea would obviously be entirely incompatible with Aquinas' conviction concerning the divine simplicity. Further, we can apply in this connexion what he says about Averroes' hypothesis of one intellect in all men. Were there, he says, only one intellect in all men, it would be quite impossible to explain the diversity of our intellectual lives and activities (*S.T.*, Ia, 76, 2). Similarly, he would doubtless argue, on the hypothesis that all human minds are internal modifications of the divine mind it is impossible to explain the difference between the ideas and convictions of different men. If these differences are not explained away as illusion, there can even be contradictions in God. If they are described as illusion, how does illusion arise in God? Pantheism does nothing to diminish the difficulties which may be thought to accompany theism. It involves one in denying or in explaining away or in falsifying the foundation from which all our metaphysical reflections must start, namely the real multiplicity of distinct finite things with which we are acquainted in experience.

*

1. I mention this point because it has sometimes been asserted against theism and in favour of pantheism that if God is infinite, there can be no things really distinct from Him. If there were, it would be possible to 'add to' the absolutely infinite being. And to say that this is possible involves one in a contradiction.

In treating of the divine creative activity Aquinas speaks of God as creating in accordance with the divine ideas and of things as reflecting or expressing the divine ideas. And in doing so he retains a traditional mode of speaking with a long history behind it. The Middle Platonists and Neo-Platonists had placed the Platonic 'ideas' in the divine mind, and St Augustine took over this way of speaking, though he did not, like the Neo-platonists, make the divine mind a being subordinate to the supreme deity. Aquinas adopted the same mode of expression, though he realized very well that talk about divine ideas is apt to be misleading and set himself, therefore, to analyse what is meant by the proposition that there are ideas in God. On the one hand, the term 'idea' can be taken to mean a modification of the mind. And if the term is taken in this sense, the proposition that there are ideas in God is false. On the other hand, God eternally knows the divine perfection as imitable externally by a plurality of creatures. And we are therefore justified in talking about ideas in God if we mean that He knows His own perfections, His own essence, as the exemplar of many possible things. 'The term *idea* does not signify the divine essence as such but in so far as it is the likeness or principle of this or that thing.... It is not contrary to the simplicity of the divine intellect to understand many things; but it would be contrary to its simplicity to be informed by a plurality of subjective determinations' (*S.T.*, Ia, 15, 2, *ad* 1 and *in corpore*).

This is an illustration of a not infrequent procedure on Aquinas' part. He takes over a traditional mode of speaking, which had been used somewhat loosely by his predecessors, and attempts to analyse the meaning which it must have in order to be compatible with what he regards as true and established philosophical principles. This is one reason, of course, why a considerable amount of his philosophy appears to concern terminology and questions of language. So indeed it does. For the matter of that, all philosophy is largely concerned in some sense with questions of language. But the questions in which Aquinas was interested are not always those which interest philosophers today. If one does not believe in God at all, one is unlikely to take much interest in the analysis of the proposition that there are ideas in God or that God creates in accordance with the divine ideas. And this is partly the reason why a considerable number of people may feel inclined to say that medieval philosophers were concerned with 'talk about words', this phrase being here intended in a pejorative sense. These critics may forget, however, that concern with language is not peculiar to medieval thinkers.

*

There is, however, one problem which inevitably arises for a theistic philosopher and which has always excited interest. And it can hardly be called a purely linguistic problem, though, like any other philosophical problem, it necessarily involves concern with language. For no problem can be profitably discussed without this concern. I refer to the problem of evil. This problem does not, it is true, arise in an atheistic philosophy in the form in which it presents itself to the theist. But the problem, even considered as a purely theoretical one, is not without interest even for atheists. For atheism has not infrequently been defended on the ground that the existence of evil prevents any clear-sighted and honest thinker from believing in a personal, good and infinite God, possessing the attributes of omniscience and omnipotence.

If we are going to discuss the problem of evil, Aquinas would insist, we must first decide what is meant by evil. And his own view was this; evil is not a positive thing, but a privation. In holding this view he followed the Pseudo-Dionysius, who had developed the Neo-platonic analysis of evil. But we need not concern ourselves here with the history of this theory: the important question is, what is meant by calling evil a privation. And it should be made clear from the start that by 'privation' Aquinas does not mean precisely the same as 'absence'. An illustration will show what this distinction signifies. Inability to see is not a privation in a stone. If a stone could see, it would simply not be what is meant by a stone. The perfection of being able to see is absent from the stone, in the sense that the latter does not possess it; but the stone cannot properly be said to be 'deprived' of the power of vision. In a human being, however, blindness is a privation: the blind man is deprived of a faculty which pertains to human nature. On the other hand, blindness is not a positive entity like a piece of cake or a drop of water. 'Evil denotes the absence of Good. But it is not every absence of good that is called *evil*. For absence of good can be understood either in a privative sense or in a purely negative sense. And absence of good in the latter sense is not evil. . . . Otherwise it would follow that a thing is evil if it lacks the good which belongs to something else. For instance, man would be evil because he lacks the swiftness of a wild goat or the strength of a lion. It is absence of good in the privative sense which is called evil. Thus privation of sight is called blindness' (*S.T.*, Ia, 5, 48, 3). And the same can be said of moral evil. It is a privation in the human free act of the relation which it ought to have to the moral law promulgated by reason or to the divine law.

It must at once be added, however, that when Aquinas calls evil a 'privation', he does not mean to assert that evil, either physical or moral, is an illusion or that it is not real. Blindness in a human being is a privation and not a positive entity; but it does not follow that it is unreal or an illusion. For it is a real privation. The analysis of evil as privation is not, therefore, an attempt to make out that there is no real evil in the world at all. The description of evil as privation does not diminish the evil in the world, and still less does it do away with it. For the matter of that, if we point out that darkness is not a positive entity like a rock, we do not thereby turn night into day.

But something further must be said about this analysis of evil. For the natural reaction of many people would be to say: 'What nonsense! A tumour on the brain is a physical evil. But it is certainly something positive. Cruelty is a moral evil. But it is certainly not a privation.' This reaction is perfectly understandable. But it must be remembered that Aquinas is looking for the formal essence or nature of evil. He does not wish to forbid us saying in ordinary speech that a tumour is a bad thing. But he asks in what this badness precisely consists. Does it consist in the tumour considered as a positive entity? In his opinion it does not. An excised tumour is no more an evil thing than the man's brain from which it was excised. The evil involved in a tumour on the brain consists essentially in the disorder which its presence introduces. And disorder is the privation of right order. To say this is not to say that the effects of having a tumour on the brain are not positive effects. If the presence of the tumour causes blindness, for example, the effect is positive; but blindness is a privation of the power of seeing which 'ought' to be there. If the tumour causes stumbling movements, the movements are positive effects; but the evil consists essentially, Aquinas might say, not in the movements as such but in the privation of the power to co-ordinate one's movements in the normal manner. As for cruelty, this is certainly something positive in the sense that it involves desires, feelings, and actions or words, or both. Aquinas does not mean to say that the action of shutting up Jews in the gas-chamber at Auschwitz concentration camp was a privation. To shut up Jews in a gas-chamber because they were Jews was certainly a positive action, and it was equally certainly a morally evil action. But to say this does not settle the question, in what precisely does the evil of this positive action consist? We may be inclined to reply that it consists precisely in putting Jews in a gas-chamber because they are Jews, and in nothing else. But Aquinas would comment that though it is undoubtedly true that to shut up Jews in a gas-chamber because they are Jews is morally wrong, to say that it is morally wrong is to say that the human act involved is contrary to the moral law; and lack of conformity in human actions, which should be conformed to the moral law, is a privation. And to say this in no way alters the fact that the action in question was something positive.

But, it may be said, even if Aquinas' analysis of evil as a privation is not quite so silly as it sounds at first hearing, how does it affect the problem of evil? For if, as has been admitted, the technical analysis of evil as privation does not deny or even diminish the reality of evil and the extent to which it is found in the world, it is difficult to see how it can be in any way relevant to the problem of evil. It seems to leave things precisely where they were.

The relevance of the analysis in Aquinas' eyes to the problem of evil can be shown in this way. If God created all things, and if evil is a thing, we should have to say that God created evil directly. And rather than say this we might be inclined to follow the Manichaeans in ascribing the creation of evil to an evil deity, thus asserting a metaphysical dualism. But if evil is a privation, it is not necessary to speak of it as having been created by God on the ground that God created all things. As a privation, evil can exist only in a being: it is 'incidental' or a 'by-product' (*De potentia*, 3, 6, *ad* 3). Aquinas does not mean that it is unimportant, but simply that there is no sense in talking about a privation which is not the privation of a perfection in a positive entity. The latter comes first, so to speak; before there can be any corruption or disorder there must be something to be corrupted or disordered. And according to Aquinas every being, considered as such, is good. If we consider a flea in relation to its unpleasant effects on us we can call it evil. But in itself, considered simply as a being, it is good. For every being is actual so far as it is being, and actuality involves perfection. And a perfection is 'desirable' either by the thing which possesses it or by something else. The flea has a tendency to its own self-preservation; and to this extent we can say that it 'desires' its own being. Being and good (when the word is used in this ontological sense) have the same denotation, though 'good' here signifies being considered in relation to will, desire, or natural inclination or tendency. If, therefore, every being is 'good', there is no need to postulate an evil deity as creator of evil; for evil is not and cannot be the direct term of creative activity. Nor, indeed, could there be an evil deity, if by this we mean a sheerly evil being. For sheer evil is an impossibility. Aquinas does not mean to deny the existence of Satan. But for him Satan is not an ultimate being at all, but a creature. Created good, he remains good, if considered simply as a being. He does not constitute an exception to the validity of a metaphysical analysis which allows of no exception. And if we once accept Aquinas' use of terms, it is obvious that no being can be completely evil. For this follows from the use of the terms.

But if metaphysical dualism of the type mentioned is excluded, it may appear that the problem of evil is rendered all the more acute. For is not the responsibility thrown back entirely on God? Even if God cannot be said to have directly created evil, He 'foresaw' it and, if He is omnipotent, He could prevent it. Must we not say, therefore, that God is ultimately responsible for evil?

Let us take physical evil first. Aquinas certainly maintains that God did not will physical evils for their own sake; but he points out that God undoubtedly willed the creation of a universe in which physical evil was in some way involved, as far as the natural order of events is concerned.[1] For example, to create sensitive beings means creating beings capable of feeling pain. Capacity for experiencing pleasure cannot naturally be separated from the capacity for experiencing pain. At the very least, therefore, God permitted the occurrence of physical evils. But Aquinas talks as though God willed certain evils for the sake of the perfection of the whole universe. For instance, he speaks as though the perfection of the whole universe requires the existence of mortal beings, subject to death, as well as of beings which cannot undergo bodily death, namely the angels. This

1. It is necessary to add this qualification, since Aquinas believed that under certain conditions (if there had been no Fall) the physical evils consequent on the Fall of man would not have occurred. But this theme belongs to dogmatic theology, not to philosophy. And in any case it is clear that God 'foresaw' what the world would in fact be like.

applies, however, only to those physical evils which, given the natural order, are inevitable, and not to those which owe their origin to human stupidity or to human wickedness. This picture of God as a kind of artist and of the universe as a work of art, requiring shadows as well as lights, is apt, in spite of its traditional character, to appear disconcerting and unhelpful to many minds. It certainly is not an anthropocentric view of the matter.

As for moral evil, this was in no sense positively willed by God. It was, however, permitted by Him for the sake of a good, namely that man might be free, participating in his own limited degree in the divine freedom and capacity for creative activity. It may appear at first sight that if God can be said to will certain physical evils, like death, not for their own sake but for the sake of the perfection of the universe, He should also be said to will moral evil that moral good might shine more brightly in contrast. But there is an obvious difference. There is nothing morally disreputable about bodily death. It is a natural phenomenon, which in the natural order of events is inevitably associated with animal and human existence. And when Aquinas says that God willed death for the sake of the perfection of the universe, though not for its own sake, he means that God willed the creation of animals and men for the sake of the perfection of the universe, animals and men being naturally mortal creatures. But moral evil is not an inevitable accompaniment of the development of human nature; nor is it necessary that the exercise of freedom should involve actual morally evil choices. Nor could God positively will that human beings should act immorally. But without supernatural intervention on God's part man's power to act morally involves in this life the power to choose immorally. And so God, in creating man, must be said to have permitted moral evil, though He did not will that man should choose to act immorally and though in fact He gives man the means of choosing rightly.

The comment may be made that these considerations do not solve the problem of evil. The question is not whether

God permitted evil, since it is obvious that He must have done so if He created the world, but rather how, if He is good, He could create a world which would involve the presence of so much evil. Quite apart from those physical evils which are inevitable in the natural course of events, moral evil and all those physical evils which are due to human stupidity and wickedness were foreseen and permitted by God. And the question is how He could permit this if He is both good and omnipotent. It may be said that nobody can suggest a detailed picture of affairs in which evil would be absent. And this may be so. But it does not alter the fact that, according to Aquinas, God freely chose to create a world in which He foresaw as present all those evils which are in fact present.

To this question, why God chose this world, foreseeing all the evils which would in fact occur, no answer, I think, can be given. That is to say, no answer can be given which would be accepted by an objicient as a 'solution' to the problem of evil. St Bonaventure remarked that if anyone asks why God did not make a better world or make this world better, no answer can be given except that He so willed and that He Himself knows the reason. And I do not see that Aquinas could say much more than this. Christian theological dogmas are doubtless relevant in some way to the problem of evil, but they do not constitute a theoretical solution of it. The doctrine of the redemption, for example, throws light on the way in which suffering can be made of value by the sufferer, but it does not solve the metaphysical 'problem of evil'.

It is important, however, to bear in mind the following points. First, it is not the case that Aquinas was blind to the problem of evil. Though he certainly adopts a less anthropocentric attitude towards suffering and death than many would be inclined to adopt, he remarks, for example, in the prologue to his commentary on the Book of Job that nothing is more difficult to reconcile with divine providence than the sufferings of the innocent. At the same time he was convinced that the metaphysician can prove the existence of God independently of the problem of evil, and that we therefore know that there is a solution to the problem even though we cannot provide it. And this, of course, is one of the ways in which he differs from the modern agnostic who is inclined to start with the problem in mind rather than to regard evil as something which has to be reconciled, so far as this is possible, with an already established truth. In conclusion it may be worth while pointing out that to say that God permitted evil for the sake of a greater good, which is to a great extent veiled from us, is not to say that human beings should do nothing towards diminishing the amount of evil in the world. We have to distinguish between the practical problem of alleviating suffering and diminishing its extent and the theoretical problem of evil which arises in a metaphysical or theological context. There is no reason for depicting Aquinas as suggesting that human beings should adopt a purely passive attitude towards evil. It is obvious that he held nothing of the kind with regard to moral evil. Nor did he make any such suggestion with regard to physical evil. He would say, of course, that though God foresaw and permitted evil, He also foresaw, and indeed willed, man's efforts to diminish its extent.

CHAPTER FOUR

Man (1): Body and Soul

THERE are two possible extreme views of the psycho-physical constitution of man. On the one hand it may be held that the 'real' man is the soul, or even simply the mind, which inhabits the body, the latter being regarded at best as an instrument of the soul and at worst as the soul's prison-house or mortal tomb. This view appears to have found expression in the so-called exoteric writings of Aristotle, of which only fragments have come down to us and which have been attributed by Werner Jaeger and other scholars to an early period in Aristotle's life when he was still strongly under the influence of Plato. Certain critics have maintained that there is no sufficient evidence for attributing these 'exoteric writings' to a youthful and transitory phase in the philosopher's intellectual development; but it would be out of place to embark on this controversial question here. It is sufficient to point out that in writings published at some period during his lifetime Aristotle expounded an even sharper dualism than that which had been taught by Plato. Plotinus too, the Neoplatonist, placed all the emphasis on the human soul. As he believed, like Plato, in the soul's, or at least in the mind's, pre-existence and in reincarnation, the logical consequence of his position was that the soul can be united successively with different bodies and that it is therefore an independent thing or substance in its own right. The same view is, of course, implied by those eastern philosophies and religions which maintain the doctrine of reincarnation. In Christian thought the idea of the soul's pre-existence does not appear, except in the case of a few early thinkers like Origen who had been much influenced by Neo-platonism. But a quasi-Platonic view of the relation between soul and body is implied, for example, by St Augustine's description of man as 'a rational soul using a mortal and earthly body' (*De moribus eccl.*, 1, 27, 52) or as 'a certain substance participating in reason and fitted for ruling a body' (*De quantitate animae*, 13, 21). And a similar view of the relation of soul to body finds popular expression in a great deal of Christian ascetic literature. In post-Renaissance philosophy this dualism appears in the philosophy of Descartes, as customarily interpreted at least.

On the other hand attempts have been made to do away with this dualism, notably by a reduction in some sense of the soul to the body. In Greek philosophy we find, for example, the view of the atomists, followed by the Epicureans, that the soul, like the body, is composed of atoms, even if of somewhat 'superior' atoms. In later thought the monistic account of the relation of soul to body ranges from the materialism expressed by some of the writers of the Enlightenment, particularly by some French writers, to the much more sophisticated epiphenomenalism of more recent times. The epiphenomenalists do not deny the reality of mind, nor do they describe psychic activities as material processes in any ordinary sense: they maintain rather that when the organism has reached a certain stage of development mind supervenes. And though they may regard thinking, for example, as in some sense a function of material processes they do not state that it is nothing but a material process. However, mind, even though a reality, depends in such a way on the body that there is no question of its existing apart from the body.

One may note that neither extreme view is put forward without some empirical grounds which appear to support it. Plato, for example, argued that the soul cannot be a mere 'harmony' of the body, on the ground that it can rule the body. And he and other philosophers have argued that the mind's activities transcend the capacities of matter. Self-consciousness, too, which enables us to distinguish between 'me' and 'my body' has been invoked as evidence in favour of dualism. On the other hand the dependence of psychic activities on the body is also an evident fact. Not only do

we depend on sense-perception for the acquirement of knowledge, but a certain correlation can also be traced between
psychic processes and physical conditions, as in the case, for
example, of memory. Physical disturbances can produce
psychic disorders, and some psychic disorders at least can be
ameliorated by physical treatment or operation. One can
say in general that those philosophers who have concentrated their attention on the higher psychic activities and on
man's religious and moral like have inclined to some form of
dualism, while those who have paid special attention to the
dependence of psychic processes on physical conditions
have inclined to a monistic interpretation of the relation of
soul to body. Both extreme dualism and outspoken monism
may go beyond the empirical data; but there is certainly
something to be said in favour of either position.

This suggests that the truth is to be found in a middle
position, in doing justice to all the empirical data and in
avoiding a one-sided concentration on this set of data to the
exclusion of that. And in point of fact we find Aquinas pro-
posing such a middle position. He will not allow that the
soul is an independent complete substance which could just
as well inhabit this body as that, and he speaks of the soul
in Aristotelian terminology as the 'form' (Aristotle's *entele-
cheia*) of the body. On the other hand he maintains that the
soul does not depend on the body for its existence and that
it survives the death of the body. We may therefore be
tempted to say that Aquinas' middle position amounts to an
attempt to combine the Aristotelian psychology with the
demands of Christian theology. But though there is truth
in this statement it stands in need of qualification. For in
utilizing Aristotelianism Aquinas at the same time developed
it, and his theory of the soul is not exactly the same as the
theory expounded in Aristotle's *De anima*. In his endeavour
to show that Aristotelianism was not irreconcilable with
Christianity, or at least that Aristotle's principles did not
necessarily lead to conclusions which were incompatible
with Christian theology, Aquinas rather played down the
differences between his own psychology and that of the

historic Aristotle.[1] He was the reverse of the type of writer who is always careful to lay claim to originality of thought. But the differences are there none the less, and an attentive reading of the *De anima* on the one hand and of Aquinas' own philosophy of the soul on the other quickly reveals them.

Like Aristotle, Aquinas uses the word 'soul' in a wide sense. Soul is 'the first principle of life in living things about us' (*S.T.*, Ia, 75, 1). If we understand the word in this broad sense, it obviously follows that all living things have 'souls'. This would seem ridiculous, of course, if we took the word 'soul' in the sense in which it is usually taken today; but Aquinas' *anima* is equivalent to Aristotle's *psyche*. It is the principle or component factor of a living thing which first makes it a living thing and which lies behind, as it were, all that thing's vital activities. A plant is capable of nourishing itself and of reproduction. Neither activity is itself a soul, but it is the 'vegetative soul' or vital principle in the plant which makes these activities possible. The range of activities of a living thing reveals the kind of soul which is present in it. Animals are capable not only of nourishing themselves and of reproduction, as plants are, but also of sensation and of other activities of which plants are not capable. To animals, then, we must attribute 'sensitive souls', and not simply 'vegetative souls'. Again, human beings are capable of other activities, such as thinking and choosing freely, of which animals are not capable. We must therefore attribute to them a higher kind of soul, namely 'rational soul'. We have therefore a hierarchy of souls or vital principles. This does not mean that an animal possesses a vegetative and a sensitive soul or that a human being possesses three souls. An animal possesses only one soul, a sensitive soul, and a human being possesses only one soul, a rational soul. But in

1. When I speak of the 'historic' Aristotle in this connexion, I refer to the actual doctrine, though this is by no means always clear or perhaps even consistent, of the *De anima*. I do not intend by using this phrase to commit myself to the view that Aristotle was personally responsible for the whole of the *De anima*.

virtue of its sensitive soul the animal can exercise not only the vital activities which are found in plants but also an additional range of activities; and it is therefore superior to the vegetative soul. Similarly, in virtue of his one rational soul the human being can exercise not only the vital activities of plants and of animals but also a still higher range of vital activities, namely those which are linked with the possession of mind.

Still keeping to this wide sense of the word 'soul', one can go on to note that for Aquinas the soul in each case stands to the body as form to matter. The human soul is therefore the form of the human body. Something has been said earlier about the form-matter or 'hylomorphic' theory; but it may be as well to explain here that to call the soul the 'form' of the body is for Aquinas to say that the soul is what makes the body a human body and that soul and body are together one substance. The human being is not composed of two substances, soul and body; it is one substance, in which two component factors can be distinguished. When we feel, it is the whole man who feels, neither the soul alone nor the body alone. Similarly, when we understand something we could not do so without the soul, but it is the man who understands. Aquinas does not mean that soul and body are not distinguishable realities; he calls them 'incomplete substances'; but together they form one substance, the human being, to which all human activities are properly ascribed. The body without the soul is not strictly a body at all; it is an aggregate of bodies, as is speedily manifested by the disintegration that sets in after death. And though the human soul survives death, it is not strictly speaking a human person when it is in a state of separation from the body. For the word 'person' signifies a complete substance of rational nature.

Holding this view of man's psycho-physical unity, Aquinas naturally rejects the theory which he ascribes to Plato. 'Some have said that no intellectual substance can be the form of the body. But because the nature of man seemed to contradict this position, since man seems to be composed of an intellectual soul and of a body, they thought out certain ways by which they could preserve (the unity of) human nature. Plato, therefore, and his followers held that the intellectual soul is not united to the body as form to matter, but only as mover to thing moved, saying that the soul is present in the body as a sailor in a ship. . . . But this theory does not seem to fit the facts. For according to it man would not be one thing simply. . . . He would be one thing only "accidentally" (*per accidens*). . . . To avoid this conclusion Plato held that the human being is not a thing composed of soul and body, but that he is the soul itself, using a body, just as Peter is not a thing composed of a man and his clothing, but a man using clothing. But this can be shown to be impossible. For animals and men are sensible and natural things; and this would not be the case if the body and its parts did not belong to the essence of man and animal. . . .' (*C.G.*, 2, 67). And Aquinas goes on to argue that sensation is an act of the whole psycho-physical organism, not of the soul alone, using a body. Thus he rejects any theory according to which the soul is in the body as a pilot in a ship, and he refuses to admit that the analogy of an agent employing an extrinsic instrument like an axe provides an accurate picture of the relation of soul to body.

Furthermore, Aquinas applied to the soul his general theory of matter as the principle of individuation within the species. He did not think that the soul exists as a kind of universal before union with the body : it does not exist at all before union with the body. Nor did he mean that the human soul depends for its existence on the body. For he held that each human soul is created by God. But he did believe that a human soul depends on the body for the acquisition of its particular natural characteristics. Indeed, this follows from his theory, which has been mentioned earlier, that the mind is originally like a wax tablet capable of receiving impressions but not yet possessing them. 'According to the order of nature the intellectual soul occupies the lowest position among intellectual substances. For it has no naturally inborn knowledge of truth, as the angels have, but it has to piece together its knowledge from material things perceived by the senses. ... Therefore the intellectual soul had to have not only the power of understanding but also the power of sensing. But sensation does not take place without a corporeal instrument (organ). The intellectual soul had therefore to be united to a body which could be an appropriate organ of sense. Now, all the other senses are based on touch. ... Among the animals man has the most highly-developed sense of touch; and among human beings themselves those who possess the most delicate sense of touch have the finer minds. A sign of this is that we see superiority of understanding going with refinement of body' (S.T., Ia, 76, 5). Whether all this is true or not is another matter; but in any case it is clear that Aquinas was strongly influenced by Aristotle's pronouncements in the De anima concerning the dependence of psychical activities on physiological conditions. But it is not only in his commentary on the De anima that Aquinas says that people with a good sense of touch have clearer minds and that rough-skinned and coarse-textured persons are mentally inept: he makes similar remarks in the Summa theologica, as in the passage which has just been cited. Similarly, he asserts that 'a man is made apt of understanding by the good disposition of the interior powers (of the organism), in the production of which the good dispositions of the body has a part to play' (S.T., Ia, IIae, 50, 4, ad 3). In the commentary on the De anima he shows that while he follows Aristotle in thinking the purely physical (or 'behaviouristic') definition of anger as 'inflammation of the blood round the heart' to be insufficient he also follows him in thinking that the physical aspect should not be neglected. Much of what Aquinas has to say on these matters may be crude, but it clearly suggests that he would not have been astonished or dismayed at modern research into the close association between psychical and physical factors. Modern discoveries would simply appear to him as so many additional empirical confirmations of his general position.

Given this view of the psycho-physical unity of man, it is

understandable that Aquinas did not favour theories according to which the soul is united to the body as a punishment for sin or that it would be far better off if it had no body at all. The human soul has the power of sensing, but it cannot exercise this power without the body. It also possesses the power of understanding; but it has no stock of innate ideas, and it depends for the acquisition of knowledge on sense-experience. 'And thus it is clear that it is for the good of the soul to be united with a body' (S.T., Ia, 89, 1). Again, 'Origen thought, like Plato, that the human soul is a complete substance, and that the body is united to it accidentally. But since this is false, as has been shown above, it is not to the detriment of the soul that it is united to a body, but for the perfection of its nature' (Quaestio disputata de anima, 2, ad 14).

*

It might well appear that the preceding account of the soul's relation to the body does not favour the view, also held by Aquinas, that the human soul is separable from the body, in the sense that it survives death and is naturally immortal. But his insistence on the dependence of psychical on physical conditions and activities represents only one aspect of Aquinas' theory of the soul-body relationship, and it is necessary to say something of the other aspect as well.

Aquinas believed that there are distinct faculties. A dog, for instance, possesses exterior faculties or powers, like sight and hearing, and interior faculties, like sensitive memory. All of these, however, belong to the level of sensitive life, and they depend for their existence on that of the organism. To call them distinct faculties does not mean, of course, that they are independent of the sensitive soul or vital principle of the animal: on the contrary, they are rooted in it and exist only when the sensitive soul exists. But since the sense of sight, for example, has a different 'formal object', namely colour, from that of the sense of hearing, namely sound, the two senses must be distinguished from one another. Now, each of these faculties is seen to be intrinsically dependent on the body; there can be no seeing, for instance, except in a metaphorical or analogical sense, apart from a bodily organ. And since activity follows, that is manifests, being (*operatio sequitur esse*), this dependence of sensitive activities and of the sense-faculties on the body shows that the sensitive soul or vital principle itself depends intrinsically on the body, in the sense that it cannot exist apart from the body. In the human being, however, we find activities which, considered in themselves, transcend the power of matter. For example, the mind or intellect can conceive and know other than purely material things, and this shows that it is not itself material. 'If the intellect were corporeal, its activity would not reach beyond the order of bodies. So it would understand only bodies. But this is patently false. For we understand many things which are not bodies. Therefore the intellect is not corporeal' (*C.G.*, 2, 49). We should not be able to pursue pure logic or mathematics or work out an abstract theory of physical science, were the mind corporeal. Still less should we be able even to raise the problem of God, let alone develop a metaphysical theology. Again, self-consciousness is a sign of the immaterial character of the human mind (*ibid.*). And the same can be said of free choice. All these activities manifest the immateriality or spirituality of the mind, and so of the human soul, the nature of which is made clear by its higher activities (again *operatio sequitur esse*).

It is worth noting that though Aquinas argues from acts or activities to faculties and from faculties to the soul which possesses these faculties, the theory of really distinct faculties is not essential to the line of argument, in the sense that the same line of argument could not be pursued, were the theory of really distinct faculties called in question or rejected. For the line of argument is from the character of what can be observed in introspection and known by analogy to the character of that which cannot be observed in itself. If some of the activities or operations of the human soul transcend the power of matter, then the soul itself, which manifests its character in these activities, must itself transcend matter.

It is also to be noted that Aquinas is not concerned here with proving the existence of a soul in man, in the wide sense of a vital principle or principle of vital activities and functions; he is concerned with the character of that principle. That there is a soul in man, he believed to be evident from the fact, known to everybody and constantly expressed in or implied by ordinary language, that man is a living thing. Moreover, the unity of man and the oneness of the human soul is recognized, implicitly at least, by everybody. For while everyone speaks of 'my idea' or 'my conviction' and uses such phrases as 'I choose' or 'I decided', everyone also recognizes as his own, as belonging to himself, activities like eating or sleeping, seeing or hearing, remembering or imagining. Aquinas believed in distinct faculties, but he had no use for the suggestion that there are distinct souls in man, corresponding to the different levels of vital activity. Acceptance of this suggestion would make nonsense of the common experience of human beings, which finds constant expression in ordinary language. Moreover, even those activities which we share with non-human beings take on special characteristics when they are found in man. 'Sensitive life (literally, the operations of the sensitive soul) is much higher in man than it is in brutes, as is clear in the case of touch and in that of the interior senses' (*De potentia*, 3, 11, *ad* 1). And this too is evidence for there being only one soul in man.

At the same time, even though the presence of a soul in man is sufficiently evident, the character of this soul is not immediately evident. Aquinas was quite well aware that it is possible to admit the presence of a soul in some sense and yet to maintain that the soul is a function of matter, in the sense that it depends intrinsically on the body. And so he was convinced that its spiritual or immaterial character has to be proved. No doubt he thought that its character is implicitly known by all, in the sense that reflection on the data of consciousness leads to the conclusion that it is immaterial. The 'discovery' of the spiritual character of the soul is not like the discovery of a hitherto unknown island which an explorer may suddenly come across in his travels. But the soul is not perfectly self-luminous. What I am conscious of is my acts as mine; I do not observe my soul apart from its acts. Nor am I immediately conscious of a faculty like the mind, if it is considered apart from concrete mental activities. By introspection I am aware of myself thinking, for example, as I am aware of my acts of choice; but I do not immediately observe my mind apart from its operations or my will apart from all acts of choosing. Aquinas therefore argues from the immediately 'observable' to the character of the soul. On the other hand, this is not for him an inference from the known to the completely unknown, from the manifest to the completely hidden. For, as we have seen, his fundamental position is that all are conscious of their activities and operations as theirs; and the data of consciousness contain implicitly an awareness of the soul's character, though systematic reflection is needed to render this implicit awareness explicit. We can speak, if we like, of Aquinas' process of reflection as 'analysis': it was certainly not for him 'speculation', if by this term is meant a wild leap into the realm of the completely unknown.

The question arises, however, whether Aquinas is not involved in holding simultaneously two incompatible positions. For on the one hand he holds, as we have seen earlier, that all human natural knowledge depends on sense-experience, while on the other hand he maintains that man's highest psychical activities are intrinsically independent of the body. And it may be asked whether he does not say at the same time that the human soul is dependent on and independent of the body.

Aquinas' position is this. The human soul is able to exercise some activities which transcend the power of matter, and this shows that the soul itself is not material. And that which is not material does not depend intrinsically on the body for its existence. At the same time the soul is naturally the form of the human body, and it is natural for it to gain its knowledge in dependence on sense-experience. (Indeed, strictly speaking it does not gain knowledge: it is the man, composed of soul and body, who gains knowledge.) While united with the body it has no other natural means of gaining knowledge than in dependence on sense-experience. But this does not mean that its higher activities are absolutely incapable of being exercised in independence of the body. After death, when it is separated from the body, it cannot exercise its sensitive powers, but it can know itself and spiritual objects. Even in this state of separation, however, the soul is naturally the form of the body, and it follows that the state of separation is not its natural state. It is what Aquinas calls *praeter naturam* (beyond nature); and he draws the conclusion that the soul in this condition of separation from the body is not strictly a human person. For the word 'person' means the full human being, body and soul. Aquinas was convinced both that the human soul depends in this life on sense-experience for all its natural knowledge and that its highest activities transcend the capacity of matter. In other words, the highest activities of the soul, and so the soul itself, are intrinsically independent of the body, in the sense that they can be exercised in the state of separation from the body; but at the same time they are extrinsically dependent on the body, in the sense that while the soul is united with the body it is dependent for its natural knowledge on sense-experience.

This does not mean, as we have seen when treating of the knowledge of God, that man is incapable of knowing anything but corporeal things. It means rather that sense-experience forms the starting-point for all his knowledge, and that in this life he cannot know anything, even what is divinely revealed, without the use of images. This dependence of the mind on images is, however, extrinsic rather than intrinsic. In this life we cannot know anything without the use of images; but when the soul is separated from the body its mental activity does not depend on the senses and the imagination. We should not conclude, however, that the state of separation is better than the state of union, absolutely speaking at least. From the theological point of view one can say that the soul of the man who has achieved salvation by dying in a state of grace is better off after death than it was when exposed to the moral perils of this life; but, absolutely speaking, it is better for the soul to be united to the body than not to be united to it, since it is naturally the form of the body. This line of thought tends to suggest that the resurrection of the body is to be expected; and Aquinas was prepared to admit this. 'It is therefore contrary to the nature of the soul to be without the body. But nothing which is contrary to nature can be perpetual. Hence the soul will not for ever be without the body. Therefore since the soul remains for ever, it should be united again with the body, and this is what is meant by rising (from the dead). The immortality of souls seems then to demand the future resurrection of bodies' (*C.G.*, 4, 79). But he showed, by a preceding paragraph, that this argument did not amount to a proof of the resurrection of bodies, if it was taken by itself, without, that is to say, the resurrection of Christ and the Christian revelation. However, the point which I have been trying to make is that Aquinas would answer the accusation of holding two incompatible positions about the dependence of man's higher activities on the body by making a distinction between extrinsic and intrinsic dependence.

As Aquinas insisted that there is only one soul in man and that the whole soul survives death (which means precisely the separation of the soul from the body), his position was not the same as that of Aristotle. It is true that for Aristotle there is only one soul (*psyche*) in man, which is the entelechy or form of the body; but this psyche does not include the immortal intellect (*nous*) or mind. Aristotle does indeed sometimes speak as though the immortal mind were a separable part of the soul; but his general position is made fairly clear in the *De anima*. The human psyche is the principle of biological, sensitive and certain mental functions, and it is the form of the body; but precisely because it is the form of the body it cannot exist in separation from the body. To say of something that it is the form of the human body is, for Aristotle, to say that it is inseparable from that body. And he draws the conclusion that if anything in man is immortal, it is not the form of the body. There is indeed an immortal intellect; but immortality did not mean for Aristotle what it meant for Aquinas. For the latter the human soul is created by God as the form of the body when the body comes into being as a human body in the natural way, and it survives death. Immortality therefore means persistence in existence after the dissolution of the composite being. For Aristotle, however, the immortal mind is eternal, existing before as after its presence in the body. And he therefore speaks of it as coming 'from outside'. Hence it cannot be considered as a part of the soul. Aristotle, it is true, stresses the difficulty of the whole matter and avoids dogmatism; but it is clear that he made, or at least was inclined to make, a sharp distinction between the human psyche and the immortal mind. When therefore Aquinas propounded the view that the whole soul of man survives death, though it cannot exercise all its potentialities in separation from the body, he was saying that it is possible for something to be the form of the body and yet to survive death, that is, the dissolution of the composite being. And this was not the position of Aristotle, even though Aquinas does not himself make this point very clear. Hence it is not true to say that he slavishly reproduced Aristotle's theories, however much he may have been influenced by them.[1]

If the word 'form' in the context meant 'shape' or 'figure', it would obviously be absurd to say at one and the same time that the human soul is the form of the body and that it survives bodily death. But although it is clear from what has been already said that Aquinas is not using the word in this sense, it may none the less appear that he is trying to have things both ways. On the one hand he asserts not only that the human soul is the form of the body in the sense that it makes the body a living body, capable of exercising sensitive activities, but also that to 'inform' the

1. I am aware, of course, that the interpretation of Aristotle which I have given above is not universally accepted. But it seems to me to be the correct one, though I cannot argue the matter here.

body is natural to the soul. On the other hand he asserts that the human soul is naturally immortal. And the combination of these two assertions may appear to be an attempt to have the best of two worlds, so to speak; to combine the 'Platonic' doctrine of immortality with an Aristotelian view of the relation of soul to body. This criticism is understandable. But Aquinas' contention is that among forms which inform bodies the human soul alone is a spiritual principle. He admits that it follows from the doctrine that the soul is naturally the form of the body that in its state of separation between death and the resurrection it is not in its natural condition and that it is not strictly a human person, since the word 'person' signifies the whole complete substance, the unity of soul and body. But he contends that the human soul is in spiritual form, which, as spiritual, cannot be affected by the disintegration of the body. To assert that the soul is naturally the form of the body is not to assert that it cannot exist in separation from the body; it is, however, to assert that when it is separated from the body it is not in its natural condition and retains a natural orientation towards informing the body.

It is clear, therefore, that the crucial point in Aquinas' argument in favour of immortality is his argument in favour of the incorporeality or spirituality of the soul. For if it is spiritual in the sense that its existence is not tied to the existence of the bodily organism or to any corporeal organ, its persistence after death seems to follow. And when William of Ockham denied that the presence in man of an immaterial or spiritual form can be proved by philosophic reflection, he naturally went on to deny that the immortality of the soul can be proved. (According to Ockham, the truth of both propositions is known by revelation, not by philosophical reasoning.)

Aquinas' argument in favour of the human soul's spiritual character is based, as we have seen, on the contention that man exercises psychical activities which are not intrinsically dependent on a corporeal organ. He then argues that this fact shows that the 'form' which exercises these activities is

itself spiritual. His position would not involve him in denying that intellectual activity has a physical aspect, in the
sense that it is accompanied, for instance, by movements in
the brain. It would, however, commit him to denying not
only that intellectual activity can be identified with movements of the brain but also that it is intrinsically dependent
on these movements, in the sense that there cannot be intellectual activity of any kind without them. In other words,
he is committed to denying not only the outdated form of
materialism which is represented by Hobbes' idea that
thought is a motion in the head or by Cabanis' dictum that
the brain secretes thought as the liver secretes bile, but also
the doctrine of epiphenomenalism according to which the
mind, though not a corporeal thing, supervenes when the
brain has reached a certain degree of development in the
evolutionary process and cannot exist apart from it. He is
also committed, of course, to denying the validity of the
analysis according to which the word 'mind' is no more
than a collective name for psychical events. But by denying
the truth of such views Aquinas would deny the truth of
interpretations of the empirical data, not the empirical data
themselves. For example, it is doubtless true that intellectual
activities are found only when a corporeal organ has attained a certain stage of development. But to say that mind
is a kind of epiphenomenon or efflorescence of the brain is to
enunciate a theory about the facts, an interpretation of the
facts, the meaning of which is by no means altogether clear
and which is in any case open to dispute. Again, the statement that 'mind' is no more than a collective term for
psychical events expresses a theory or interpretation, the
validity of which is open to question. True, Aquinas' account
of the nature of the soul also involves interpretation and
theory; for on his own admission we have no direct intuition
of the soul as a spiritual 'substance'. But my point is simply
that his interpretation cannot be ruled out simply because
it is an interpretation. The question is which is the most
adequate interpretation. I do not for a moment suggest that
what Aquinas says on the subject of the human soul is all

that needs to be said. Apart from any other consideration, he was primarily a theologian, not a philosopher or a psychologist. But one might perhaps ask oneself whether our ability to form any theory about the soul really fits in with a phenomenalistic analysis of man's psychical life.

*

In Aquinas' treatment of immortality we do not find the impassioned accents of a Miguel de Unamuno. It gives the impression of being extremely academic and dry. Even when he is speaking of the desire for everlasting life there are no emotional overtones: at least they are far from obvious. But this objectivity of treatment is characteristic of Aquinas' philosophical and theological writings: indeed, it is characteristic of a large number of medieval thinkers. And this is perhaps one of the features of their writing which makes their works appear to some readers to be extremely remote from human life and existence. This impression of remoteness and aloofness from concern for human existence and destiny can, of course, be sometimes misleading; and the present instance is doubtless a case in point. For discussion of the question whether death completely terminates human existence or not is a discussion which, by definition, concerns human existence, in however dry and objective a manner it may be conducted. Moreover, one must bear in mind the fact that Aquinas was always concerned with truth, and he thought that knowledge of truth is better obtained by dispassionate consideration of evidence and arguments than by appeals to the heart or to the emotions. In addition we have to recall to mind the fact that Aquinas lived in a milieu which was very different from our own. For he lived in a society which, though certainly not Christian in the sense that all lived up to the demands of the Christian life, was Christian in the sense that the doctrines of Christianity were commonly accepted. I do not mean to imply that all the inhabitants of Christian Europe were firm believers. But it is obvious that Christianity was commonly accepted; and this means that people already believed in immortality. They did not, for the most part, look to philosophers to provide them with reasons for believing what they already accepted as revealed doctrine. It is also as well to remember that Aquinas, as a Christian theologian, was not primarily interested in the question of mere survival after death. For him, as for any orthodox Christian, the purpose of human existence is the supernatural vision of God, which cannot be achieved by philosophic reflection or by any merely human effort, and eternal life in the full sense involves the integration of the whole human personality and its elevation to a higher plane. Obviously, there could not be any eternal life if the human being were completely destroyed at death, and Aquinas paid attention to philosophic reasons for saying that the human soul survives death. But the mere survival of a disembodied soul is not at all the same thing as eternal life in the full Christian sense. And as it is by revelation and not by philosophic reflection that the Christian knows of man's supernatural destiny, it is easy to understand that Aquinas did not write with poetic enthusiasm about the subject of mere survival, considered in abstraction from Christian revelation. In his eyes the important question for any man would be whether he was prepared to fulfil his supernatural destiny by cooperating with divine grace, not simply whether he was going to survive or not as a kind of disembodied mind.

Aquinas argues from the spirituality of the soul to its incorruptibility. A human being is capable of knowing all bodies. But if the mind were corporeal it would have to be a particular kind of body. And in this case it would not know or be capable of knowing other kinds of bodies. A human being would be in the position of a sick man to whom all things taste bitter. Just as the eye sees colours and cannot hear sounds, so the mind would be confined to the knowledge of the type of body corresponding to itself. 'It is clear that a man can know by his mind the natures of all bodies. But a cognitive principle must have in its own nature nothing of the nature of its objects. Otherwise that which was naturally present in it would prevent the knowledge of other things. Thus we see that the tongue of a sick man which is infected by a choleric and bitter humour cannot perceive anything sweet; but all things seem bitter to it. Therefore if the intellectual principle had in it the nature of any body, it could not know all bodies. It is thus impossible that the intellectual principle should be a body' (S.T., Ia, 75, 2). Nor can we suppose that the actual organ of cognition is corporeal, for a similar reason. If water is poured into a coloured vase and we look at the water through the glass, it appears to be of the same colour as the glass (ibid.). If the mind knew by means of a purely corporeal organ, this organ would be a particular kind of body, and this would prevent the knowledge of other kinds of corporeal things. The intellectual soul of man must therefore be incorporeal. But in this case it must also be incorruptible. It makes no sense to speak of an immaterial principle or form becoming worn out, as it were, and as falling to pieces or disintegrating. Nor, if it is not intrinsically dependent on the body, can it cease to exist when the body disintegrates. The human soul, in fine, can be corrupted neither per se, by reason of some factor inherent in itself, nor per accidens, by reason of the disintegration of the body (S.T., Ia, 75, 6).

The human soul is thus 'naturally' immortal, not in the sense that it is impossible for God to annihilate it but in the sense that, unless God withdraws His conserving activity, an event which there is no reason for expecting, it continues to exist without any miracle being required. Some later medieval philosophers, such as Duns Scotus, maintained the view that even if we grant that some of man's activities transcend the power of a material agent it does not necessarily follow that the human soul survives the dissolution of the composite being. Aquinas' line of reasoning amounts, according to them, only to a probable argument, and not to a strict proof. But it is clear, I think, that Aquinas himself considered that it could be strictly proved that the human soul is spiritual in character and that it therefore persists after bodily death. In this case the validity of the argument would be independent of previous acceptance of God's existence.

Perhaps the same can hardly be said of the argument which follows. 'And a sign of this (that the soul is incorruptible) can be gathered from the fact that each thing naturally desires existence in its own way. Now, in things which are capable of knowing desire follows knowledge. The senses do not know existence except here and now. But the intellect apprehends existence absolutely and without temporal limit. Therefore every thing which possesses intellect naturally desires to exist for ever. And a natural desire cannot be in vain. Therefore every intellectual substance is incorruptible' (S.T., Ia, 75, 6). In the Summa contra Gentiles the argument is expressed in this way. 'It is impossible that a natural desire should be in vain. But man naturally desires to remain in perpetuity. This is clear from the fact that it is existence which is desired by all things. Moreover, man apprehends existence intellectually, not simply existence her and now, as the brutes may be said to apprehend it, but existence as such. Man therefore attains perpetual existence in his soul, by which he apprehends existence as such and without temporal limit' (C.G., 2, 79). On the level of purely sensitive life existence is apprehended only 'here and now', not in abstraction from particular circumstances, and death is shunned here and now, instinctively. But man conceives and desires perpetual existence. And since this desire is the form which a natural desire takes in an intellectual being, it must be fulfilled.

In this argument, which incidentally was a traditional one, Aquinas is obviously not talking simply of an instinctive impulse to conserve life by shunning or shrinking back from what is felt as threatening security and life. If he were, the argument would prove too much, namely that animals are immortal. He is talking of a conscious desire for immortality, a desire which presupposes the idea of existence in perpetuity. This desire is natural in the sense that it is the form taken in an intellectual being by the impulse towards the conservation of life which is naturally implanted in living things. But can we conclude from a 'natural desire' to its fulfilment unless we presuppose the existence of a creator who, having implanted these natural desires, sees to it that they are not frustrated? Perhaps Aquinas thought that we could. But in this case must it not first be shown that the human soul is capable of surviving death? This at least was Duns Scotus' comment. However, in the *Summa theologica* Aquinas simply gives this argument as a 'sign' of the incorruptibility of the human soul. And this may imply that man's power of conceiving continued existence after death and his desire for it help to show the spiritual character of the soul and so to confirm the argument on which Aquinas lays most emphasis. He was accustomed, when trying to prove a point, to give various lines of argument, without at the same time providing any very clear indication whether he regarded a particular argument as a strict proof or as a probable or a persuasive argument. Hence it is difficult to know what precise weight he attached to the argument to immortality from the 'natural desire' for it. It is clear, however, that he regarded as fundamental the argument based on an examination of the soul's nature in the light of its higher activities. He was not the man to base an affirmation of human immortality simply on 'intimations of immortality' or to say with Schiller that 'what the inner voice says does not deceive the soul which hopes',[1] though he may very well have regarded the desire for immortality as a sign of the spiritual character of the soul. If this is what he meant it is a pity that he did not say so more clearly. An argument which proceeds simply from a desire to its fulfilment does not seem convincing to me, even if the desire is said to be 'natural'.

When Aquinas talks about immortality, he is talking, of course, about personal immortality. The Islamic philosopher, Averroes, had interpreted the rather obscure statements about immortality in the third book of Aristotle's *De anima* as meaning that there is one immortal intellect which enters into temporary union with, or performs a function in, individual men. There is therefore no personal

1. Und was die innere Stimme spricht,
   Das täuscht die hoffende Seele nicht.

immortality. We could not say that John and Peter, considered as individuals, are in any way immortal; for the immortal, or more properly eternal, intellect which functions both in John and in Peter during their lives is not peculiar to John or Peter. When this active intellectual principle is functioning in John and working, as it were, on John's capacity for receiving ideas, a kind of personal intellect is produced, which belongs to John. But in so far as this personal intellect or mind survives death it is only as a moment in the one active intellectual principle. We might speak, then, of the human race being in some sense immortal and of individuals as sharing in some sense in an impersonal immortality; but there would be no question of John or of Peter surviving death as recognizable individuals.

This strange theory was expounded in Aquinas' time by a group of lecturers in the faculty of arts at the university of Paris. They did not maintain that the theory was in fact true; but they maintained at any rate that it represented the teaching of Aristotle and that it followed from his principles. This was held for a time by Siger of Brabant (c. 1235–c. 85), though he later changed his views. The expounders of this theory, when charged by theologians with defending an unorthodox opinion, replied, therefore, that they were speaking as historians, as exegetes of Aristotle, and that they were not affirming the theory to be true. It appears, however, that some of them, in their devotion to Aristotle, maintained that it would have been true had God not managed matters otherwise. In other words, philosophic reflection alone, represented by Aristotle, leads to the conclusion that there is only one immortal intellect; but revelation assures us that what the philosopher, left to himself, would expect to be the case is not in fact the case.

Aquinas attacked this group on two counts. In the first place he maintained that the theory of one immortal intellect in all men did not follow from Aristotle's principles and that it was wrongly ascribed to him by exegetes who misinterpreted the text. Into this purely historical question it is unnecessary to enter. In the second place he maintained that the theory is in itself ridiculous and unsupported by any evidence. And in maintaining this view he was at one with many other theologian-philosophers with whom he did not see eye to eye on some other matters. He argued, for example, that on the theory of one intellect in all men it is quite impossible to explain the different ideas and intellectual lives of different human beings. It might be possible to explain the presence of different images in different people; but it would not be possible to explain the presence of different concepts and convictions. 'If there were one intellect in all men, the different images in different men would not be capable of producing the different intellectual operations of this and that man, as Averroes pretends that they could. It remains, therefore, that it is altogether impossible and inappropriate to postulate one intellect in all men' (*S.T.*, Ia, 76, 2). In the *De unitate intellectus contra Averoistas* he argues at length that the theory of Averroes makes nonsense of all statements in which we say 'he thinks . . .' or 'I think . . .'. Yet the propriety of this way of speaking is confirmed by all the available data. Similarly, if the theory of Averroes were true, it would be nonsensical to attribute moral responsibility for voluntary actions either to ourselves or to other individuals. Yet we do attribute moral responsibility, and we know that we are justified in principle in doing so. Aquinas evidently felt strongly about the theory which he was opposing, for he ends the *De unitate intellectus*, after observing that in writing against it he has had recourse to rational argument rather than to appeals to authority, by challenging the unconvinced to stop muttering in corners with lads who have no judgement in such matters and to publish their replies, so that the question can be properly debated.

*

Aquinas' general theory that our natural knowledge is gained in dependence on sense-experience has already been stated. But something more must be said about his analysis of the process by which we come to know, even if it is not possible to pursue the analysis into all its details.

The first stage in the acquisition of knowledge is sense-perception. Our organs of sense are affected by external objects, and we receive sense-impressions. The eye, for example, sees colours or colour-patches; but it would not do so unless it were affected by its object acting on it through a medium. It receives an impression, therefore, and undergoes a physical alteration. The process of sensation cannot, however, be reduced to a mere physical change. 'If physiological change sufficed for sensation, all natural bodies would have sensations when they underwent change' (*S.T.*, Ia, 78, 3). Sensation is a psycho-physical process in which a sensible 'form' is received.

If we consider the level of the individual external senses in itself, it is true to say that there are only discrete sense-impressions. The sense of sight, says Aquinas, is able to distinguish one colour from another (the impression of green is different from the impression of blue); but the sense of sight is quite unable to compare and distinguish colours from sounds, since it does not hear. It is obvious, however, that even animals synthesize their sense-impressions. The dog perceives a man and achieves a synthesis of the different sense-impressions of sight, hearing, smell and touch. It is therefore clear that even at the level of purely sensitive life there takes place a synthesis of the data of the different external senses. Aquinas therefore postulates interior 'senses' by means of which this synthesis is achieved. The word 'sense' may seem peculiar, because we are accustomed to use the word only in reference to what Aquinas calls the five external senses; but by using the word he intends to indicate that the power or faculty of which he speaks belongs to the level of sensitive life and is found in animals as well as in human beings.

The function of distinguishing and collating the data of the various external senses is performed by the general sense (*sensus communis*). We must also postulate an imaginative power which conserves the forms received by the senses.

Again, the animal is able to apprehend, for example, that something is useful to it. A dog apprehends that a particular man is friendly or unfriendly. We shall thus have to postulate a power or disposition to apprehend these facts (the *vis aestimativa*) and a power of conserving such apprehensions (the *vis memorativa*). In postulating all these powers or faculties Aquinas relied very largely on Aristotle, and we may well ask in what precise sense, if any, we are justified in speaking of different 'faculties' or 'interior senses'. But the point to which I wish to draw attention is Aquinas' insistence on the work of synthesis that goes on in cognition. The synthesis of which I have been speaking takes place at the level of sensitive life, and it must not be taken to mean a conscious, deliberate synthesis; but that a synthesis does take place is a fact which scarcely admits of doubt.

Although, however, the synthesis which takes place on the sensitive level is in some sense common to animals and to men, this does not mean that sensitive cognition is identical in both. I have already quoted a passage from the *De potentia* (3, 11, *ad* 1), where Aquinas says that sensitive life, though generically the same in animals as in men, is not specifically the same, since it is 'much higher' in the latter, 'as is clear in the case of touch and in the case of the interior senses'. Thus according to Aquinas what corresponds in human beings to the *vis aestimativa* in animals deserves a special name, since more than instinct is involved; and he calls it the *vis cogitativa*.[1] He was aware that in human perception sense and reason are both involved. But it does not follow that an attempt to abstract or isolate what belongs to the level of sense-life from what belongs to the level of reason is misguided or useless.

For Aquinas an explanation is needed of the transition from sensitive to rational or intellectual cognition. The

1. This power belongs to the level of sensitive life in man, and 'the physicians assign to it a definite organ, namely the middle part of the head' (*S.T.*, Ia, 78, 4). But it lies, as it were, on the confines of reason, and Aquinas also calls it 'particular reason' (*ibid.*), since it does not conceive universals, as reason proper does.

senses apprehend particular objects, and images, even if confused, are particular. The mind, however, has universal concepts; it apprehends in abstraction the forms of things. We therefore have on the one hand sensitive apprehension of the particular and on the other intellectual cognition of the universal. This does not mean that universals as such have any extra-mental existence. There are, for example, only particular human beings; there is no such thing as an existent universal man, nor can there be. But individual human beings possess, Aquinas was convinced, specifically similar essences, and this similarity of essence is the objective foundation of the universal concept of man, which enables us to predicate the same term of individual human beings, saying, for example, that John is a man and that Peter is also a man. But even when we suppose this view of universals, namely that universals as such exist in the mind and not extra-mentally, the problem still remains, how is the universal concept formed? What is the process by which the universal concept is formed? It cannot be explained as a purely passive process, passive, that is to say, on the mind's part. For the mind, being immaterial, cannot be directly affected by a material thing or by the image. It is necessary to postulate an activity on the mind's part, in order to explain how the universal concept is formed from the material provided by sense-experience. In other words, on the rational level there takes place a further stage of the process of synthesis involved in human cognition, and an analysis of this further stage is required.

Aquinas employs the Aristotelian distinction between the active and passive intellects, two distinct functions of the mind. According to him the active intellect 'illumines' the image of the object apprehended by the senses; that is to say, it actively reveals the formal and potentially universal element which is implicitly contained in the image. It then abstracts this potentially universal element and produces in the passive intellect what Aquinas calls the *species impressa*. The passive intellect reacts to this determination by the active intellect, and the result is the *species expressa*, the universal concept in the full sense. This language is certainly unfamiliar and therefore difficult to follow; but what Aquinas has in mind is more or less this. The human intellect has no store of innate ideas: it is in potentiality to possessing ideas or concepts. Considered in this light, the intellect is passive. And its concepts must be derived in some way from the data provided by the senses, exterior and interior. But the senses provide particular impressions of particular objects, together with the images to which these impressions give rise, whereas concepts are universal in character. We must suppose, then, that the intellect as active picks out, as it were, the potentially universal element in the image, the synthesized reproduction in the imagination of the data of the different senses. Thus the intellect as active abstracts the universal essence of man from a particular image, leaving out the particularizing notes which confine the image to being the image of this or that particular man, and impresses it on the intellect as passive. And so the universal concept is born.

In the process of synthesis and abstraction there is therefore continuity, from the primary sense-impressions up to the universal concept. The mediating point between the data of sense and the universal concept is for Aquinas the image. And it is important to realize that when he talks about images in this connexion he is not speaking of arbitrarily constructed images like the image of a unicorn. In our sense-experience of, say, Peter, the eye sees colour-patches, the ear hears sounds, and so on. These sense-impressions are, however, synthesized in the form of the 'image'. And it is from this synthesis that the universal, 'man', is, according to Aquinas, abstracted. That which is primarily known by the mind is, however, the universal, that is the form, as apprehended in Peter. Peter is known as a man. It is only secondarily that the mind apprehends the universal precisely as universal. That is to say, it is only secondarily that it apprehends the universal as predicable not only of Peter but also of James and John and every other individual human being. To speak of 'abstraction' is not, therefore, for Aquinas to cut off the life of the intellect from that of the senses and to say that the mind knows only its own ideas. The universal concept is primarily the modification of the intellect by which a thing (Peter for example) is known according to its form or essence.

As we have seen earlier, Aquinas held that the mind is dependent on the image, not only in the formation of its ideas but also in their employment, in the sense that there is no thinking without the use of images or symbols. Since the mind is active and possesses the power of active reflection, it is not confined to the knowledge of material things; but at the same time it can know immaterial things only in so far as material things are related to them and reveal them. Moreover, in thinking about immaterial things we cannot dispense with the use of images or symbols. We can recognize the inadequacy of the images based on sense-experience, but we cannot get rid of them. We cannot conceive immaterial things, even when their existence is known by revelation, except on an analogy with visible things, though we can attempt to purify our ideas of them. 'Images necessarily accompany our knowledge in this present life, however spiritual the knowledge may be: for even God is known by us through the images of His effects (in creatures)' (*De malo*, 16, 8, *ad* 3). Again, 'the image is a principle of our knowledge. It is that from which our intellectual activity begins, not simply as a transitory stimulus, but as a permanent foundation of intellectual activity. . . . And so when the imagination is impeded, so also is our theological knowledge' (*In librum Boethii de Trinitate*, 6, 2, *ad* 5).

A point to be noticed is that truth and falsity are predicated primarily neither of sense-impressions nor of concepts but of judgements. We can hardly speak of error in the case of a particular sense apprehending its own proper object, unless perhaps the organ is impaired; but inasmuch as Aquinas is prepared to speak of the senses 'judging', he is also prepared to speak of truth and falsity at the sense-level. We might say, for example, that an animal misjudged the distance, distance being only indirectly apprehended by the senses. But though a 'judgement' of sense may be true or false, according as it corresponds or not with reality, its truth or falsity is not reflectively apprehended at the sense-level. 'Truth is primarily in the mind. . . . It is defined as conformity between the mind and the thing. Hence to know this conformity is to know truth. Sense, however, does not know truth as such. For although sight has the likeness of a visible thing it does not know the correspondence between the thing seen and its perception of it. The mind, however, can know its own conformity with an intelligible thing, not simply by apprehending its essence, but it makes a judgement about the thing. . . . It is then that it first knows and enunciates truth. . . . And so, strictly speaking, it is in the mind's judgements that truth is found and not in sensation, nor in the intellectual apprehension of an essence' (*S.T.*, Ia, 16, 2). I may have a true perception of Peter as white; but it is not of this perception as such that truth is primarily predicated. It is the judgement that Peter is white which is strictly speaking 'true'. Aquinas does, indeed, speak of things as 'true', as, being, for example, conformed to the mind of the Creator. But in the *De veritate* and elsewhere he carefully distinguishes the various senses in which he uses the word 'true' and states that truth is primarily found in the mind's act of judging.

*

Aquinas has been called an 'intellectualist'. But the question whether the name is appropriate or not obviously cannot be answered without a previous clarification of its meaning. If by 'intellectualist' is meant someone who lays great emphasis on knowledge and on rational activity, there are certainly grounds for applying this name to Aquinas. After all, one would expect him as a university professor to emphasize rational reflection and to exalt knowledge. In the Middle Ages there was a dispute concerning the faculties of the soul, the question being which was the 'noblest' faculty. This is not a dispute in which any enthusiastic interest can be expected today; but it is worth remarking that Aquinas was convinced of the pre-eminent claims of the intellect. For he maintained that whereas the will tends towards its object the intellect possesses it in cognition, and possession is better than tending towards. In knowledge, he said, knower and known are one; that is, the knower becomes the known by mental or spiritual assimilation, without, however, ceasing to be himself. Natural knowledge is thus a faint anticipation of the vision of God in heaven, which is the final end of man.

But if by 'intellectualist' is meant a man who is blind to or who disparages aspects of human life other than the reflective activity of the intelligence, the name certainly cannot be applied to Aquinas. When he said that the final happiness of man consists primarily in the intellectual vision of God as He is in Himself, he did not mean to exclude love. Complete love was for him the fruit of complete knowledge. And when he emphasized man's intellectual activity in this life, he certainly did not mean to disparage, nor was he blind to, other aspects of human activity. If for no other reason, he could not do this either as a devout Christian or as a theologian. But also as psychologist and philosopher he was aware of the importance of the appetitive and voluntary aspects of human nature. And something must be said of his views on this subject.

In every thing there is an inclination or propensity to a particular form of behaviour. The word 'inclination' suggests a conscious tending towards an object; but Aquinas uses it in a very general sense which would cover, to use his example, the natural upward movement of fire. This natural and unconscious 'appetite' is determined by the form of the thing, and it is invariable. In things which are capable of knowledge, however, we find an appetite which follows apprehension of an object as good or desirable. As present on the level of sensitive life this appetite is called the animal or sensitive appetite. When a dog sees its food, it is impelled towards it by its sensitive appetite, which Aquinas also calls 'sensuality'. But this last word must not be taken in the sense which it often bears today, as when we speak of a sensual person. For Aquinas it means simply 'the appetite which follows sensitive apprehension' (S.T., Ia, 81, 1). To call it 'sensuality' is not to say that it is disordered. The sensitive appetite for food is not something disordered. On the contrary, it is natural and tends to the objective good of the thing which possesses it.

This sensitive appetite is found, of course, in man. But in man there is also a rational or intellectual appetite, by which he desires a good consciously apprehended by the reason and which is called 'will'. According to Aquinas, these two, the sensitive appetite and the will, are distinct powers. 'We must say that the intellectual appetite is a power distinct from the sensitive appetite. . . . For objects apprehended by the intellect are different from those apprehended by sense' (S.T., Ia, 80, 2).

Behind and in all choice Aquinas sees the desire or love of the good. 'The first movement of the will and of any appetitive power is love' (S.T., Ia, 20, 1). And this inclination of the will towards the good is natural and necessary, in the sense that the will is set by its very nature towards the good and that this inclination is not subject to free choice. Different people may desire different things. 'Some men seek riches as the supreme good, others pleasure, others something else' (S.T., Ia, IIae, 1, 7). But whatever they desire and seek, they desire and seek it under the guise of good, that is, as being good or at least as being thought of as good. Aquinas does not mean that all human beings necessarily seek and choose that which is objectively good for man from the moral point of view. But whatever a man seeks is sought as being good or as being thought of as good, that is, as meeting or fulfilling some need of human nature or as actualizing and perfecting some potentiality of human nature.

Another way of putting this is to say that all human beings desire and necessarily desire 'happiness'. But this statement lends itself to misunderstanding. According to Aquinas all human beings necessarily desire and seek what he calls *beatitudo*. And this term, which corresponds to some extent to Aristotle's *eudaimonia*, is traditionally translated by the word 'happiness'. One might use instead 'well-being' or perhaps 'blessedness' or 'beatitude'; but whatever term is used some explanation of its use is required. And perhaps the chief point to remember is that whereas the word 'happiness' is normally used only for a subjective state, the psychological condition of feeling happy, the word *beatitudo* has a much wider meaning for Aquinas. When used in an objective sense, it connotes that the possession of which actualizes a man's potentialities, thus rendering him satisfied or happy. When used in a subjective sense, it means fundamentally the activity of enjoying the possession of that which perfects a man's potentialities, though it can also mean the state of satisfaction or happiness which accompanies this activity. Or one can put the matter in this way. *Beatitudo* in the objective sense connotes that good which, being possessed, perfects the potentialities of man as man. Used in a subjective sense it connotes the activity of possessing this good and the satisfaction or happiness (in the ordinary sense) which accompanies this activity. To say therefore that all men necessarily desire 'happiness' (*beatitudo*) is to say that all men necessarily seek that which perfects and satisfies the needs of their nature or is thought of as doing so, and that all their particular choices are informed by this natural inclination of the will. In every particular choice the object is chosen because it contributes to or is thought of as contributing to the attainment of the supreme good for man, the possession of which is happiness or *beatitudo* in the subjective sense.

Now, Aquinas had a quite definite idea of what constitutes the supreme good for man. And this idea was a Christian idea. The supreme good for man, objectively considered, is God: considered subjectively, it is the possession of God. It is the possession of God, who is the supreme being and so the supreme good, which perfects man's potentialities in the highest possible way and which confers perfect happiness in the psychological sense. And inasmuch as all seek the good in the possession of which happiness lies, all can be said, in an interpretative sense, to seek God. But this does not mean that every human being consciously seeks God, which would be patently untrue. If God as He is in Himself were revealed to us, it would be impossible for the will not to go out towards Him. But God is not so revealed to us. Indeed, even though God is in fact the concrete supreme good, He can appear to a human being as 'evil', as, for example, the being whose law checks and restrains the expression of a man's impulses. We do not possess that vision of God which alone could exercise an inevitable attraction on the will. To us every concrete good, even God Himself, can be looked at under some aspect or other as being disadvantageous to us, as not being wholly good and desirable from every point of view. Hence in this life the will is not bound by necessity to choose any particular concrete good. Physiological and psychological factors peculiar to oneself, the influence of environment and so on may incline one to desire some particular kind of good, to consider some particular kind of thing as desirable; but the will is not necessitated simply because it is the will to desire and seek a particular concrete good. To say therefore that the will is necessarily set towards the good and that all men necessarily seek happiness is to make a very general statement. It is to say that whatever a man chooses he chooses as a good, real or apparent, and that all men seek the actualization of their potentialities and the fulfilment of their needs.

One or two comments on this theory of the fundamental dynamic inclination of the will may be appropriate here. In the first place the statement that all human beings necessarily seek happiness may not seem to fit the empirical facts. When a man commits suicide, for example, is he seeking happiness? He may very well believe that death means the final and complete cessation of his existence as an individual human being. And if this is what he believes, it would surely be queer and paradoxical to say that he is seeking happiness when he commits suicide. Again, is it not a fact that some people leave the pursuit of happiness on one side, preferring, for example, the pursuit of fame or the pursuit of power?

Aquinas would answer, of course, that if a man commits

suicide because, for example, his life is wretched or unhappy or because he is threatened with some public disgrace
which he is not prepared to meet, he does not desire extinction as such but rather escape from present or threatening
evils, this escape appearing to him under the guise of something good. Even if he thinks of extinction as something
desirable, he pictures it to himself as having some desirable
characteristic; as being, for instance, a state of complete and
final rest and tranquillity. When one desires, one always
desires something. As for the man who chooses the pursuit
of power rather than the pursuit of happiness, his case really
presents no difficulty. It seems to do so only because the
word 'happiness' is given a particular meaning, the enjoy-
ment of sense-pleasure, for example, or the leading of a tran-
quil life undisturbed by ambition and the lust for power.
But the man who seeks power rather than sense-pleasure is
also seeking happiness: he is seeking what appears to him
as desirable and good, as actualizing his potentialities and
fulfilling the needs of his nature.

But, it may be objected, if the theory that whatever the
will chooses it chooses as being a good, real or apparent,
and that all men seek happiness, is able to cover all possible
empirical facts, this can only be because the terms 'good'
and 'happiness' are given so wide a connotation that they
are to all intents and purposes evacuated of meaning. If the
person who states the theory is saying something to which
nobody can really take exception, he cannot be uttering
any more than a triviality. 'Good' in the general sense means
for Aquinas being in its relation to will, that is, being considered as desirable or as capable of perfecting the agent.
And to say that all men desire the desirable or what appears
to them as desirable does not tell us very much, though it is
doubtless true.

This objection is perfectly understandable. But before I
make some brief remarks on the subject I wish to explain
what Aquinas does not mean by saying that whatever the
will chooses, it chooses as being a good, real or apparent.

If this statement were understood as meaning that nobody

ever deliberately does what he believes to be morally wrong, we would hardly be inclined to call it a 'triviality' or a 'tautology'; but we would say that it is patently untrue. For it is clear not only that people do sometimes act in a way which they believe to be morally wrong but also that they do so deliberately and consciously. But Aquinas did not intend the statement to be understood in this sense. His contention was that though a man may know that some action is wrong and yet do it, what he wills is not the evil as such but something which appears to him as desirable, and so as good, even though he may be well aware that the attainment of the apparent good involves him in moral guilt. We have to distinguish between the objectively good and the 'apparently good'. The former is in the context that which perfects man considered as a totality, as a human person. The good which is good merely 'apparently' is that which answers to some particular craving or desire in man but which does not perfect his nature considered as a totality. For example, a person who sets off on the path of taking a dangerous habit-forming drug does not choose what is objectively good for him as a human being; but he would never take the drug at all unless he thought of the action of taking it as in some way satisfying, as being in some way good or desirable. He may believe that to take heroin is morally wrong and yet do it; but he would not start the habit (which he may afterwards, of course, be unable to break by himself) unless he thought of the action as 'perfecting' his nature in some way. Objectively it does not do so; and the man may know this. But the fact remains that the action is felt to answer some need. The man may know that it is only an apparent good; but if he chooses to do it he is choosing an object which appears to him as desirable, even though he may believe it to be morally wrong. 'Similarly, a fornicator seeks a pleasure which involves him in moral guilt' (S.T., Ia, 19, 9). What the fornicator seeks, Aquinas contends, is a pleasure, something positive which answers to an instinctive craving. He may know that fornication is morally wrong and not objectively good, and in this case he is involved in moral guilt. But though he may know that the action is evil or morally bad, he does not choose the evil or badness as such. At least he does not choose it directly. What he chooses directly is a pleasure, though he can be said to choose evil indirectly, inasmuch as he chooses to do an action which is morally bad and which he may know to be morally bad.

It may seem that though Aquinas' account of human choice will cover the case of the fornicator who is primarily concerned with doing a pleasurable action even though he may believe it to be morally wrong, it will not cover those people who seem to make a kind of cult of evil. It may be said, for example, that it will not cover cases of diabolism or the case of a person who appears to desire to sink himself into the depths of corruption for its own sake. But even in these cases Aquinas would insist that the primary and direct object of choice is something positive, not a privation (namely moral evil as such), though this may be chosen 'indirectly'. For instance, an apostate priest who celebrates the Black Mass may desire to commit sacrilege and blasphemy; he does what is wrong and what he knows to be wrong. Indeed, there would be little point in celebrating a secret blasphemous rite unless he believed that it was blasphemous and sacrilegious, in fact as well as in name. But what he primarily and directly chooses, Aquinas might say, is something positive which appears to him as desirable; the assertion, for example, of his complete independence over against God, the defiance of God. The privation of right order is, indeed, inseparable from this action; and the man may choose the action because it is evil. But what he directly chooses is the action itself. Yes, we may say, but it is possible for a man to go about looking for evil to do. This is at least a conceivable case. Aquinas would presumably reply that such a man does not directly choose evil as such, that is to say a privation, but that he seeks primarily the satisfaction of some impulse or drive, the psychological origins of which may be hidden from the man himself.

But though these considerations may serve to prevent one

from supposing that Aquinas was blind to the fact that people can do not only what is wrong but what they know to be wrong, they serve at the same time to make more acute the original objection against the statement that whatever the will chooses it chooses as being a good, real or 'apparent'. For it seems in the end to amount to the statement that we desire the desirable. If Aquinas does not intend to say that we always choose to do morally good actions (a statement which, as has been remarked, would be false), what else can he be saying than that when we choose we always choose, not a privation as such, but something positive, which appears to us as being in some way desirable? And when the meaning of this statement is explained in such a way that it can be made to cover all the empirical facts about human choice, it turns out in the end to be tautological or, at best, a triviality.

But is Aquinas really saying quite so little as that we desire the desirable or that men seek what they seek? If we take the statement that whatever the will chooses it chooses *sub specie boni* in isolation, it does seem to me to lend itself to the accusation of being a triviality or a tautology. But if we look on the statement in the light of Aquinas' moral theory and as one of the foundations of this theory, it gains in significance. 'Good' in the context of human choice means the development or 'perfecting' of human nature, the actualization of man's potentialities as a human person, or that the possession of which actualizes these potentialities and perfects man's nature. And to say that the will always chooses *sub specie boni*, that it always chooses a good, real or apparent, is to draw attention to the fundamental drive behind all our conscious choices, the drive or impulse to self-development and self-perfection, to 'happiness'. As this natural impulse does not depend on or necessarily carry with it an explicit conception of man's objective good in the concrete, it is possible to form a mistaken idea of it. Moreover, since this good does not in any case present itself to us in this life in such a clear light that it inevitably secures the adhesion of the will, it is also possible to know what it in fact is and yet to concentrate on the satisfaction of one particular impulse or tendency in a way which is incompatible with the attainment of the objective good for man. Aquinas therefore sets out to determine what is the objective good for man, that is to say, what it is in the concrete. And this theme will be discussed in the next chapter, in connexion with his moral theory. In the meantime I suggest that the statement that whatever the will chooses it chooses *sub specie boni*, as being a good, real or apparent, gains in significance when looked at in the perspective of Aquinas' complete moral theory. As in some other cases, he starts from the admitted, the familiar, and in a sense the trivial, and proceeds to develop what seem to him to be its implications. This development helps to unfold the meaning of the original statements. I suggest, therefore, that whether we agree or not with Aquinas' point of view he is in fact saying something more than he may appear to be saying if we take a particular statement in isolation from a theory which is at least partly designed to unfold its implications and develop its full meaning.

*

We have seen that according to Aquinas no concrete good, not even God, is presented to us in such a way in this life that the will is bound of necessity to choose it. Hence we can say that with regard to the choice of particular goods the will is free. But it does not follow from this that all the acts performed by a human being are free acts. The word 'free' is properly applied only to acts which proceed from the reason and the will, and these acts are called by Aquinas 'human acts' (*actus humani*). They may, of course, be purely interior, as when a man deliberately chooses to think of a mathematical problem. But there are also acts which proceed from a human being as their cause, though they are not deliberate acts. What we call reflex acts are of this kind. They are called by Aquinas 'acts of a man' (*actus hominis*) to indicate that they are truly a man's acts but to distinguish them at the same time from 'human acts'. 'Those acts alone are properly called "human" of which a man is master. Now, a man is master of his acts through his reason and will. Therefore free will is said to be a faculty of the will and the reason. Thus those acts are properly called "human" which proceed from deliberate choice' (*S.T.*, Ia, IIae, 1, 1). Scratching done without attention, says Aquinas, is not properly speaking a human act; that is to say, it lies outside the sphere of freedom. Aquinas is very far from maintaining that all a man's acts are free, and there may well be dispute about the propriety of calling this or that particular act 'free'. But he was convinced that all sane persons do at any rate sometimes choose and act freely. And we therefore have to consider what he meant by freedom and the sense in which he understood free will (*liberum arbitrium*).

Aquinas' analysis of freedom is markedly intellectualist in character, in the sense that a strong emphasis is laid on the reason's function in free choice. Every act of free choice is preceded by a judgement of the reason, and Aquinas speaks of choice as being 'formally' an act of the reason. And if we assume his doctrine of distinct faculties, this at first sight appears to be a very queer statement. For in the faculty-language it would seem that choice should be associated with the will rather than with the reason. Some explanation of Aquinas' meaning is therefore required. Failure to understand his use of technical terms leads naturally to misinterpretation of his doctrine.

The mind or reason can regard any particular good under different aspects or from different points of view. Take going for a walk, for example. I can regard it as something good, as the fulfilment of a need for exercise, for instance, or as a pleasurable recreation on a sunny afternoon. Or I can regard it under another aspect as 'evil', as likely to be a hot and dusty business, for example, or as taking up time which should be spent on writing letters to catch the evening post. I can regard it from this point of view or that as I like, and in this sense my judgements about it are free; but I am still thinking about going for a walk and looking at it from various angles; I have not yet, as we say, 'made up my mind'

whether to go for a walk or not. But in the end I make a
final judgement: for example, 'the letter really ought to be
written now, and I ought not to shirk the job and go for a
walk'. And in accordance with this judgement, let us suppose, I will or choose not to go for a walk. The act of choice
is an act elicited by the will: in Aquinas' language it is
'materially' or 'substantially' an act of the will. But it is
elicited under the command or judgement of reason, and is
therefore said to be 'formally' an act of the reason. 'If anyone performs an act of courage for the love of God, the act
is materially an act of courage, but formally an act of
charity. Now, it is clear that reason precedes the will in
some way.... Therefore, the act by which the will tends
to something proposed as good by the reason is materially
an act of the will, but formally an act of the reason.... And
so choice is substantially an act of the will and not of the
reason; for choice is accomplished in a certain movement
of the soul towards the good which is chosen. Hence it is
clearly an act of the appetitive power' (*S.T.*, Ia, IIae, 13, 1).
Free will (*liberum arbitrium*) is not a faculty distinct from
the will. 'It is the will itself, though it designates the will,
not absolutely, but in relation to that act which is called
"choosing" ' (*De veritate*, 24, 6). Aquinas does indeed say that
liberum arbitrium is 'the power by which a man can judge
freely' (*De veritate*, 24, 6), and this statement may seem to
contradict the statement that the term designates the will.
For judging is naturally associated with the mind rather than
with the will. Aquinas himself notes this objection and
answers that 'although judgement belongs to the reason, yet
freedom of judging belongs immediately to the will' (*De
veritate*, 24, 6, *ad* 3). Choice is free in regard to particular
goods, which we can look at from different points of view;
but I should not look at a good from this point of view
rather than from that unless I willed to do so. In free choice
there is an interplay of reason and will, and that is why
Aquinas says that in the definition of *liberum arbitrium* in-
direct allusion is made to both faculties (*De veritate*, 24, 6,
ad 1). His intellectualism is shown in the statement that free-

dom is 'formally' in the intellect or reason; but this intellectualism is corrected or supplemented by the statement that freedom is 'materially' in the will. Free choice is an act of the will resulting from a judgement of reason.

Aquinas remarks that, if man were not free, 'counsels, exhortations, precepts, prohibitions, rewards and punishments would be pointless' (S.T., Ia, 83, 1). He obviously thought that free choice implies the power to choose otherwise than one actually does choose. If one freely chooses A rather than B, one might have chosen B: if one is offered a choice between tea and coffee, one might choose either or neither. As human beings act for the most part 'in character', according to disposition, habit and so on, many acts are, from a practical point of view, predictable. But we cannot predict infallibly all a person's acts; in the case of a fully free choice the agent might have chosen otherwise, even if it was highly probable that he would choose as he did. Are we to say, then, that for an infinite mind, God, all man's acts, including his free acts, are predictable? This is really a false problem in Aquinas' eyes. For the question implies that some events are future to God. 'Although contingent events take place successively, God does not come to know them successively, as we do, but simultaneously; for His knowledge is measured by eternity, and eternity being simultaneously entire, comprises all time. Therefore all things which take place in time are eternally present to God . . . and are known by Him infallibly' (S.T., Ia, 14, 13). 'When I see Socrates sitting down, my knowledge is certain and infallible, but no necessity to sit is imposed on Socrates by this fact. So God knows with certainty and infallibility all those things as present which for us are past, present, or future. And yet no necessity is thereby imposed on contingent events' (De rationibus fidei ad Contorem antiochenum, 10).

It was maintained, then, by Aquinas that man is free in choosing this or that particular good. The choice of some particular goods may be necessary as a means to the acquisition of the final end, happiness; but even when we know theoretically that this is the case, it is not so evident to us that we are unable to regard them from another point of view or under another aspect. It may be objected, however, that our choice of this or that particular end, sense-pleasure for example, or power or knowledge, is determined by our character, which in turn is determined by physiological and psychological factors, by environment and upbringing. It is useless, of course, to look to Aquinas for a discussion of the influence on human character and conduct of, say, the endocrine glands. We should be guilty of an obvious anachronism if we expected anything of the kind. But in view of the fact that Aquinas himself stressed the dependence of psychical characteristics on physiological conditions, we can justifiably expect some allusion at least to the bearing of this dependence on human choice. And in point of fact we find him saying that 'an end appears choiceworthy to a man in accordance with his physical make-up; for by a disposition of this kind a man is inclined towards choosing or rejecting something' (S.T., Ia, 83, 1). The important word in the present context is 'inclined'. Aquinas immediately adds: 'But these inclinations are subject to the judgement of reason.... Therefore they do not destroy freedom of the will.' And he says the same of acquired habits and passions. In his view all these factors influence human conduct, but they do not, except in pathological cases, determine it. Of course, when he says that passions and acquired habits are subject to the judgement of reason, he does not mean that they can be shaken off at a moment's notice. A man who has acquired certain undesirable habits may require a long time to get rid of them. But it was not necessary for him to acquire them, and when he has acquired them he can with perseverance get rid of them; unless, indeed, he is in an abnormal pathological condition.

The point of view of Aquinas on this matter represents, then, what we may call the point of view of common sense. He was convinced that our ordinary way of speaking about ourselves and others implies the recognition of freedom as a fact, and he endeavoured to explain freedom of choice with the aid of the categories of means and end. This does not mean, however, that Aquinas regarded free acts as entirely arbitrary and capricious, as 'causeless' events. If by 'cause' is meant a determining factor free acts are, of course, 'causeless'. But every free act is done for an end, in accordance with a judgement of the reason; and it is thus an instance of final causality, and it is not purely capricious or gratuitous. As for Aquinas' theory of the relation between divine efficient causality and human free acts, its interpretation is a matter of controversy, and it would in any case take us further into the sphere of theology than I care to go here.

CHAPTER FIVE

Man (2): Morality and Society

AQUINAS' moral theory is to be found mainly in the two divisions of the second part of the *Summa theologica* and in the third book of the *Summa contra Gentiles*, though moral questions are also treated or touched on in some of the *Quaestiones disputatae* (in the *De virtutibus in communi*, for example) and the *Quodlibeta*. His commentary on Aristotle's *Ethics* is certainly of value for ascertaining his own ideas; but the main purpose of the work is obviously to explain the teaching of the Greek philosopher. If therefore we are looking for Aquinas' own ideas about human moral conduct, we have to turn chiefly to two works one of which was explicitly designed as a systematic treatise on theology while the other, as we saw earlier, cannot be called a purely philosophical work with regard either to its purpose or to its content.[1]

To say this is not to suggest that Aquinas has no moral philosophy or that he forgets his own distinction between philosophy and theology based on Christian revelation. When discussing sins and vices he remarks that 'the theologian considers sin principally as an offence against God, whereas the moral philosopher considers it as being contrary to reason' (*S.T.*, Ia, IIae, 71, 6, *ad* 5). He does not say that there are morally bad acts which are not offences against God or that there are offences against God which are not contrary to right reason. What he says is that the theologian and the moral philosopher consider morally bad acts from rather different points of view or under different aspects. No doubt when he mentions the 'moral philosopher'

1. I use the phrase 'purely philosophical' in the sense indicated by Aquinas' own distinction between philosophy and dogmatic theology.

he is thinking chiefly, though not exclusively, of Aristotle; but his words show that he was well aware when he was talking specifically as a Christian theologian. He did not, however, attempt to work out a moral philosophy in complete abstraction from Christian doctrines. Indeed, it would be absurd to expect him to have done so in either of the *Summas*. For in the *Summa theologica* he was writing for students of theology, while in the *Summa contra Gentiles* one of his aims was to show how the Christian religion, though it is not deducible from philosophical truths, not only harmonizes with the latter but completes them, as it were, and sheds a fresh light upon them. Aquinas was perfectly well aware that a Greek philosopher like Aristotle was capable of distinguishing between morally good and morally bad actions, and he himself adopted a great deal of the Aristotelian ethical analysis. But he was also convinced that without revelation we can have only an imperfect and inadequate knowledge of the purpose of human life and of man's supreme good. It is only natural that when he is discussing man's final end he starts with the Aristotelian conception of 'happiness' and ends with the Christian doctrine of the beatific vision of God in heaven and that when he is discussing the virtues he completes his treatment of them by talking about the 'theological virtues' of faith, hope and charity.

In the following pages, therefore, I shall not attempt to prescind altogether from Christian doctrines; for to do this would be to give an unreal impression of Aquinas' thought. He was a theologian-philosopher of the thirteenth century, not the holder of a chair of moral philosophy in a modern British university who might think it his business to avoid presupposing the truth of his private religious beliefs. On the other hand, I do not want to give the impression that Aquinas made no distinction between what can be known about human life and destiny by a non-Christian philosopher and what cannot be known apart from revelation. For this was not in fact the case. But Aquinas certainly believed in the harmonious relation between all truths, however attained, and he wished to exhibit and illustrate this harmony.

*

In the last chapter we saw that Aquinas distinguished between 'human acts' (*actus humani*) and 'acts of a man' (*actus hominis*). It is only the former, namely free acts proceeding from the will in view of an end apprehended by the reason, which fall within the moral sphere and are morally good or bad. A purely reflex act, for example, is not a 'human act' in Aquinas' technical use of the term. For though it is the act of a human being, in the sense that is performed by a human being, it does not proceed from him considered precisely as a rational free being. And acts of this kind do not fall within the moral sphere. 'Moral acts and human acts are the same' (*S.T.*, Ia, IIae, 1, 3).

A modern reader might be inclined to understand the word 'act' in this connexion as meaning an action which can in principle be observed by other people, the action, for example, of giving money to a needy person or the action of stealing jewellery. So it may be as well to remark at once that Aquinas makes a distinction between the 'interior act' and the 'exterior act'. Obviously, if we are talking about human acts in the technical sense, there cannot be an exterior act without an interior act; for a human act is defined with reference to the will. In every human act the will is directed towards an end apprehended by the reason. Therefore in every human act there must be an interior act of the will. But there can be an interior act without what would ordinarily be reckoned as the corresponding exterior act. A man might, for instance, make up his mind to steal a watch, though he never actually does so, perhaps because a good opportunity for doing so does not occur. When therefore Aquinas talks about morally good and morally bad acts he refers primarily to interior acts. If, however, the interior act issues in an exterior act or is considered as doing so, the word 'act' signifies the total complex unless some qualification or the context shows that the word is being used in a more restricted sense.

Now, as we saw in the last chapter, Aquinas maintains that in every human act the will is directed towards an end, towards something apprehended as or thought to be good, that is, something which is known or thought to perfect in some way the subject who desires and chooses. And in accordance with his finalistic conception of nature Aquinas goes on to argue that the human will is necessarily set towards the final or ultimate good of man as such, and that it is under the impulse of this dynamic and innate orientation of the will that we make our particular choices. And the question arises what is the good of man as such, the object which alone can satisfy completely man's desire and striving. What is the object, the possession of which perfects man in the highest and completest way and by doing so confers happiness in the psychological sense?

It may be objected, of course, that the question assumes illegitimately that there is such an object. But Aquinas maintained that we would desire nothing at all, were there not an ultimate or supreme good for man, since all particular ends or goods are desired and sought after as means to the attainment of the ultimate or final end. It might indeed still be objected that even if we grant the existence of a natural desire for a complete and all-satisfying good, it does not necessarily follow that the desire is capable of fulfilment. But it must be remembered that Aquinas presupposes the existence of a God who has created things with innate tendencies towards the development of their own real potentialities. He presupposes, as proved elsewhere, that human nature has been created by a personal God who would not have created it with an unavoidable impulse towards a non-existent good or a good incapable of being attained.

The question, what is the supreme good or final end of man, is a real question in view of the empirical fact that different people have different ideas of what this good is. Every human being strives after the actualization of his potentialities, after the possession of a good which will satisfy the will, after 'happiness'; but it does not follow that all agree about the nature of this good. 'All desire the final end, because all desire their perfection, which is what the final end signifies. But they do not all agree about the concrete nature of the final end' (*S.T.*, Ia, IIae, 1, 17). By saying that all desire their perfection Aquinas does not mean that all human beings make a point of striving after moral perfection, which would be patently false; he means that all tend towards the actualization of the potentialities of their natures, even though they may never make use of terms like 'supreme good' or 'final end'. For him all created things tend towards the actualization of their potentialities; human beings do so not only instinctively but also by means of intellect and will. But since there is neither an innate idea nor an intuition of the supreme good in the concrete, people's ideas of what constitutes the supreme good or final end can be, and indeed are, different. Very often we can tell what this idea is only by observing a man's actions and seeing by the way in which he organizes his life what is his guiding purpose or operative ideal. One man may devote himself to obtaining the greatest possible amount of sensual pleasure, another to the pursuit of power, another to the attainment of knowledge, and so on. Aquinas would not see any difficulty against his theory in modern psychological investigations which show that the ideal or end which a man professes to follow is by no means always coincident with his operative ideal, that is, with the end in view of which he actually organizes his life. But since he believed that in spite of all differences between individuals there is such a thing as human nature, the question, what is the objective supreme good or final end of man as such, was for him a real question.

Aquinas proceeds to consider the claims of various goods to be the ultimate good of man as such.[1] Sense-pleasure, for example, cannot be man's supreme good because it perfects the body only: it actualizes the potentialities of, and satisfies only a part of the human being. Moreover, sense-pleasure can be enjoyed by animals as well as by human beings, and it is the good for man as such, as a 'rational animal',

1. Cf. *S.T.*, Ia, IIae, 2, 1 f.; *C.G.*, 3, 27 f.

that we are looking for. Again, power cannot be man's supreme good. For it would be absurd to speak of the supreme good as capable of abuse and of lending itself to the fulfilment of evil or unworthy purposes; and it is clear that power can be used to serve either good or bad purposes. Nor can scientific or speculative knowledge constitute man's supreme good or final end. The pursuit and attainment of scientific knowledge may satisfy this or that exceptional individual in the sense that it is what he desires and that to which he sacrifices the development of other sides of his nature; but it cannot achieve the objective perfecting of the whole personality. Not even the metaphysical knowledge of God can do this. Indeed, it is deficient even on the level of knowledge. For by philosophical reflection we come to know rather what God is not than what He is. Even the knowledge which we can have of God by faith falls short of the knowledge which alone can satisfy the human mind. To find the ultimate good or final end of man we have to turn to the supernatural vision of God which is attainable only in the next life.

It may appear that Aquinas here falls victim to his intellectualist tendencies and that he makes knowledge the ultimate good of man. And it is certainly true that he finds the essence of *beatitudo* in the intuitive knowledge or vision of God. But this does not mean that he excludes love, for example. According to him, the complete satisfaction of the will and of other elements in the human personality are part of 'happiness' in the wide sense, but this satisfaction follows from the vision of God; and it is therefore in the intellectual vision of God that he finds the formal essence of *beatitudo*. However, though he lays most emphasis on the intuitive vision of God he is thinking in terms of the Christian doctrine of the risen and transfigured human personality in its completeness. Nor does he forget the Christian doctrine of the communion of saints.

Beatitudo can mean, therefore, either God Himself or man's possession of God, according as one is thinking of the object, the possession of which confers happiness, or of man's possession of this object. For Aquinas it is this possession of God which actualizes man's potentialities in the highest possible degree and in the completest manner. But since he was convinced that this possession is impossible without supernatural grace, that it transcends the natural powers of man and that without revelation we cannot know that it is attainable and constitutes the actual final end of man, the conclusion inevitably suggests itself that the moral philosopher in a narrow sense cannot be sure what man's supreme good or final end really is. And this conclusion would obviously create considerable difficulties in a teleological ethic in which the concept of a final end plays such an important part. For human acts are declared to be morally good or bad in so far as they are or are not compatible with the attainment of this end.

Aquinas, however, did not think that without revelation it is impossible to have any knowledge of the good for man. Even if a philosopher knows nothing about the beatific vision of God, he is perfectly capable of seeing that some acts conduce to man's perfection, to the development and perfecting of his nature as man, and that others are incompatible with it. Hence he did not say that Aristotle in his teaching about the good for man was simply wrong or that he was a benighted pagan who could know nothing of morality. Aristotle, he said, was concerned with that imperfect and temporal happiness which man can attain in this life by his own efforts. In his admiration for Aristotle and in his desire to show that the general lines of the latter's philosophy were not incompatible with Christianity he may have tended to play down those aspects of Aristotelianism which seemed in the eyes of some critics to stamp it as a closed and purely naturalistic system. But Aquinas was convinced that Aristotle's outlook on the world and on human life was incomplete and inadequate rather than simply wrong or untrue. Grace perfects nature but does not annul it: revelation sheds further light, but it does not cancel out the truths attainable by purely philosophic reflection.

*

However great may be the differences between Aristotle's and Aquinas' conceptions of man's final end or ultimate good, it is clear that both men developed teleological theories of ethics, the idea of the good being paramount. For both of them human acts derive their moral quality from their relation to man's final end.

According to Aquinas, every concrete human act is either morally good or morally bad. But the term 'human act' must be taken in his technical sense, and the word 'concrete' is important. For if we consider human acts purely in the abstract some of these can be morally indifferent. Going out into the garden, for instance, can be called morally indifferent if it is considered purely in the abstract. But a concrete or individual human act is either morally good or morally bad, since it is either compatible or incompatible with the attainment of man's supreme good or final end. If we consider the act of going out into the garden purely in the abstract, we are not in a position to call it either morally good or morally bad: we cannot do this until we come to talk of a concrete or individual act of going out into the garden, an act informed by a certain purpose and characterized by certain circumstances. 'Any individual act has some circumstance by which it is drawn into the class either of good or bad acts, at least in virtue of the intention. . . . But if an act is not deliberate . . . (such as stroking the beard or moving a hand or foot), it is not properly speaking a human or moral act. . . . And so it will be indifferent, that is, outside the class of moral acts' (S.T., Ia, IIae, 18, 9).

The phrase 'informed by a certain purpose' has just been used. And it is important to understand the importance attached by Aquinas to intention. When he considers the interior act and the exterior act as component parts of a single whole, he likes to apply an analogy taken from the hylomorphic theory. Thus he compares the interior act with 'form' and the exterior act with 'matter'. Now intention belongs to the interior act. And it informs the whole act, in the sense that absence of a good intention and presence of a bad intention vitiates the whole act and renders it morally bad. If a materially good act is done with a bad intention the total human act, consisting of both elements, is rendered morally bad. 'For instance, we say that to give alms for the sake of vainglory is bad' (S.T., Ia, IIae, 20, 1). The action of giving alms is materially good, but the bad intention gives a 'form' to the individual human act of almsgiving which renders it morally bad. And, in general, in order that a human act should be morally good, a number of factors have to be present; and the absence of any one of them, of a right intention for instance, is sufficient to prevent our calling it good in an unqualified manner.

It does not follow, however, that for Aquinas intention is everything. 'Goodness of the will, proceeding from intention directed to an end, is not sufficient to make an exterior act good' (S.T., Ia, IIae, 20, 2). For, as Augustine says, there are some things which cannot be justified by any alleged good intention (ibid.; sed contra). The fact that a bad intention vitiates a human act, even though the external complement of the interior act is materially good, does not justify the view that a materially bad act is turned into a good act by the presence of a praiseworthy intention. For a human act, considered as a whole, to be morally bad, the absence of one single requisite factor is sufficient. But for a human act to be good without qualification the presence of one single requisite factor, like a good intention, is not sufficient. If I steal money from a man in order to give it in alms to someone else, my action is not justified by my good intention.

It is therefore not possible to father on Aquinas the view that the end justifies the means in the popular understanding of this proposition. When he says that human acts derive their moral quality from their relation to man's final end or supreme good, he does not mean that one is justified in doing anything at all provided that one has a certain intention. In order that a human act in the full sense should be morally good it must be compatible both 'formally' and 'materially' with the attainment of the final end. What is done, as well as the intention with which the act is performed and the way in which it is performed, must be compatible with attainment of the final end. Aquinas does not mean, of course, that an act cannot be morally good unless there is an explicit and actual reference to the final end or supreme good of man. If a man performs an act of kindness he may not consciously advert to anything else but the other person's needs and his own ability to meet that need. But his act is either compatible or incompatible with the attainment of the good for man: it must have some relation to it. And according to Aquinas it is from this relation that it ultimately derives its moral quality.

Every concrete or individual human act, therefore, must be either morally good or morally bad. But it does not necessarily follow that because a human act is morally good it is also morally obligatory. An act is morally obligatory only when not to do it or to do something else would be morally bad. If, for example, I see a child fall into a river and start to drown and I am the only person who can save it, to walk away and leave the child to die because it would be an inconvenience to me to get my clothes wet would be a morally bad action. I am under a moral obligation to perform the one action which, we will suppose, is capable of saving the child. But it sometimes happens that one is under moral obligation to choose among several possible lines of action without being morally obliged to choose this or that particular line of action. Suppose, for example, that a man has to support a family by adopting a profession and that he can do so by becoming either a porter or a postman. To choose one or other profession would be, in the circumstances imagined, a moral obligation; but the man would not be under a moral obligation to become a porter rather than a postman or a postman rather than a porter. Morally obligatory acts are thus a subdivision of morally good acts. In Aquinas' ethical theory the concept of the good remains paramount.

Although it means anticipating what will be said later in connexion with Aquinas' idea of the moral law, one can put the matter in this way. Reason sees that some acts are necessary for the attainment of the good for man. According to

Aquinas reason sees, for example, that it is necessary to take reasonable means to preserve one's life. Reason therefore orders the taking of food (we are talking about normal circumstances, of course). But this does not mean that one is under a moral obligation to eat beef rather than mutton or either of them rather than fish. Any one of these actions is morally good in so far as it conduces to the attainment of the end; but we cannot say of any particular one of them that it is morally obligatory unless some special circumstances intervene which make it so.

There are, of course, obvious objections to this sort of theory. People, it may be said, do not really argue in this way. There are indeed cases of moral perplexity when one has to reflect and take time to decide what is the right thing to do; but even then ordinary people do not refer to any 'final end' or 'supreme good'. In any case we generally see immediately what is the right thing to do; we feel that this is what we ought to do in the circumstances. Furthermore, we feel that certain actions ought never to be performed, whatever the consequences may be. To treat people, for example, in the way in which political prisoners were treated at Dachau or at Auschwitz is simply wrong in itself: it is not wrong because it is incompatible with some end beyond itself. An analysis of moral obligation in terms of means and end is incompatible with the moral consciousness.

It is true that our natural reaction to reading a description of the tortures inflicted on political prisoners at Dachau is to say that such actions are wrong and that they cannot be justified by any appeal to consequences like increase of scientific knowledge. We feel immediately a repugnance to such actions, and we may very likely go on to say that a man who does not see immediately that they are wrong is deficient in moral sense. But Aquinas did not deny that we can be aware of the wrongness of some actions without having to go through an explicit process of argumentation. He certainly did not think that there is adequate ground for saying that all human beings see intuitively the rightness of all those actions which are right and the wrongness of all those actions which are wrong. This is a point to which I shall return later. But at the same time he did not think that when the ordinary man judges that an act is wrong this judgement must be the result of his having asked himself whether the act is compatible with the attainment of the supreme good for man and of his having come to the conclusion that it is not compatible. Since man has an innate tendency to perfection, that is, to the development of his potentialities as a rational being, it is only natural that many men should see in a quasi-instinctive manner that to treat other human beings as people were often treated in the Nazi concentration camps is an offence against human personality and that it expresses and promotes the degradation of the agent. The acts are wrong in themselves, in the sense that they cannot be excused by political expediency or by desire for increasing scientific knowledge; but it does not follow that there is no reason why they are wrong. We ought to distinguish, Aquinas might say, between the way in which a person comes to believe or to recognize that an act is wrong and the objective reason why the act is wrong. In whatever way or ways people come to recognize the wrongness of wrong acts, the acts have this in common, that they are wrong and ought not to be performed. And it is only natural for a philosopher to inquire whether what they have in common, namely wrongness, is an unanalysable quality which we can recognize but about which nothing more can be said or whether it is a characteristic which can be analysed.

Aquinas' analysis of good and bad, right and wrong, in terms of means and end can be misunderstood if we fail to distinguish the various senses in which we can speak of means and end. If an artist paints a picture, the brushes can be called means or instruments in the production of the picture, but they do not form part of it. On the other hand, the lines which the artist traces on the canvas and the patches of colour which he successively applies form part of the picture itself. They can be called 'means' in some sense; but the end, namely the picture, is not something entirely beyond them or external to them. It is, however, external to the artist. But in the teleological ethic of Aristotle morally obligatory acts are not means to an end which is simply external to these acts, since they are already a partial fulfilment of it; nor is the end something external to the agent. If we take the word *beatitudo* in the sense in which Aquinas sometimes uses it, namely as signifying the object the possession of which confers happiness, the end is certainly 'external' to the human agent; but if the word is taken in the other sense in which he uses it, namely as signifying the activity by which the object is possessed, the final end is not external to the human agent. Aquinas followed Aristotle in holding that the final end of man consists in activity, and activity is obviously not external to the agent in the sense that a picture is external to the artist. It may be said that for Aquinas the whole world, including human beings with their potentialities and activities, exists for the glory of God, so that human moral conduct is necessarily subordinated to an end outside itself. Good acts and obligatory acts have value only through their relation to an extrinsic end. But the perfecting of creatures, the development of their natures, is for Aquinas the glorification of God. We cannot justifiably make a dichotomy between human moral conduct on the one hand and the glory of God on the other, as though this were some *tertium quid* apart from both God and man. God is glorified by the highest possible development of man's potentialities as a rational being, and every moral act of man has therefore an intrinsic value. But this is not to say that they have value purely atomistically, so to speak; they have intrinsic value within the total context of man's movement towards his final end, which is in concrete fact, though not by a necessity of nature, the supernatural possession of the infinite good.

The foregoing remarks do not amount, of course, to a proper discussion of the controversy between the upholders and the critics of teleological ethics. Nor do they constitute a proof of the truth of Aquinas' position. Their purpose is simply to show how a problem arises in connexion with his ethical theory and at the same time to suggest some considerations which may help towards the understanding of the theory. Further light will, I hope, be shed by the outline which will be given later of his theory of the natural moral law.

*

As we have seen, Aquinas emphasized the place and function of reason in moral conduct. He shared with Aristotle the view that it is the possession of reason which distinguishes man from the animals, to whom he is in many ways similar. It is reason which enables him to act deliberately in view of a consciously apprehended end and raises him above the level of purely instinctive behaviour.

Now, every normal human being acts deliberately in view of consciously apprehended ends. And in this sense every normal human being acts, at least sometimes, rationally. And to act for an end is to act for a good. But it does not follow that the good which a man chooses for the attainment of which he takes particular means is necessarily compatible with the objective good for man. There is therefore room for the concept of 'right reason', reason directing man's acts to the attainment of the objective good for man. Both the burglar and the seducer can be said to be acting 'rationally' if they take the appropriate means to the fulfilment of their respective purposes. But since neither burglary nor seduction is compatible with the attainment of the objective good for man, the activities of the burglar and the seducer are not in accordance with 'right reason'. If it is said that moral conduct is rational conduct, what is meant is that it is conduct in accordance with right reason, reason apprehending the objective good for man and dictating the means to its attainment.

But though Aquinas laid emphasis on man's possession of reason he did not look on man as being either in fact or in ideal a kind of disembodied intellect. And though he emphasized the function of reason in moral conduct he was not insensible to the place of emotion and passion in human life. The passions,[1] he says, are common to human beings and to animals, and if they are considered simply in themselves they do not enter the moral order; that is to say, one cannot properly talk about them as being either morally good or morally bad. It is only when they are considered in relation to the human reason and will that we can speak of them as good or bad in a moral sense. When they are in accordance with right reason and subject to its control they are good, when they are allowed to obscure reason and to lead us into acts, not necessarily external acts, which are contrary to right reason, they are bad. But it is false to say that man would be better off without any passions or emotions; for without them man would not be man. We have no right to say that all passions are evil.

When treating of this matter Aquinas alludes to the dispute between the Stoics and the Peripatetics or Aristotelians. 'The Stoics said that all passions are evil, whereas the Peripatetics said that moderated passions are good' (*S.T.*, I*a*, II*ae*, 24, 2). And he makes the following characteristic comment. 'Although as far as words go the difference between them seems to be considerable, in actual fact there is no difference, or at any rate very little, if, that is to say, one bears in mind what each party meant' (*ibid.*). For the Stoics, according to Aquinas, meant by 'passions' the motions of the sensitive appetite unregulated by reason, and in condemning all passions as evil they were really condemning what the Peripatetics also condemned, namely unhealthy upsurges of emotion, unregulated by reason and tending to lead man into acts contrary to right reason. And Aquinas goes on to say that if one understands the word 'passion' in the sense given it by the Stoics, it is true to say with them that the presence of passion or emotion diminishes the moral value of an act. But if one does not under-

1. In the ordinary language of today the word 'passion' generally signifies an emotion unregulated by reason, as in the sentence 'She flew into a passion.' But Aquinas uses the word in a neutral sense, to mean emotions and affects.

stand the word in this restricted sense, the statement that the moral goodness of an act is necessarily impaired by the presence of passion or emotion is false. Indeed, 'it pertains to the perfection of moral goodness that a man should be moved towards the good not only by his will but also by his sensitive appetite' (S.T., Ia, IIae, 24, 3). Aquinas was well aware, of course, that the doing of one's duty may be some times extremely unpleasant; and he was also aware that the strength of the moral character is tested in precisely these situations. But his ideal of the completely integrated human being did not permit him to share the view, not infrequently ascribed to Kant, that it is in itself better to do one's duty without or even contrary to inclination than to do it with inclination. Needless to say, Aquinas thought that it is better to do an act of kindness even though it goes against the grain than not to do it. And he would doubtless take a poor view of doing acts of kindness simply and solely to obtain a pleasurable feeling from doing them. But he also thought that it is in itself better to do acts of kindness with pleasure than to do them with set teeth, as it were. Ideally, the whole man should be attracted by the good.

*

One of the main factors in human moral activity is thus the passions or emotions. The whole moral life is founded on the will's movement towards the good, and particular emotions can greatly help or hinder moral choice and action. Another influential factor is habit. Aquinas recognized, of course, the presence of innate 'habits' in the sense of innate bodily dispositions which incline us to act in one way rather than another. But in his technical use of the word he meant by 'habit' an acquired habit, acquired, that is to say, by acts, rather than innate bodily predispositions. Acquired habits, or simply habits, are for him qualities which in accordance with his distinction between different faculties or powers he describes as qualities of the latter. Thus there can be habits not only in the powers of the sensitive part of man but even in his intellectual faculties. These habits are caused by acts, though we obviously cannot say how many acts are required to form a habit. Generally speaking, repeated acts of the same nature are required, though 'it is possible for bodily habits to be caused by one act, if the agent is powerful enough, as when a strong medicine immediately causes health' (*S.T.*, Ia, IIae, 51, 3). And habits dispose a man to act readily and easily in certain ways.

The word 'habit', however, is a neutral word from the ethical point of view; for there can be both good and bad habits. Good operative habits are called by Aquinas 'virtues' and bad operative habits 'vices'. But he was not content with this distinction, and he followed Aristotle in distinguishing between the moral virtues, which incline a man's sensitive appetite to act in accordance with right reason, and the intellectual virtues, which perfect a man's rational powers. We can have certain intellectual virtues without possessing the moral virtues. It is possible, for example, to be a competent metaphysician or pure mathematician without being a moral man in the colloquial sense of the term. And it is obviously possible to have the habit of self-control with regard to the passions of anger or lust without being a metaphysician or a mathematician. But it is not possible to have the moral virtues without the intellectual virtue of 'prudence' which inclines us to choose the right means to the attainment of the objective good or to have prudence without the moral virtues.[1] We cannot therefore dissociate altogether the moral from the intellectual virtues.

Aquinas writes at length about the virtues, and I do not propose to follow him into his analysis of them. A great deal of what he has to say on the subject is taken from Aristotle, though he was also influenced, of course, by the Christian Fathers who had themselves been influenced by Cicero and

---

1. It is possible, of course, to have prudence without the moral virtues if the word is used in a neutral sense, to cover, for example, the forethought of the skilful thief and his power of choosing apt means to secure the attainment of his purpose. But Aquinas is thinking of the habit of choosing the objectively good means to the objectively good end for man.

by the Stoics. But it was not merely the example of Aristotle and of other writers on moral topics that led him to treat so extensively of the virtues. For he was convinced that 'we need virtuous habits on three counts' *(De virtutibus in communi,* 1), namely that we may be able to act uniformly, readily, and pleasurably in accordance with right reason. Man perfects himself and develops towards the attainment of the objective good in and through activity; and habits are one of the most important influential factors in activity. Without virtuous operative habits a man will not be able to act in accordance with right reason in the way in which he should be able to act, namely in a quasi-spontaneous manner. It is true that 'some are disposed by their bodily constitution to chastity or to gentleness or to something of this kind' *(S.T.,* Ia, IIae, 51, 1); but none the less human beings are in a state of potentiality in regard to moral and immoral activity, and it is through the acquisition of good operative habits or virtues that they acquire a relative, though not absolute, stability in acting morally.

It is clear that for Aquinas there is an ideal type of man, an ideal of human development and integration, a notion which has been flatly rejected by, for example, existentialists like M. Sartre. And the possession of the natural virtues, moral and intellectual, belongs to this ideal type. But the concrete ideal for man is not for Aquinas simply the ideal of the fully-developed natural man. For under the action of divine grace man can rise to the life of supernatural union of God. And for this higher sphere of life he needs the infused virtues of faith, hope, and charity. 'Faith, hope and charity transcend the human virtues, for they are virtues of a man in so far as he is made a sharer in divine grace' *(S.T.,* Ia, IIae, 58, 3, *ad* 3). While building, therefore, on a largely Aristotelian foundation, which represents what we may call the 'humanistic' element in his ideal for man, Aquinas proceeds to discuss the theological virtues, which are not acquired in the same way as the natural virtues, and the gifts of the Holy Spirit. However much he may have borrowed from

Aristotle and other ancient writers, his complete picture of the fully-developed human being is very different from that which we find in the *Nicomachean Ethics*.

It may appear all the more surprising that Aquinas adopted the Aristotelian analysis of virtue as a 'mean'. That Aristotle propounded this theory is easily intelligible by any-one who knows the history of Greek medical theory and of its influence on ethical thought. But that a Christian theolo-gian should adopt it may seem strange. In what sense can St Francis of Assisi, for instance, be called an example of 'the mean'?

For Aquinas, as for Aristotle, a virtue like courage is con-cerned with passions or emotions, and it inclines a man to act in such a way that he avoids the extremes represented by two contrary passions. The courageous man is not carried away by fear, as is the coward; nor on the other hand does he go to the extreme of foolhardiness and rashness. Courage can thus be said to be a 'mean' between cowardice and rash-ness, in the sense that it reduces passion to the rule of reason and inclines a man in his actions to steer his way easily and readily between extremes. 'According to its substance', to use Aquinas' terminology, courage combines the foresight of the coward with the boldness of the rash or foolhardy man, and it is thus a mean. But if it is looked at from the point of view of excellence, it is an extreme. To fall into excess or defect is relatively easy: to follow the path marked out by right reason is not so easy. There is only one such path; and though it lies between the pitfalls of excess and defect and is thus a middle way, it is an extreme when regarded from the valuational point of view.

This Aristotelian doctrine of the mean was doubtless con-genial to Aquinas' temperament. He was not an admirer of fanaticism or of rigorous Puritanism any more than he was of moral slovenliness. At the same time he evidently felt that there was some difficulty at least in reconciling it with Christian ideals; for he himself raises the question whether giving away all one's goods and following a life of poverty does not constitute an excess (*S.T.*, Ia, IIae, 64, 1, *obj.* 3).

His answer is more or less to the effect that such actions would constitute an excess if they were done out of superstition or out of a desire to make a name for oneself, but that if they are performed in response to the invitation of Christ they are in accordance with reason and cannot be called excessive. The doctrine of the mean does not refer to a mathematical middle-point like the middle-point in a finite line, which can be calculated mathematically. That which is in accordance with right reason is the mean in the sense intended by the doctrine: it does not signify a middle-point between two extremes which can be calculated arithmetically. At the same time, however, Aquinas recognized that there can be such a thing as heroic virtue which can scarcely be fitted into the doctrine of the mean without stretching the latter to breaking-point. Thus in his commentary on the fifth chapter of St Matthew's Gospel he remarks that 'when a brave man fears what should be feared he is virtuous, and not to fear would be vicious. But when, trusting in divine help, he fears nothing in the world, that is superhuman. And virtues of this kind are called divine.' And when treating of the theological virtues he admits that from one point of view the doctrine of the mean cannot be applied to them. If we are talking about the virtue of love considered in itself, it is not possible to love God too much; there can be no question of an excess, though there can be defect. But he goes on to say that if we are considering man's condition and the ways in which he should manifest love for God, we can talk about a 'mean' even in this connexion. He evidently felt that the doctrine of the mean had a certain universal application in that it represented respect for the rule of right reason and for the proportion and measure demanded by right reason; but at the same time he saw that its literal application was restricted to cases where it made sense to speak of possible excess and defect. It may be that his Aristotelianism led him to apply the doctrine so widely that the use of the 'mean' in some of its applications was forced and artificial. But I do not think that his use of the doctrine was simply due to a determination to follow Aristotle. For it represents, as I have said, his own dislike of one-sided exaggerations and his own respect for the rule of reason.

*

In the foregoing sections we have considered Aquinas' idea of man as drawn by an innate impulse of the will towards the good. And mention has been made of 'right reason', that is, of course, reason considered as directing man's acts to the attainment of his objective good or end. But little has been said about obligation and the concept of the moral law. And I wish to deal now with these topics. Discussion of them should also help to throw some light on what has gone before.

When he turns to the subject of law Aquinas begins, as is his custom, with some general remarks. Law in general, he says, is a measure or rule of human acts, a measure or rule conceived by reason and promulgated with a view to the common good. And he defines law as 'an ordinance of reason made for the common good by him who has charge of the community, and promulgated' (S.T., Ia, IIae, 90, 4).

This definition obviously suggests the thought of human positive law, the law of the State; and in view of this fact it might seem natural to start with law in this sense and then to go on to the idea of the natural moral law, leaving to the end the problem of the metaphysical foundations, if any, of the moral law. In actual fact, however, Aquinas starts with the idea of the eternal law of God. And I prefer to follow him in his order of treatment rather than to change it. But it may be as well to remark at once that if Aquinas starts with the concept of the eternal law of God this does not mean that for him the moral law depends on God's arbitrary choice. This point will, I hope, be made clear in what follows. The reason why he starts with mention of God is that moral law is for him one of the ways in which creatures are directed towards their several ends. He sees the moral life in the general setting of the providential government of creatures. For him the moral law is not something without any relation to anything other than itself; it is a special case of the general principle that all finite things move towards their ends by the development of their potentialities. If Aquinas were writing an ethical treatise today, he might very well start at a different point. But actually he places the moral law in a metaphysical setting from the very beginning, and I propose to adhere to his arrangements of the matter.

Aquinas speaks of God as an artist or an artificer who has an idea of the work to be created or done and of the means to its fulfilment. God conceives eternally all creatures according to their different kinds: He conceives their ends and the means to the attainment of these ends. And the divine wisdom, considered as moving all things according to their several ends in subordination to the end of the whole created universe, the communication of the divine perfection, is the eternal law. 'Hence the eternal law is nothing else than the plan of the divine wisdom considered as directing all the acts and motions' of creatures (S.T., Ia, IIae, 93, 1). But this does not mean that God settles arbitrarily, as it were, the means which will lead to the perfection of creatures. He sees eternally in human nature, for example, the activities which constitute its objective development or unfolding; and though He created man freely He could not both create man and contradict the exigencies of human nature. For the eternal idea of human nature is, for Aquinas, the divine perfection conceived by God as imitable in a certain way in creation. To say, therefore, that God could not conceive human nature and at the same time alter the fundamental ways in which the potentialities of this nature are to be actualized is not to say that His freedom is restricted by an essence existing apart from Himself. Rather it is to say that God, precisely because He is God, cannot act irrationally and contradict Himself.

The eternal law is thus the plan of divine wisdom directing all things to the attainment of their ends. Now, inanimate bodies act in certain ways precisely because they are what they are, and they cannot act otherwise; they cannot perform actions which are contrary to their nature. And animals are governed by instinct. In fine, all creatures below man participate unconsciously in the eternal law, which is reflected in their various natural tendencies, and they do not possess the freedom which is required in order to be able to act in a manner incompatible with this law. But man, as a rational and free being, is capable of acting in ways which are incompatible with the eternal law. It is therefore essential that he should know the eternal law in so far as it concerns himself. Yet how can he know it? He cannot read, as it were, the mind of God. Is it, then, necessary that God should reveal to him the moral law? Aquinas answers that this is not necessary in the strict sense of the word. For although man cannot read off, as it were, the eternal law in God's mind, he can discern the fundamental tendencies and needs of his nature, and by reflecting on them he can come to a knowledge of the natural moral law. Every man possesses the natural inclinations to the development of his potentialities and the attainment of the good for man. Every man possesses also the light of reason whereby he can reflect on these fundamental inclinations of his nature and promulgate to himself the natural moral law, which is the totality of the universal precepts or dictates of right reason concerning the good which is to be pursued and the evil which is to be shunned. By the light of his own reason, therefore, man can arrive at some knowledge of the natural law. And since this law is a participation in or reflection of the eternal law in so far as the latter concerns human beings and their free acts, man is not left in ignorance of the eternal law which is the ultimate rule of all conduct. 'The natural law is nothing else but a participation of the eternal law in a rational creature' (*S.T.*, I*a*, II*ae*, 91, 2).

It is sufficiently obvious that the term 'natural law' does not bear the same sense here that is borne by the term 'law of nature' when the law of gravitation, for example, is spoken of as a law of nature or as a natural law. Irrational things do indeed reflect the eternal law in their activities and behaviour; but if we talk about them as obeying a natural law the word 'law', insists Aquinas, is used analogically. For law is defined as an ordinance of reason, and irrational creatures, being irrational, cannot recognize and promulgate to themselves any natural law. Human beings, however, can do so. And the term 'natural law' is applicable in the strict sense, not to the natural tendencies and inclinations of man on which his reason reflects, but to the precepts which his reason enunciates as a result of this reflection.

For Aquinas, therefore, it is the human reason which is the proximate or immediate promulgator of the natural moral law. This law is not without a relation to something above itself; for it is, as we have seen, the reflection of or a participation in the eternal law. But inasmuch as it is immediately promulgated by the human reason we can speak of a certain autonomy of the practical reason. This does not mean that man can alter the natural moral law which is founded on his nature. But it means that the human being does not receive the moral law simply as an imposition from above: he recognizes or can recognize its inherent rationality and binding force, and he promulgates it to himself. This is one reason why in outlining Aquinas' ethical theory one could start with the concept of the natural moral law, though I have preferred to begin, as he began, with its eternal and transcendent foundation, the eternal law of God.

According to Aquinas 'the primary precept of the law is that good should be done and pursued and evil avoided; and on this are founded all the other precepts of the law of nature' (S.T., Ia, IIae, 94, 2). But the precept that good should be done and evil avoided, the truth of which is said by Aquinas to be known intuitively, obviously tells us very little about human conduct: we want to know what 'good' and 'evil' mean in the concrete. And as it is the good for man which is under consideration Aquinas proceeds to give content to the term by examining the fundamental natural tendencies or inclinations of man. For an inclination or tendency is directed towards an object as good, and a natural tendency or inclination, arising from the fact that a thing is a being of this or that particular kind (a sensitive thing, for example, or a rational being), is directed towards an object

222

or end as a natural good of that thing. Hence by examining man's nature and natural inclinations one can discern the good for man in the natural order.

'The order of the precepts of the law of nature follows the order of natural inclinations. First, there is present in man an inclination towards the good considered in relation to his nature in so far as this nature is shared by all other substances. For every substance tends to conserve its existence according to its own kind. And as a consequence of this inclination those actions by which a man's life is conserved and death avoided belong to the natural law' (S.T., Ia, IIae, 94, 2). Together with all other substances man has a natural tendency to preserve his being, and reason reflecting on this tendency as present in man promulgates the precept that life is to be preserved. 'Secondly, there is present in man an inclination according to his nature in so far as it is shared by other animals' (ibid.). This naturally implanted inclination, shared in a measure by all things which enjoy sensitive life, is an inclination to propagate the species and bring up offspring. And reason reflecting on this natural inclination promulgates the precept that the species is to be propagated and children educated. 'Thirdly, there is present in man an inclination to his good as a rational being. Thus man has a natural inclination to know the truth about God and to live in society' (ibid.). Reason, reflecting on man's nature as that of a rational being, promulgates the precept that he should seek truth and avoid ignorance, especially about those things knowledge of which is necessary for the right ordering of his life, and that he should live in society with other men.

In view of the fact that Aquinas not only accepted the institution of clerical celibacy and the ideals of the religious life but was himself a Dominican, it may appear odd that according to him there is a fundamental precept of the natural moral law to the effect that the human species should be propagated. His answer to a comment like this is as follows: 'The natural precept about taking nourishment must necessarily be fulfilled by every individual; for otherwise he could not be preserved. But the precept about generation bears on the human community, which ought not only to be multiplied corporeally but also to make spiritual progress. And so sufficient provision is made if some only attend to generation, while others give themselves to the contemplation of divine things for the enrichment and salvation of the whole human race. Similarly, in the case of an army some guard the camp, others bear the standards, and others fight. All these things ought to be done, but they cannot all be done by one man' (S.T., Ia, IIae, 152, 2, ad 1). And it is no more incumbent on married people to have as many children as possible, regardless of circumstances, than it is for a man to eat as much as possible. It is reason reflecting on human nature that is the guide to conduct, not reason working in pure abstraction. And reason sees the irrationality not only of racial suicide, which would contradict a natural impulse implanted by God, but also of the statement that every human being is bound to marry and have children. The precept about the propagation of the human race is vague, Aquinas might say, in the sense that we cannot deduce from it that a particular individual is bound to marry and have children; but it is not so vague that it says nothing at all. We can deduce from it, for instance, that anyone who agreed to or promoted a policy of racial suicide would be acting wrongly. However, the conception of a law which obliges people in general but nobody in particular obviously presents some difficulty.

Before we proceed any further it may be as well to make the following remarks. Aquinas thought of man as tending naturally and inevitably towards his perfection, towards the actualization of his potentialities as man, towards his final end or good. And he thought of the practical reason [1] as discerning the acts necessary to the attainment of this end and

1. 'The practical reason and the speculative reason are not different powers' (S.T., Ia, 79, 11). The latter is reason as concerned simply with the knowledge and consideration of truth, while the former is reason as concerned with the application of what it apprehends either in moral conduct or in artistic or technical production.

as ordering them while forbidding their contraries. In this sense, obligation is imposed by the practical reason, binding the free will to perform the acts necessary for the attainment of the final end or good for man and to abstain from the acts which are incompatible with its attainment. The moral imperative is not, therefore, a problematical hypothetical imperative, to use Kantian terminology. It does not say, 'If you want to attain this end (to become a competent carpenter or a successful burglar), you must take these means.' It is not a technological imperative or an imperative of skill. The moral imperative says, 'You necessarily seek this end because you are what you are, a human being; therefore you ought to do this and not to do that.' In this sense the imperative is unconditional and absolute. Kant would call it an assertoric hypothetical imperative, and he considered that this imperative was not equivalent to the categorical imperative recognized by the moral consciousness. But Aquinas was obviously convinced that though the moral imperative is in a real sense unconditional and absolute a rational analysis and account of obligation can be given which shows the part it plays in human life and in the general scheme of things. According to him, all seek 'happiness' in an indeterminate sense. And the moral imperative directs the taking of the means to this end. But among the means are the discovery of what 'happiness' signifies in the concrete and the conscious willing of it as thus concretely conceived.

We have so far three primary precepts of the natural law, relating to man considered on the biological, animal or sensitive, and rational levels. And Aquinas thought that reason reflecting on human nature as manifested in experience can discover less general and more particular precepts. For example, he thought that from the second precept, relating to the propagation of the species and the education of children, one can derive the law of monogamy, on the ground, among others, that this is required for the proper care and upbringing of the children (*G.C.*, 3, 124). The natural moral law in its totality therefore consists of a multiplicity of precepts of varying degrees of generality. But at the same time all these precepts are virtually contained in the fundamental precept that good is to be pursued and evil avoided.[1]

*

The foregoing outline of Aquinas' theory of the natural moral law gives rise to a number of questions. I can comment, however, only very briefly on a few selected questions. And I begin with the one which is perhaps most likely to present itself to the reader's mind.

Aquinas believed that actions which are contrary to the natural moral law are not wrong simply because God prohibits them; they are prohibited by God because they are wrong. Suicide is wrong and eating meat on Friday when one is bound by the ecclesiastical law of abstinence is also wrong. But while there is nothing wrong in itself in eating meat on Friday, so that to do so is wrong only when and because it is forbidden, suicide is contrary to the natural moral law and so is wrong in itself. Ecclesiastical precepts like the law of abstinence on Fridays can be suspended or changed, but the natural moral law is unalterable. It is true that Aquinas distinguishes between primary and secondary precepts, derived from the first, and says that the last can be 'changed' for special reasons in a few particular cases. But what he means is that in some particular cases the circumstances of an act may be such that it no longer falls under the class of actions prohibited by the precept. For instance, we can say in general that if someone entrusts his property to us for safe keeping and asks for it back we ought to return it. But no sensible man would say that if someone entrusts us with a knife or a revolver and asks for it back when he is in a state of homicidal mania we are obliged to return it. In its general form, however, the precept remains

1. The two parts of this precept have to be taken together. As we saw earlier, Aquinas held that we are morally obliged to perform not all possible good acts but only those the omission of which would be evil.

valid. And we can say with truth that Aquinas believed in a set of unalterable moral precepts.

The question arises, however, whether this theory is compatible with the empirical fact that different people and different social groups have held divergent moral convictions. Do not the empirical facts suggest that the moral law is not unalterable but changeable? Or, to use the value-language, do not the empirical facts suggest that values are historically relative and that there are no universal and absolute values? Believing in a human nature which is constant Aquinas was led to postulate an unchangeable moral law; but some of the precepts which he regarded as forming part of its content have not been regarded by many people in the past and are not now regarded by many people as moral precepts at all. Is it not reasonable to conclude that Aquinas simply canonized, as it were, the moral convictions and standards of his time or at least of the society to which he belonged?

This is a far-reaching problem, and I must content myself with making the following relevant point, namely that differences in moral convictions do not by themselves constitute a disproof of the theory that there is an unchangeable moral law. For there might be an unchangeable moral law and at the same time varying degrees of insight into the content of this law, these differences being explicable in terms of the influence of a variety of empirical factors. To use the value-language, there might be objective and absolute values and at the same time different degrees of insight into these values. I do not mean to imply either that the existence of an unchanging moral law was for Aquinas an uncertain hypothesis or that the explicability of differences in moral conviction on the theory that there is such a law proves of itself that the theory is true. My point is that differences of opinion about moral precepts and moral values do not constitute a proof of the relativist position. And this point is one that should be taken into consideration in any discussion of the problem.

Aquinas himself was not ignorant of the fact that different

groups have held different moral convictions. According to him all men are aware of the most fundamental principles in their most general form. All men would agree that in some sense good is to be pursued and evil avoided. If a man denies this principle he is probably denying not the principle itself but that what another man or a given society calls good is good. But when we come to less general and more particular conclusions, derived from the fundamental principles, ignorance is certainly possible. 'In the case of some the reason is blinded by passion or by bad habits or by physical conditions. For example, according to Julius Caesar robbery used not to be considered wrong among the Germans, although it is expressly against the natural law' (S.T., Ia, IIae, 94, 4). A fortiori there can be differences of opinion about the application of precepts to particular cases. Conscience may be erroneous, whether through our own fault or through some cause for which we are not responsible.[1] And if our conscience tells us that we ought to perform a particular act, it is our moral duty to perform it. 'Every conscience, whether it is right or wrong, whether it concerns things evil in themselves or things morally indifferent, obliges us to act in such a way that he who acts against his conscience sins' (Quodlibetum, 3, 27). This does not mean that there is no such thing as right reason and no such thing as an objectively correct moral conscience; but ignorance and mistakes are possible in moral matters, and the nearer we come to particulars the greater is the field for error.

But though the reader may be prepared to admit that differences in moral convictions do not by themselves alone constitute a disproof of Aquinas' theory of an unalterable moral law, he may easily feel that the latter's whole approach to the subject of moral precepts is extremely artificial and excessively rationalistic. For Aquinas talks as though people derive or deduce less general from more general moral precepts and then proceed to apply these pre-

1. Aquinas called the habitual knowledge of the primary moral principles *synderesis* and the act of applying moral principles to particular actions *conscientia* (cf. S.T., Ia, 79, 12–13).

cepts to particular actions. But surely, it may be said, this picture does not represent the facts. Moral precepts seem to be ultimately reducible to the expression of feelings of approval or disapproval of certain actions or of certain types of action. True, we do enunciate general moral precepts; and moral philosophers have not unnaturally tried to rationalize their own moral convictions or those of the group or society to which they belonged. But feeling comes first: it is the whole basis of ethics. It may indeed appear that ethical disputes can be settled by rational argument, and in a certain sense they can sometimes be so settled. For example, if two men can agree on a definition of murder they can discuss in a rational manner whether the action of killing someone who is dying from a painful and incurable disease falls under the definition or not. Each man points out to the other features of the action in question which he thinks that the other has overlooked, and it is at any rate possible that in the end one will succeed in convincing the other. But rational argument is possible only when there is already a certain measure of moral agreement. Is it not a notorious fact that if two people disagree about fundamental moral issues or defend sharply opposed sets of values, neither can be convinced simply by the arguments advanced by the other? They will either agree to differ or they will end in anger and even abuse. Moreover, the function of any arguments which may be advanced by one of them seems to be that of facilitating a change of feeling or of emotional attitude. And perhaps the same can be said of discussions concerning the moral quality of particular actions or types of action when these discussions cannot be reduced to a quasi-logical problem of classification. If two men discuss the question whether so-called 'mercy killing' is right or wrong, the one maintaining that it is right, the other that it is wrong, the function of drawing attention to aspects of the action which the one man believes to have been overlooked by the other seems to be that of facilitating a change of emotive reaction in the other. The one man desires to substitute in the other man a feeling of approval for a feeling of disapproval or *vice versa*, as the case may be; and the arguments and appeals to reason which are employed are techniques used to facilitate this change of emotive response. In fine, morality is 'more properly felt than judged of', to use Hume's words (*Treatise*, 3, 1, 2).

It can hardly be denied that Aquinas' language sometimes seems to imply an extremely rationalistic interpretation of the way in which people form their moral judgements. But we have to look at what he means by the statements which he makes. He compares, for example, the precept that good is to be pursued and evil avoided with the proposition that the whole is greater than any one of its parts. And while he thought that this proposition is known to all human beings once they have had experience of material things he did not mean to say that every human being explicitly enunciates it to himself in so many words, even though he would certainly assent to it if it were proposed to him. 'In the cognitive powers there can be inchoate habits. . . . And the understanding of (first) principles is termed a natural habit. For it is owing to the very nature of the intellectual soul that once a man knows what is a whole and what is a part he knows that every whole is greater than any one of its parts, though he cannot know what is a whole and what is a part except through ideas derived from images' (*S.T.*, Ia, IIae, 51, 1). Directly a human being has experience of material wholes he recognizes immediately the relation between whole and part, and that he knows this can be seen by the fact that he never assumes that any part is greater than the whole of which it is a part. But it does not necessarily follow that he ever says to himself in so many words that a whole is greater than any one of its parts. Similarly, a human being obtains the idea of good, of a thing considered as perfecting or as satisfying his nature in some way, only through experience of actual objects of desire and sources of satisfaction. But because of his innate inclination to the good in this sense he immediately apprehends it as something to be pursued, while he apprehends evil, considered as that which is opposed to his nature and natural inclinations, as something to be avoided. The fact that he does apprehend the good or the perfection as something to be pursued and the evil, that which is opposed to or thwarts his natural inclinations, as something to be shunned and avoided is shown by the whole of his conduct. For every human being naturally shuns whatever appears to him as opposed to his nature. But it does not necessarily follow that he ever explicitly enunciates to himself the proposition that good is to be pursued and evil avoided. One may be tempted to say that all this belongs to the instinctive level and the level of feeling rather than the level of rational apprehension. But Aquinas would doubtless comment that a man does not shun death, for example, simply in the same way that an animal can be said to do so. For he shuns it not only instinctively but because and in so far as he apprehends it with his reason as destructive of his nature. And since he shuns it and avoids it as evil, knowledge that evil is to be shunned and avoided is implicitly presupposed. Though we could have no idea of evil except through experience of things opposed to our natural inclinations, apprehension of the principle that evil is to be avoided is logically presupposed by recognition of the fact that this particular thing is to be avoided because it is evil.

As regards deduction, Aquinas did not think that we can deduce the proposition that to have sexual intercourse with someone else's wife[1] is wrong from the precept that good is to be pursued and evil avoided simply by contemplating, as it were, this latter precept. We can no more do this than we can deduce from the principle of non-contradiction the proposition that a thing which is white all over cannot at the same time be red all over. We obtain our ideas of whiteness and redness from other sources than an analysis of the principle of non-contradiction. At the same time we reject the proposition that a thing can be simultaneously white all

1. I avoid the word 'adultery' here because this word, though it can be used in a purely technical or legal sense, may suggest from the start the idea of wrongness. And to say that a wrong action is wrong is to utter a tautology.

over and red all over precisely because it involves a contradiction. Similarly, we do not obtain our ideas of other people
and of wives and of sexual intercourse simply by analysing
the precept that good is to be pursued and evil avoided. But
once we have obtained those ideas we reject, if we do reject,
the proposition that it is right to have sexual intercourse
with someone else's wife because we apprehend actions of
this sort as being evil. The word 'deduction', therefore, can
be very misleading; and what Aquinas actually says is that
other precepts of the natural law are 'founded on' or 'based
on' the precept that good is to be done and evil avoided. The
concrete good for man can be known only by reflection on
human nature as known in experience.

It has been said above that we reject, 'if we do reject', the
proposition that it is right to have sexual intercourse with
someone else's wife because we apprehend actions of this
sort as being evil. As we have seen, Aquinas thought that the
nearer we come to particulars the more possible becomes
ignorance or error concerning the objective good for man,
and so concerning the particular precepts of the natural
moral law. But some particular types of action are practically always apprehended as evil, as opposed in some way or
other to human nature. For example, even at the lowest
level of civilization some acts will be immediately 'felt' to
be destructive of social cohesion in the group and so opposed
to human nature considered under its social aspect. And they
will awaken disapprobation in a quasi-instinctive manner. I
have put the word 'felt' in inverted commas and I have
spoken of a 'quasi-instinctive' manner because I think that
while Aquinas might agree that the term 'feel' has a use in
drawing attention to the difference between, say, a primitive man's apprehension of an act as evil and a moral philosopher's reflective appreciation of its moral quality he would
still maintain that the primitive man mentally apprehends
the act as evil and that the term 'feel' is inappropriate in so
far as it suggests the absence of any mental activity.

One can put the matter in this way perhaps. Aquinas
thought that all men share some very vague ideas about the

good for man, precisely because they are men and possess certain natural tendencies and inclinations in common. For instance, men see that knowledge of the truths required for life should be sought for. And if one wishes to draw attention to the immediacy of the perception one might perhaps say that they 'feel' this. But Aquinas would doubtless insist that mental activity is involved and that some word like 'apprehend' or 'understand' is more appropriate.

But when it comes to apprehending what are the truths necessary for life and, in general, to determining in a concrete way what is the good for man and to forming moral judgements which are less general than what Aquinas calls the primary principles of the natural law in their widest form, there is room for prolonged reflection and discussion. There is room also for the intervention of a variety of factors other than rational reflection, which can exercise an important influence in the formation of a man's moral outlook and set of determinate values. And these factors can be internal, physiological and psychological, as well as external, like upbringing and social environment.

Finally, when there is question of applying principles to individual cases, of deciding whether a given action belongs to this class or that class, and is right or wrong, Aquinas recognizes (cf. his commentary on the *Ethics*, 2, c. 2, *lectio* 2) that though the moral philosopher can provide some help, by drawing attention, for example, to different features of the action, he cannot settle a person's perplexity by a process of sheer logical deduction. Ultimately a man has to make his own decision. And Aquinas observes that a man's actual decision may be perfectly correct even though the abstract problem has not been satisfactorily settled. Perhaps we might say that in such cases the man 'feels' that the action is right or wrong, as the case may be, in order to emphasize the difference between the immediacy of the judgement and a piece of logical or mathematical deduction. But Aquinas would doubtless say that the virtue of 'prudence' often enables a man to discern the objective moral quality of an action even when he is unable to give adequate reasons, which would satisfy a moral philosopher, for saying that the action is right or wrong. An action is right or wrong for Aquinas in virtue of its relation to the good for man, and this relation is discerned by the mind, even though the immediacy of the discerning may be such as to incline one to use the word 'feeling'. And the (or at least a) fundamental difference between Aquinas' theory and a purely emotive moral theory is that the former asserts an objective and determinable relationship in virtue of which actions are good or bad, right or wrong, whereas the latter does not.

In this section I have mentioned ideas suggested by the relativist and emotive theories of ethics. My purpose in doing so, however, was clarificatory rather than polemical, and to avoid misunderstanding I want to explain this point. It was not my intention to 'expound' these theories; and therefore I have carefully avoided mentioning the name of any philosopher save that of Hume, who was mentioned as the author of a proposition which it is usual to quote on these occasions. Nor was it my intention to refute the theories by means of Aquinas' philosophy. My purpose was simply that of using some ideas suggested by these theories to clarify the latter's position. The chief plank on which the relativistic theory of morals rests is probably the empirical fact that different people have held divergent views about moral matters. And as facts are facts whatever conclusions may be drawn from them, it is important to ask whether Aquinas had any idea of these facts and whether his ethical theory is capable of accounting for them or of allowing for them. Similarly, in the moral life of ordinary people deduction, as this is understood in logic and mathematics, does not seem to play any very conspicuous rôle, whereas something that might plausibly be described as 'feeling' appears to be an important factor. It is therefore a pertinent question to ask whether Aquinas thought that everyone forms his or her moral convictions by a process of logical deduction and whether his theory can account for the factor of immediacy in our moral and valuational judgements. In other words, my purpose was simply that of making a brief contribution to the clarification of Aquinas' position with the aid of ideas suggested by later ethical theories.

*

As far as the most general precepts of the natural moral law are concerned, they are known by all, if, that is to say, they are considered simply as general universal truths. But 'reason may be hindered by concupiscence or by some other passion from applying a general principle to the case of some particular action' (*S.T.*, I*a*, II*ae*, 94, 6). And the binding force of 'secondary' or more particular precepts may be unknown, even in their universal form, by some men or groups of men 'either on account of false beliefs or because of evil customs and corrupt habits, as when robberies, or even sins against nature, were not considered by some to be sinful' (*ibid.*). Aquinas argues, therefore, that it was desirable, or even in some sense morally necessary, that God should reveal even those moral precepts the binding force of which is capable of being discovered by the human reason. For many people are led more by sense than by reason, and even when rational reflection is at work it does not work in a vacuum. The philosopher is not a disembodied mind but a man with prejudices and passions of his own which can influence his intellectual life. And Aquinas believed that a revelation of this kind had been made to the Jews in the Ten Commandments.

We have already seen, however, that for Aquinas, the Christian theologian, man has a supernatural final end or supreme good the attainment of which transcends his natural powers. True, human nature is not destroyed or annulled by the fact that man is called to the beatific vision of God, and so the human mind is not rendered incapable of discovering the natural moral law. But it cannot discover by itself either that man actually has a supernatural destiny or the means appointed by God for its attainment. This knowledge is acquired by revelation, and the latter is therefore required not only to make it easier for men in general to know those moral precepts the binding force of which reason is capable of discovering but also to impart to man the knowledge of the supernatural means, like the use of the Sacraments, which God wills him to take in order to receive and grow in supernatural grace. In addition, therefore, to the natural moral law we have the positive divine law. Law in the sense of human positive law, the law of the State, will be considered in the next section, in connexion with political society.

*

The identification of the good for man with 'happiness' or with self-perfection may easily give the impression that Aquinas' ideal was purely individualistic and even egotistic in an unpleasant sense. Yet he regarded life in society as being prescribed by the natural law. That is to say, he recognized in the human being a natural tendency to live in society with his fellows, not only in the smaller group of the immediate family circle but also in those larger groups which in their developed form are called States or political communities. Social life is thus founded on human nature itself, and the family and the State are both natural communities. Reason, reflecting on man's fundamental inclinations and tendencies, says that these societies ought to be formed, inasmuch as they are necessary for the development of man's potentialities. 'It is natural for man to be a social and political animal, living in community; and this is more true of him than of any other animal, a fact which is shown by his natural necessities' (De regimine principum, I, I). And Aquinas goes on to illustrate his point. For example, Nature has provided other animals with food, clothing, and means of defence; but man has to procure these things by using his reason, and the individual cannot satisfy all these needs by himself except at a very primitive level. The adequate satisfaction of man's economic and bodily needs requires organized society, and this shows that society is natural to man. Again, man's social nature is shown by the development of language. Other animals express feelings by sounds, but man alone seems capable of developing language as an expression of thought and a means of communication. In fine, society is required for the satisfaction of man's bodily and spiritual needs. It is therefore not a purely artificial construction but a natural institution which follows from man being what he is. And as founded on human nature it is willed by God who created man. This does not mean, of course, that the historical divisions into nations and States are dictated by God. A given State owes its historical origins to a variety of empirical factors which can be investigated by historians. But that there should be civil or political society or societies is willed by God, as is shown by the fact that He created man who cannot attain his full stature without society.

Furthermore, every society requires direction and government. It is a mistake to think that government exists simply in order to keep the peace and punish evildoers. According to Aquinas, government would be required even if there were no evildoers and even if no one was inclined to break the peace. St Augustine had been inclined to speak as though the State were a result of the Fall of man and as though political authority existed primarily because fallen human beings stand in need of a coercive power to restrain their evil tendencies and to punish crime. But this was not at all Aquinas' point of view. 'Man is by nature a social animal. Hence in a state of innocence (if there had been no Fall) men would have lived in society. But a common social life of many individuals could not exist unless there were someone in control to attend to the common good' (S.T., Ia, 96, 4). One can illustrate the point in the following rather banal fashion. Even if no one was disposed to infringe the traffic regulations, the latter would still be necessary; and so there must be an authority to settle and prescribe them. Government exists primarily to care for the common good. Like society, it is a natural institution, and as a natural institution it is, like society, willed by God.

The different points of view of Augustine and Aquinas

can, of course, be explained historically up to a point. The former, looking back on kingdoms like Assyria and Babylon and their relations with the Jewish people and on the pagan Roman empire and its relations with Christianity, was inclined to regard the State as a regrettable necessity due to the Fall of man and capable of being redeemed, as it were, only through subordination in some way to the Church. Aquinas, however, living in the Middle Ages, was used to the idea of the Christian State and to the concept of the division of powers. But we must also bear in mind the influence of Roman legal theory on the medieval political theorists and, so far as Aquinas is concerned, the influence of the Aristotelian theory of man's social nature and of political society.

Given this view of the State, it is obvious that Aquinas could not regard the State as having been absorbed by the Church or as possessing no positive function of its own. The State existed before the Church and, as a natural institution, it co-exists with the Church, exercising its own function. Aquinas speaks of this function as the promotion of the common good. 'For the good life of the community three things are required. First, that the community should be established in the unity of peace. Secondly, that the community, united in the bond of peace, should be directed to good action.... Thirdly, that through the ruler's diligence there should be a sufficient supply of the necessities for a good life' (De regimine principum, 1, 15). The government therefore exists to preserve internal peace and to care for the defence of the community, to promote the moral well-being of the citizens, so far as this can be done by legislation supported by sanctions, and to ensure them a sufficient supply of material necessities. If, then, we wish to speak of the government and governmental apparatus as 'the State', we must say that for Aquinas the State possesses a positive function. On this point he was at one with Aristotle, and like the latter he speaks of the moral function of the State as promoter of the 'good life'. To represent Aquinas as participating in the political and economic controversies of the nineteenth century would be an anachronism. But we can say that the policy of *laisser-faire* would not be compatible with his view of the purpose and function of political society and government. The task of the State is actively to produce the conditions under which a full human life can be lived.

It would also, of course, constitute an anachronism, were one to depict Aquinas as making pronouncements about twentieth-century totalitarianism. But if one means by the latter term the theory of an absolute State, fountain of morality and sole arbiter of right and wrong, truth and falsity, one must say that totalitarianism is incompatible with Aquinas' political theory. It is true that he sometimes speaks of the individual as a 'part' of the community, considered as a 'whole', and that he draws a comparison between the subordination of a physical member, like an arm, to the whole body and the subordination of an individual citizen to the good of the whole community. But he certainly did not regard the rights of the State over its members as absolute. For one thing, his belief in man's supernatural destiny and in the position of the Church would effectually prevent his accepting the notion of the absolute power of the State. But quite apart from his belief in the divine and independent mission of the Church his theory of legislation would in no way lend itself to employment in a totalitarian political theory. For he regarded the function of human positive law as being primarily to define clearly and support by temporal sanctions the natural law, in all cases at least where this is required by the public good. For example, if we take the precept of the Decalogue 'Thou shalt not kill', its vagueness is obvious. What actions are to be considered 'murder' and what killings are not to be classed as 'murderous'? One of the functions of human positive law, the law, that is, of the State, is to define such concepts as clearly as possible and to provide those temporal sanctions which are not provided by the natural law. Of course, this does not mean that legislation should be confined to defining prohibitions which can be more or less clearly deduced from the moral law. But legislation must be compatible with the moral law. Since the function of legislation is to promote the common good, the criterion of goodness and badness in legislation is its relation, as discerned by reason, to that end. It does not follow that every precept and prohibition of the natural moral law should be embodied in legislation; for there may be cases in which this would not conduce to the public good. It might do more harm than good. But in no case is the State entitled to pass legislation which runs counter to the natural law. 'Every human law has the nature of law in so far as it is derived from the law of nature. If in any case it is incompatible with the natural law, it will not be law, but a perversion of law' (*S.T.*, Ia, IIae, 95, 2). And Aquinas naturally demanded of Christian rulers that they should respect the divine positive law, interpreted by the Church.

From this view of the relation of human positive law to the natural moral law it naturally follows that just laws are binding in conscience. On the other hand, unjust laws are not binding in conscience. A law is unjust, says Aquinas, if it imposes burdens on the citizens, not for the common good, but to satisfy the cupidity or the ambition of the legis- lator; if in enacting the law the legislator goes beyond the powers committed to him; or if burdens (taxes, for ex- ample) are imposed in an unfair and disproportionate manner. 'Laws of this kind are acts of violence rather than laws . . . they do not bind in conscience unless observance of them is required in order to avoid scandal or public dis- turbance' (*S.T.*, Ia, IIae, 96, 4). Laws can also be unjust by contravening the divine positive law, 'and laws of this sort ought not to be obeyed' (*ibid.*). As for those who persist in enacting unjust laws, they are 'tyrants', and rulers of this kind can legitimately be deposed on the ground that they are guilty of abusing their position and power unless, indeed, there is reason for thinking that rebellion would result in as bad a state of affairs as the one which it was designed to remedy.

The view that it is legitimate to depose tyrants suggests

that the ruler has a trust to fulfil, and that this can be abused. And this was in fact Aquinas' view. But we cannot justifiably conclude without more ado that he thought of sovereignty, derived like all legitimate authority ultimately from God, as coming to the sovereign via the people. He may, indeed, have held this view. Remarks to the effect that the ruler represents the people (S.T., Ia, IIae, 90, 3) or that the prince has legislative power only in so far as he stands in the place of the community (S.T., Ia, IIae, 97, 3, ad 3) seem to suggest that he did. But in the second passage referred to he seems to be speaking of elected governments and not to be making a universal statement. In any case it is difficult to be certain what his view was on this matter; for he does not accord it any clear explicit treatment. What is certain, however, is that though he did not regard any particular form of government as divinely ordained for all men, and though he did not attach primary importance to the form of constitution and government, he gave the palm to a 'mixed' constitution in which the principle of unity, represented by monarchy, is combined with the principle of administration by the best and with some measure of popular control, as, for example, by the people electing certain magistrates. Aquinas thought that monarchy is most conducive to unity and that it is the most 'natural' form of government, possessing analogies with God's rule over creation and with government in communities of insects like bees. But at the same time the constitution should be such that the likelihood of tyrants arising or of rulers acting tyrannically is diminished as far as possible. So we can say, if we like to use modern terms, that Aquinas favoured constitutional monarchy. But the main requirement is that, whatever the form of constitution may be, the ruler or rulers devote themselves to caring for and promoting the objective common good.

The State therefore has a positive function of its own, and Aquinas did not think of it as a department of the Church or of the ruler as a vicar of the Pope. On the other hand, he thought of the Church as an independent society, superior in dignity to the State, inasmuch as it existed to help man to secure his supernatural and supertemporal end, and of the Pope as subject only to God. But it was not very easy for him to express precisely the relations between the two societies; nor would we expect to find as much consideration given to the subject as was given it in a later historical epoch when the strong and centralized monarchies of Europe had developed. He thought, of course, of the State as dealing with material and temporal affairs, whereas the Church caters for man's supernatural well-being. But he could not say that the State cares for man's natural end and the Church for man's supernatural end, since he believed that man has in fact only one final end and that this is a supernatural end. Hence he stressed the idea of a close alliance between Church and State. It is the business of the latter, and not of the former, to concern itself with economics, for example; but in its legislation and general conduct the State (Aquinas is obviously thinking primarily of the Christian State) must facilitate, and not hinder, man's attainment of the end for which he was created. Aquinas was naturally well aware of the frequent disputes which arose in medieval Christendom between Church and State; but he did not regard the attempt by one society to deny the rights of the other as providing a remedy for the conditions of friction which occurred. Harmonious relations and mutual respect for each other's position and rights were regarded by him as the ideal to be aimed at. The secularist outlook of a Marsilius of Padua[1] was, of course, quite foreign to the outlook of the thirteenth-century theologian; but so was any extreme theory of the subordination of State to Church.

1. Marsilius of Padua, who died before 1343, is well known for his work *Defensor pacis*, in which he subordinated the Church to the State. He argued that it is only the law of the State (Aquinas' human positive law) which is law in the strict sense, and he considered that the function of the Church is to serve the State by creating desirable moral and spiritual conditions to facilitate the latter's task.

CHAPTER SIX

Thomism

TODAY the philosophy of Aquinas occupies a favoured position in the intellectual life of the Catholic Church. And it is also generally regarded, of course, as representing in the modern world the prolongation of an ancient, some would say 'antiquated', philosophical tradition. Compared with, say, neopositivism on the one hand and existentialism on the other, Thomism is looked on as being eminently conservative. But in the Middle Ages Aquinas' philosophy never came to occupy the position in the Catholic Church which it enjoys today; it was simply one philosophy among others. And mention has already been made in the first chapter of the fact that Aquinas was regarded by his contemporaries as an innovator. Indeed, some of his ideas met with opposition not only from theologians and philosophers outside the Order to which he belonged but even from some Dominicans. Thus in 1277, three years after Aquinas' death, Robert Kilwardby, the Dominican archbishop of Canterbury, followed the example of the bishop of Paris in censuring a number of propositions which included a few that had been held by Aquinas. Soon after the latter's canonization in 1323 the Parisian censures of 1277 were withdrawn, as far as they affected Aquinas, attacks from outside the Order were diminished, and the theologico-philosophical system of Aquinas soon became the official doctrine of the Dominicans. But this does not mean that his system won general acceptance. In the fourteenth century there were various 'schools', including the Thomists, who followed Aquinas, the Scotists, who followed John Duns Scotus, and the group which followed Giles of Rome. These groups, each of which followed a past and creative thinker, together formed the so-called 'ancient way' (*via antiqua*); and their influence was strongest in the Orders. This 'ancient way' was contrasted with the 'modern way' (*via moderna*) represented by the nominalist movement of the fourteenth century, the greatest figure of which was the English Franciscan, William of Ockham (d. 1349). This movement of thought was predominantly analytic and critical in character, with a marked interest in logical studies, and it bears some resemblance, sometimes a notable resemblance, to the prevailing trend in British philosophy today, though the points of similarity should not indeed be exaggerated. As one would expect with a new and 'modern' movement, it became fashionable and won widespread popularity, capturing most of the new universities which were founded in the course of the fourteenth and fifteenth centuries, though it also obtained a strong hold in the older universities such as Oxford and Paris. In time nominalism itself became a recognized tradition or school rather than a new and spreading movement of thought, and at the period of the Renaissance we find university chairs not only of Thomism and Scotism but also of nominalism. It is therefore a very great mistake to think that medieval philosophy and Thomism are synonymous terms.

In the medieval period the favourite textbook in theology and philosophy was the work to which allusion has already been made in these pages, namely the *Four Books of Opinions*, commonly known as the *Sentences*, by the twelfth-century writer, Peter Lombard. Aquinas, Duns Scotus, William of Ockham, all lectured on the *Sentences* and wrote commentaries on it. And when John Capreolus (d. 1444) wished to defend Aquinas' doctrines against the criticisms of Scotists and nominalists he did so by way of a commentary on the *Sentences*, using Aquinas' own commentary and referring to the *Summa theologica* and other works. In the course of time, however, the *Summa theologica* began to displace the *Sentences* as a textbook, and commentaries on the former began to appear. Thus a celebrated Dominican called Thomas de Vio and generally known as Cajetan wrote commentaries on this work of Aquinas between 1507 and 1522, while Franciscus Sylvester de Sylvestris (d. 1528), who is known as Ferrariensis, composed a commentary on the *Summa contra Gentiles*.

Commentaries continued to be written, but during the period of the Renaissance a freer style of writing came to be adopted. Through his *Metaphysical Disputations* the Jesuit Francis Suárez (d. 1617), the famous writer on the philosophy of law, gave a powerful impetus to the construction of systematic philosophical works in which philosophical themes alone were treated and in which the old habit of commenting on a venerable predecessor's text was dropped. The gradual growth of this newer style of writing among Scholastic authors[1] was, of course, in tune with the practice of contemporary non-Scholastic philosophers, who were composing original philosophical works of their own. Moreover, in view of what was happening outside the Schools the Scholastics were compelled to separate philosophy from dogmatic theology not simply by asserting a distinction between them but also by actually separating them in their written works. In the first half of the seventeenth century there appeared the *Thomist Philosophical Course* (*Cursus philosophicus thomisticus*) of the Dominican writer, John of St Thomas (d. 1644), and this was followed by other systematic 'philosophical courses', some based on Aquinas, others, by Franciscans, on Duns Scotus. This process of 'extracting' the philosophical system of a man who had himself never elaborated such a system in isolation from theology is sometimes spoken of in a disparaging manner, as though it constituted a distortion or perversion of the spirit of men like Aquinas and Duns Scotus. But it is very difficult to see what else the Scholastics could have done in the post-Renaissance world, when outside the Schools philosophy was being pursued as an independent branch of study. And it is only reasonable to suppose that Aquinas, had he returned to his activity on earth in, say, the seventeenth or

1. I use the term 'Scholastics' to mean in general those philosophers who consciously and deliberately adhered to one of the medieval traditions.

the eighteenth century, would have adapted his way of writing to the changed circumstances.

This activity in the composition first of commentaries and then of philosophical courses should not be taken to mean that the philosophy of Aquinas enjoyed an undisputed reign in the Catholic seminaries and educational institutions of the seventeenth, eighteenth, and nineteenth centuries. Leaving aside the devotion of the Dominicans to Aquinas and of the Franciscans to Duns Scotus and the considerable influence of Suárez both inside and outside the Jesuit Order, one can say that in many ecclesiastical seminaries and educational institutions philosophy came to consist of an emasculated Scholastic Aristotelianism, tinctured with ideas taken from other currents of thought, especially Cartesianism. More-over, this ecclesiastical philosophy was only too often out of touch not only with contemporary philosophical thought in the world outside but even with contemporary science. And it is necessary to bear this unhappy state of affairs in mind in order to appreciate the action of Pope Leo XIII when in his encyclical letter *Aeterni Patris* (1879) he asserted the permanent value of the Thomist synthesis and urged Catho-lic philosophers to draw their inspiration from Aquinas, while developing Thomism to meet modern intellectual needs.[1] He was not asking them to shut their eyes to all thought since the thirteenth century but rather to penetrate and develop the synthesis of a thinker who combined a pro-found and living belief in the Christian religion with a real trust in the power of the human mind and in the value of philosophic reflection, uniting a readiness to see truth wherever it might be found with a fidelity to fundamental rational insights which prevented any surrender to passing fashion just because it was fashionable. It is understand-able, of course, that those who have quite different ideas about religion and who think that Aquinas' philosophical convictions are obsolete should regard the papal action as

1. It is not strictly true to say that Leo XIII 'inaugurated' the revival of Thomism. What he did was to give impetus to an already existing movement.

being 'reactionary'. But when Leo XIII extolled Thomism he was not trying to put a full-stop to philosophical activity among Catholics; rather was he trying to renew it and give it a fresh impetus. And there can be little doubt that as a matter of fact the revival of philosophy among Catholics has coincided with the revival of Thomism.

Thomists insist that Thomism is acceptable on its own merits as a philosophy. And it is indeed clear that any philosophical system ultimately stands or falls by its own intrinsic merits or demerits. None the less, it would be idle to deny that there tends to be a *de facto* connexion between Thomism and Catholicism. There are indeed some philosophers who are not Catholics but whose philosophical outlook is more or less akin to that of the Thomists, and sometimes even identical with it. But it is noticeable that these philosophers are not infrequently thinkers whose religious convictions approximate to those of the Catholics. And one has only to go to an international philosophical congress to realize the truth of the observation that there is some *de facto* connexion between Thomism and Catholicism. Now, given this connexion, it is understandable that there is an inevitable tendency to use Thomism for apologetic purposes. I have no wish to question the legitimacy of this procedure. A Christian apologist who believes in the validity of the Thomist system is fully entitled to draw on it in his work. And a Thomist philosopher who believes, as Aquinas himself believed, that man's final end is supernatural and that the supreme business of life is to attain it may naturally be inclined to stress those aspects of Thomist philosophy which point beyond itself. But though the use of Thomism for apologetic purposes is easily understandable, especially in the modern world, it may not be inappropriate to stress the fact that, whatever uses it may be put to, Thomism is and remains a philosophy. Despite its *de facto* connexion with Catholicism, it is not part of the Catholic faith;[1] and if we wish to judge of its philosophical merits and its potentiali-

1. A Catholic philosopher is not committed to Thomism because he is a Catholic.

ties for fruitful development, we have to turn to those Thomists who have written as serious philosophers rather than to the somewhat slick statements of Thomist positions by popular apologists.

*

One of the first tasks of Thomist philosophers in the modern era was obviously that of showing that Thomism was not inextricably entangled with discarded scientific theories and that the validity of its general principles was unaffected by the evolution of modern science. In other words, one of their primary tasks was to show the falsity of the notion that the development of modern science had rendered meta-physical philosophy in general, and Thomism in particular, an antiquated and completely outdated mode of thought. Nowadays the existence of Thomism and the presence of Thomists in our midst is taken for granted : it represents one of the recognized currents of thought. But in the last century this was not the case. The project of reviving the philosophy of Aquinas was commonly looked on as an ex-hibition of archaism, an impossible attempt to halt the march of modern knowledge by the childish device of put-ting back the hands of the clock. How, in particular, could a revival of medieval philosophy be reconciled with an acceptance of the ascertained results of modern science and with the spirit which animated the scientists?

The fulfilment of this task is associated very largely with the university of Louvain, and especially with the work of Cardinal Mercier (1851–1926) and his collaborators. I cannot enter upon the history of Mercier's labours as a professor at Louvain; but it is necessary to emphasize the following point. Mercier was profoundly convinced of the validity of Aquinas' view that our knowledge starts with sense-percep-tion and that metaphysical reflection is based upon know-ledge of the material world. He interpreted this as implying that systematic philosophy must presuppose a knowledge of the sciences, that it must remain in contact with them, and that it must integrate their conclusions into itself. He therefore expounded the ideal not only of obtaining a thorough knowledge of scientific method and of the results obtained by scientists elsewhere than at Louvain but also of forming men who would devote themselves to the various particular sciences, in connexion with his own Institut Supérieur de Philosophies and this, as he insisted, without any apologetic purpose. Neither religion nor metaphysics, he maintained, has anything to fear from the sciences; but the metaphysician needs scientific knowledge. And scientific knowledge can be obtained only by devoting oneself to a particular science for its own sake, and not with a view to obtaining results which can be used in religious apologetics. It was in this spirit that he was instrumental in founding, for example, the laboratory of experimental psychology which won merited respect and fame under the direction of Professor Michotte, who had studied in Germany under Wundt.

Although Mercier made a distinction between the particular sciences and philosophy, and although he did not regard the latter as being simply a synthesis of the sciences, he spoke explicitly of philosophy as being the natural development and complement of the sciences. In his view the sciences begin the work of giving an explanatory account of empirical reality, and philosophy, utilizing their results, though employing also certain fundamental principles, gives the completest explanation of empirical reality which is possible for the human mind by its natural reflection. Like Aquinas, he believed in self-evident principles which the metaphysician employs in the construction of his synthesis and explanatory account of empirical reality; but he emphasized so strongly the relation of metaphysics to the sciences that he tended to substitute for the distinction between the data of ordinary experience and philosophic reflection on these data the distinction between the established results of the sciences and philosophic reflection on these results. And this represents a point of view which is not acceptable to all Thomists. Obviously, no Thomist would deny the relevance of, for example, modern discoveries in physiology and psychology to discussion of the body-mind problem and the fact that the problem has to be treated in the light of and with reference to these discoveries and theories. At the same time they prefer to stress metaphysics' independence of changing scientific hypotheses and its connexion with ordinary experience. But whichever point of view is to be preferred there can be no doubt at all that the labours of Mercier and his collaborators at Louvain contributed in a signal manner to winning respect for Thomism and to dissipating the notion that it is hostile to or suspicious or fearful of modern scientific developments and discoveries.

But the Thomists of the modern era had obviously to concern themselves not only with the relation of philosophy to science but also with the relation of Thomism to other philosophical traditions and currents of thought. And the attitudes of individual Thomists towards other philosophers have, not unnaturally, varied very considerably. While some have been inclined not only to underline differences but also to adopt a markedly polemical tone, others have consistently tried to understand the other philosophers' points of view and to discover the valuable and true elements in their thought. With those who adopted the former attitude, the concept of a 'perennial philosophy' has tended to be exceedingly narrow, while with the second group the concept has tended to take on a much wider significance. But though there are still some Thomists for whom non-Thomist philosophies seem to be little more than absurdities, it is the second attitude which has prevailed. If one attends a congress of Thomist philosophers, one can hardly fail to be struck by the fair-mindedness and sympathy with which other thinkers are discussed. Generally speaking, the present-day Thomist is concerned not only to understand what Kant or Husserl or Heidegger says and why he says it, but also to discover his real contribution to philosophic thought. For it is taken for granted that an original thinker would not say what he says unless he had got hold of some truth or apprehended some aspect of reality to which it is worth while to draw attention. If one allows for possible exceptions, it is safe to say that the serious Thomist philosopher of today is free from the sort of attitude which it seems to be incumbent upon the orthodox Marxist to adopt in regard to non-Marxist philosophers. Indeed, Marxism is likely to receive a much more level-headed and discriminating treatment from the Thomist than the latter is likely to receive from the Marxist.

One important consequence of the interest taken by Thomists in non-Thomist thought and of the sympathetic and understanding treatment which they are generally prepared or even eager to accord it is that they are inevitably influenced by other philosophies and currents of thought. This influence may not always perhaps be immediately evident. For in some cases at least Thomists have the rather disconcerting habit of finding texts in Aquinas to justify them in presenting as developments of his philosophy ideas which have certainly come to them via contemporary non-Thomist thinkers. It is odd to find, for example, a discussion which is plainly inspired by the writings of modern phenomenologists presented as a meditation on texts of Aquinas. On the other hand it is easy to understand that a philosopher who believes that Thomism is the 'perennial philosophy' should be eager to show not only that those elements in modern thought which he considers to be fruitful are compatible with the philosophy of the historic Aquinas but also that they can be regarded as being in some real sense developments of the latter and that they can be organically assimilated by a Thomism which is not looked on as a purely static importation from the thirteenth century. And in any case the point to which I wish to draw attention is that Thomists are concerned not only with understanding the non-Thomist philosophies but also with evaluating them in a positive and not simply negative manner.

In the last century the great importance and influence of Kant and the common preoccupation with epistemology or the theory of knowledge stimulated Thomists to develop their own epistemology. Yet if one speaks of 'their own epistemology', this statement can be misunderstood. For although Thomists agree about the obvious fact that Aquinas never elaborated a theory of knowledge as a separate branch of philosophy they neither have been nor are in full agreement about the function and scope of epistemology or about the way in which Aquinas' remarks about knowledge and certainty should be developed. They agree, of course, in rejecting scepticism, positivism, subjective idealism and the pragmatist account of truth and in accepting realism and the mind's ability to attain truth and certainty. They reject scepticism, for example, not merely because a philosophy of scepticism would be clearly incompatible with Aquinas' position but rather for intrinsic reasons. But there is no general agreement about the precise nature of the chief epistemological problems or about the right method of tackling them. Some of the earlier Thomists took their stand more or less on common sense and on man's spontaneous conviction that he apprehends reality and truth. This attitude, however, met with the objection that it betrayed a misunderstanding of the nature of epistemological problems and that it was consequently incapable of dealing with them. But there has been a great variety of opinions about the formulation and relative importance of these problems.

Some Thomists have regarded the problem of knowledge largely through the eyes of Descartes. They have started with what they call 'methodic doubt', have admitted the reality of Descartes' problems and have attempted to solve them in a less roundabout manner. Thus some, while taking the concrete intuition of the self as their point of departure, have endeavoured to justify by examination of this intuition both the affirmation of metaphysical principles and the assertion of the existence of material reality. By proceeding in this way they have hoped to avoid a bifurcation between ideal judgements (analytic in some sense) and judgements about existence, a bifurcation towards which Mercier is thought to have tended and which makes it difficult to bridge the gap between the order of ideas and the order of things. Others, however, have interpreted the problems about knowledge primarily in terms of the philosophy of Kant. Thus in the fifth volume of his work *Le point de départ de la méta-physique* the late Père Maréchal of Louvain undertook a prolonged critical comparison of the Thomist and Kantian positions. In the first part of the volume he developed the position of Aquinas himself in the light of the demands of the critical philosophy, stressing above all the dynamism of the intellect, its movement towards being, and developing the metaphysical implications of this intellectual dynamism. In the second part he undertook to show how if one accepts the starting-point and method of Kant one is forced in the end to proceed beyond the latter's position into metaphysics. For Maréchal, therefore, Kant was not at all the philosophical ogre which he had been for many other Thomists in particular and Scholastics in general. For him the Kantian transcendental critique of knowledge was a powerful instrument for developing the germs of a Thomist critique which were present in the writings of Aquinas. But though Maréchal's writings have exercised a wide influence there are a number of Thomists who reject in decisive terms any attempt to develop a Thomist theory of knowledge on the basis of either a Kantian or a Cartesian starting-point. Étienne Gilson, for example, will not allow that Descartes' problem of the existence of the extra-mental world is a real problem at all. At least it is a real problem only if Descartes' initial presuppositions and starting-point are accepted. As for Kant, if one starts with the presuppositions of the transcendental critique of knowledge, there can be no consistent way out in the direction of a realist metaphysics. Idealism, as it has developed historically, has drawn the logical conclusions from the premises which were initially adopted, and one cannot without inconsistency and contradiction accept the starting-point and deny the conclusions.[1] Indeed, the whole attitude which is represented by preoccupation with the theory of knowledge and by the notion that a

1. The validity of this point of view is, of course, questionable. The truth of the statement that idealism, in its historic development, is a strictly logical deduction from a given set of premisses might well be challenged.

critique of knowledge must be carried through before existential judgements can be made justifiably and before any
metaphysics of any kind is possible is both intrinsically
unjustifiable and also incompatible with Aquinas' position.
This is not to say that no Thomist theory of knowledge is
possible. But it must take the form of reflecting on the concrete act of apprehending the objectively existent and on
the metaphysical conditions and implications of this act.
M. Gilson does not, of course, deny the obvious fact that we
may be mistaken in thinking that a given judgement is true.
But he emphatically rejects any tendency to think that we
can first doubt the possibility of knowledge and then 'justify'
knowledge in some *a priori* manner. Other Thomists, however, while agreeing with Gilson that the problem of the
existence of any datum other than the subject is a pseudo-
problem, are not prepared to say that there is no critical
problem at all and that there is no place for a critique of
knowledge unless one is ready to adopt an idealist position.
The critical problem, they would say, can be stated in such
a way that its mere formulation does not prejudge the issue
between realism and idealism.

Turning to Aquinas' metaphysics we again find considerable differences of attitude among Thomists. Some of the
latter, mainly, I think, among the older generation, give the
impression of thinking that little more is required than to
repeat what Aquinas said. This impression is not entirely
justified, of course. For these writers realize the obvious fact
that the criticisms levelled against the theories maintained
by Aquinas and against his arguments in favour of these
theories have to be met. And in attempting to meet them
they do more than merely repeat the words of Aquinas. But
their point of view seems to be that though his theories and
arguments need some explanation and defence in view of
later criticism there is no justified call for development in
any other sense. It is a fallacy, they would say, to suppose
that because Aquinas lived in the thirteenth century his
metaphysics is inadequate for the twentieth century unless
it undergoes a process of 'development'. The fallacy lies in

thinking that metaphysics and the sciences are of the same type and that because the latter change and develop the former must do so too. Metaphysics deals with things considered simply as beings, and their ontological structure remains the same, whatever new discoveries may be made and new hypotheses formed by the scientists. There is thus no reason at all why Aquinas should not himself have developed the permanently valid system of metaphysics. Naturally, in another age, informed by an outlook different from that prevailing in the thirteenth century, it may be very difficult for people to appreciate and understand Aquinas' point of view and lines of thought; but this is an empirical statement of fact about people, which does not affect the metaphysical system considered in itself. It is reasonable to demand a preliminary work of explanation and clarification; but this work constitutes a pedagogical introduction to the perennially valid metaphysical system. Any development that may be called for is really extrinsic to the system: it is a development in the outlook and mental dispositions of people rather than a development of the abstract system.

To a certain extent all Thomists would agree with this point of view. If a philosopher thought that a development was called for in Aquinas' metaphysics similar to the development in astronomy from a geocentric to a heliocentric hypothesis he would have no better reason for calling himself a 'Thomist' than a Copernican astronomer would have for calling himself a disciple of Ptolemy. But many Thomists would claim that there is ample room for a development of Aquinas' metaphysics which, while remaining faithful to the latter's spirit and outlook, amounts to more than a defence of his explicitly stated positions against attack. For example, behind Aquinas' proofs of the existence of God there lies a set of presuppositions which, though alluded to here and there in his writings, stand in need of elaboration and development. It is clear that if the arguments are logically sound the conclusion must be implicitly contained in the premisses. And in this case to affirm the existence of any finite thing is to affirm implicitly the existence of God.[1] It is not surprising, therefore, that we find some Thomists interpreting the judgement in a manner which bears a marked resemblance to the view maintained by, for example, F. H. Bradley. The proofs of the existence of God do not, therefore, involve an illegitimate leap from the empirical to the transcendent, from the finite to the infinite; for they simply make explicit knowledge which is already implicitly contained in knowing that there is at least one changeable, contingent, finite being. Does not Aquinas himself say that 'all cognitive agents know God implicitly in everything they know' (*De veritate*, 22, 2, *ad* 1)? But what is meant by implicit knowledge in this connexion? Does it mean simply that though one does not know one is capable of knowing? Or does it mean something more than this? And if it does, how can this be reconciled with Aquinas' view that we have no innate idea of God and no intuition of the divine essence? Thomists point out that though Aquinas maintained that the primary natural object of the human mind is the nature of the material thing he also always held that the mind knows all that it does know as being, and that logically prior to the orientation of the human mind as human towards a particular kind of being there is the natural dynamic impulse of the mind as mind to being as such. In fact, the mind is by its nature orientated, as it were, towards infinite being: there is a dynamic impulse towards the infinite, which is the ground of the will's orientation towards the infinite good and which ultimately makes metaphysics possible. Since this impulse or orientation of the mind does not constitute an innate idea of God, and still less an intuition of the divine essence, it is possible for man to substitute for the real infinite a pseudo-infinite, to construct, for example, the idea of 'the World' as a quasi-Absolute in which finite things are

1. I presuppose, of course, the interpretation of Aquinas' argument, which was defended in the third chapter, namely that he did not regard the proposition affirming God's existence as an empirical hypothesis in the modern sense. I also presuppose the remarks about logical entailment in this context which I made in the same chapter.

situated, or even to deny the infinite altogether, though this denial does not destroy the natural orientation of the mind towards the infinite. There is always an 'implicit knowledge' of God, though this does not become what is ordinarily called 'knowledge' until it is made explicit. And the proofs of the existence of God are one way in which it can become explicit. For they focus attention on those aspects of empirical reality which act, as it were, like pointers and give free play to the natural orientation of the mind. Behind all explicit argumentation in favour of God's existence there lies the natural drive of the mind towards transcendence, which must be seen in close connexion with the will's drive towards the infinite good. Indeed, some Thomists try first to show that there is in reality this natural drive or impulse of the human mind towards the infinite and then to argue directly that this natural intellectual dynamism manifests the reality, the real existence that is to say, of the concrete infinite God. They would claim that this line of thought is in harmony with Aquinas' teaching. The latter says, for example, that 'our mind in its understanding reaches out to the infinite. A sign of this is that whatever fine quantity is given the mind can conceive a greater. Now this orientation of the mind to the infinite would be in vain (*frustra;* that is, unintelligible and inexplicable) unless there were an infinite intelligible thing. There must therefore be an infinite intelligible thing, which must be the supreme being, and this we call God' (*C.G.,* 1, 43). At the same time, these Thomists would say, the hints and remarks made by Aquinas on this subject have to be developed in order to satisfy the demands of critical reflection. And light can be shed on the way in which they should be developed by study not only of Christian philosophers like Blondel and thinkers belonging to the Augustinian tradition in general but also of the idealist current of thought.

Thomists have also shown themselves conscious of the need for exhibiting the relevance of Thomism to the modern situation of man by developing its social and political ideas and by applying Aquinas' principles to society in its present forms. In this respect Jacques Maritain has made a signal contribution. Some are inclined to think, rightly or wrongly, that in his general presentation of Thomism he lays too great an emphasis on the letter of Aquinas and on the commentaries of John of St Thomas; but in any case he has undoubtedly given a great impetus to the revival and deepening of the Thomist tradition. Indeed, Maritain and Gilson are the two best known modern Thomists. Maritain has discussed at length modern social and political developments, like totalitarianism, in the light of Aquinas' principles. In his personal political convictions he is known as standing rather to the 'Left'; but whatever his views on detailed political issues may be he always insists on the Thomist idea of the person and on society as a society of 'persons' rather than of mere 'individuals'. In his eyes Thomist social and political theory, with its emphasis on the social nature of man and on the positive function of political society and of government combined with its emphasis on the spiritual and moral aspects of the human being which make him more than a mere member of the collectivity, can point the way between totalitarianism on the one hand and atomic individualism on the other. Starting with the idea of the person he has also emphasized the humanistic aspects of Thomism, insisting that the position of Aquinas is as far removed from the pessimism of Hobbes as from the optimism of Rousseau and showing that Aquinas' insistence on the spiritual side of human personality belongs to an integral humanism which avoids the one-sided conception of man and of his needs and development which we find, for example, in the Marxist philosophy.

It is clear, therefore, that though Thomists may give to the external observer the impression of being ultra-conservative and of all saying the same thing they are indifferent neither to non-Thomist thought nor to the need for developing Aquinas' positions. And in the process of fulfilling this need they display a much greater originality of thought and variety of ideas than might at first be suspected. In other words, Thomism is not simply a museum piece; it is a living and developing movement of thought, deriving its inspiration from Aquinas but conducting its meditation on his writings in the light of subsequent philosophy and of subsequent cultural developments in general. It is worth adding, however, that modern Thomists have been predominantly interested in continental philosophy of the speculative type. One can hear a great deal in Thomist circles about Heidegger, for example; one hears a great deal less about contemporary British and American philosophers of the empiricist tradition or about what can perhaps be called the linguistic movement in Anglo-American philosophy. This can, of course, be easily explained, if one bears in mind the differences between continental and Anglo-American philosophy in general, together with the fact that Thomism is far more widespread and vigorous in countries like France, Belgium, and Germany than it is in Britain. But I think that Thomist philosophy might benefit if its adherents paid rather more attention than they do to the prevailing currents of thought in Britain and America. For one thing, the influence of continental philosophy does not invariably contribute to the maintenance of that concern with preciseness and clarity that marked Aquinas himself and has characterized many of the older Thomists. For another thing, reflection on the foundations of their metaphysics in the light of modern empiricist criticism and of linguistic analysis might lead Thomists to achieve a greater clarification of, say, the nature of 'metaphysical principles' and of their status in relation to pure tautologies on the one hand and to empirical hypotheses on the other.

If no mention has been made in this section of logical developments, the reason is that there is not very much to be said. Certain Thomists, like the Polish Dominican, I. M. Bochenski, have studied the developments in 'modern logic' and its relation to the logic used by Aquinas, and the need is felt for more work of this kind. It is certainly highly desirable that this need should be met. But though Thomists, apart perhaps from some ultra-traditionalists, feel no hostility towards or suspicion of modern logical developments

they are sceptical about the validity of any claim that
modern logic has initiated a revolution in general philosophy. And they are not, of course, alone in feeling sceptical
about this. Pioneers in a fresh line of work are only too apt
to indulge in exaggerated claims about the omnicompetence
of their pet study. At the same time it is reasonable to expect
that some at least of those who draw their inspiration from
medieval philosophy should devote particular attention to
modern developments of a line of study which was so extensively pursued in the Middle Ages.

*

It has been pointed out in this chapter that the philosophy
of Aquinas was not the only philosophical system of the
Middle Ages. And it scarcely needs saying that it is not the
only philosophy today. Indeed, the point which needs emphasizing is not that there are other philosophical systems
but that Thomism is in fact a philosophy and that any *de
facto* affiliations which it may have with Catholicism do not
destroy its philosophical character. Fundamentally it is a
sustained attempt by the human mind to understand man
and his situation, the world in which he finds himself. And
this it has in common with other systems. That which is
peculiar to it is perhaps the emphasis it places on existence,
on the act of existing, not in the existentialist sense of man
as free, as 'creating' himself, but on existence considered
as the fundamental act by which every thing is a reality.
But this emphasis does not place Thomism outside the class
of philosophical systems: it simply gives it a special stamp.
In so far as the philosophy of Aquinas was the result of the
reflection of a theologian-philosopher we can speak of it as
a Christian interpretation of the world or as an attempt to
understand empirical reality, especially on the existential
level, in the light of Christianity. At the same time Aquinas
himself distinguished clearly between philosophy and
theology, and Thomism has developed as a philosophy
which is prepared to stand or fall on its own intrinsic merits
or demerits and which appeals to reason, not to faith or to

revelation. Thomists therefore can enter and do enter into intelligent discourse on the purely philosophical level with thinkers who belong to very different traditions and schools of thought.

But if Thomism is admittedly one among other philosophies, how can it be reasonably claimed, as Thomists are accustomed to claim, that it represents the 'perennial philosophy'? How can this claim be even plausible? It may be appropriate to end this book with some brief remarks on this topic. I am not concerned with trying to prove that Thomism is in fact the perennial philosophy: I am concerned rather with trying to show that the claim is not so absurd as it sounds at first hearing.

The use of the word 'perennial' can lead to serious misunderstanding. For it suggests the idea of an acquired body of knowledge which is handed on in the form of propositions to be passively learned and accepted. And textbooks of Scholastic philosophy may seem to indicate by their structure and lay-out that this is in fact what is meant by a perennial philosophy. But it is sufficiently obvious that one does not become a philosopher by learning the propositions enunciated by Aquinas or by anyone else. It is only by personal philosophic reflection that one becomes a philosopher. And if one means by perennial philosophy a work which is accomplished once and for all by the reflection of a determinate individual or group of thinkers and which only needs to be handed on, there is no such philosophy. For in a very real sense the work has to be done all over again by every philosopher. Nor, as we have already seen, does the Thomist concept of a perennial philosophy mean that all development is excluded. The claim that there is a perennial philosophy involves the claim that there is an abiding metaphysical pattern in the changing and developing universe, which is capable of being understood and stated. But it does not follow that any given man had or has a completely adequate understanding of it. The concept of a perennial philosophy is the concept of a developing insight rather than the concept of a static and once-for-all expression of insight. Moreover, the claim that Thomism is the perennial philosophy is not intended by those who make it, at least by the more sensible among them, to exclude the possibility of fresh insights into truth being contributed by non-Thomist philosophers. It does, however, imply that these insights can be organically assimilated by a developing Thomism.

One condition for this organic assimilation is that Thomism should not be an unbalanced system which stresses one aspect of reality to such an extent that it is necessarily blind to other aspects. And it may be worth while to draw attention to one or two features of Thomism which suggest that it is in fact a balanced system. We find, for example, an 'empiricist' element and a 'rationalist' element. We find also a profound confidence in the power of the human reason coupled with a vivid consciousness of its limitations. The last mentioned factor prevents Thomism from degenerating into some form of 'Gnosticism', into professing, for example, to be able to plumb the depths of ultimate reality or, with Hegel, to read off, as it were, the contents of the divine mind.[1] Its confidence in the power of the human reason, on the other hand, divides it from those who, with Kierkegaard and with those theologians who have turned the latter's understandable attitude towards Hegelianism into an anti-philosophical dogma, would write off philosophy as a sign of human intellectual pride and as a confirmation of the powerlessness of man caused by the Fall. Thomism's confidence in the human reason enables it to enter into intelligent discourse with other philosophies, while its consciousness of the inevitable limitations of the human mind saves it from those speculative extravaganzas which incline commentators to dwell more on the psychology of their authors than on what the latter have said. In its theory of man Thomism tries to avoid materialism on the one hand

1. I do not mean to imply that Hegel was what is ordinarily thought of as a 'theist'. But it was partly, I think, his excessive confidence in the power and scope of the speculative reason which led him gradually to eliminate the belief in the divine transcendence with which he started in his early years.

and sheer dualism on the other; and in its political theory it makes its way between the Scylla of totalitarianism and the Charybdis of atomic individualism. Its humanism is a balanced humanism. The body is not declared worthless or shameful, and the sciences and the arts are not rejected in the name of religion. At the same time man is not declared, with Protagoras, to be the measure of all things.

To claim that Thomism is a balanced philosophy involves claiming that it is capable of doing justice to different aspects of reality without turning one aspect into the whole. But it does not involve the claim that the integration of philosophic truth was finally accomplished by Aquinas. And there is at least one sense in which the Thomist himself can say, 'We cannot go back to the Middle Ages; we cannot go back to Aquinas'. If we are considering Aquinas' philosophy from a purely historical point of view, the fact that he said this or that is obviously of prime importance. But if we are considering Thomism as a living and developing philosophy, it is the philosophical positions themselves which count, and the fact that Thomas Aquinas held them in the thirteenth century is not strictly relevant. At the same time the claim that Thomism as a living and developing system of philosophy can do justice to different aspects of reality would be senseless unless it is added that it can do this without ceasing to be Thomism. Similarly, if the concept of Thomism as the perennial philosophy is to have any meaning, there must be something which remains the same and permits us to speak with propriety of 'Thomism', whatever stage of development the philosophy may have reached. Otherwise the name 'Thomism' would be in obvious danger of becoming empty of meaning.

The attempt has indeed been made to draw up a list of propositions which give, as it were, the essence of Thomism and which must be held by anyone who wishes to be recognized as a Thomist. But when the emphasis is placed on the acceptance of a set of propositions, it seems to me to be misplaced. If the propositions are true, this can only be because there is a certain stable and intelligible metaphysical structure of reality which discloses itself to the reflective mind of the philosopher. And if there is such a permanent structure, it will find expression, to some extent at least, in ordinary language in the form of an implicit metaphysic. And if it can be shown not only that there is an implicit metaphysic which is not simply the reflection of linguistic forms but also that this implicit metaphysic leads naturally to an explicit metaphysic on Thomist lines, the claim that Thomism is the perennial philosophy might appear less unreasonable to philosophers at large. To those who think that philosophical theories must be erected on the changing hypotheses of the sciences, the philosophy of Aquinas can be of little but historical interest. But to those who think that philosophical reflection is grounded in common experience and that metaphysics has an intimate connexion with this experience it can be a source of constant stimulus and inspiration.

Bibliographical Notes

I

The Latin text of the Parma edition of the works of Aquinas (25 vols., 1852–73) has been reprinted at New York in 1948. Of the 'Leonine' critical edition of the works (Rome, 1882–   ) only fifteen volumes have so far appeared.

There are English translations of the *Summa theologica*, the *Summa contra Gentiles* and the *Quaestiones disputatae*, edited by the English Dominican Fathers and published by Burns, Oates and Washbourne of London. A new edition of the *Summa theologica (Summa theologiae)*, to be completed in sixty volumes, is being published at London by Blackfriars in conjunction with Eyre and Spottiswoode, with parallel Latin and English texts, introductions, notes, appendices, and glossaries.

On Being and Essence (Toronto, 1949) is an annotated translation by A. Maurer of the *De ente et essentia*. *Truth* (2 vols., Chicago, 1952–3) is a translation by R. W. Mulligan of the *De veritate*. *St Thomas On Kingship to the King of Cyprus (the Governance of Rulers)* (Toronto, 1949) is an annotated translation by I. T. Eschmann of the *De regimine principum*. There is also an English translation of *Aristotle's De anima with the Commentary of St Thomas Aquinas* (Routledge and Kegan Paul, 1951) by K. Foster and S. Humphries.

The following collections of selected passages in English can be mentioned here:

> *Thomas Aquinas, Selected Writings*, selected and edited by M. C. D'Arcy (Dent, Everyman's Library, 1934).
> *St Thomas Aquinas, Philosophical Texts*, selected and translated by Thomas Gilby (Oxford, 1951).
> *Basic Writings of St Thomas Aquinas*, edited by A. Pegis (2 vols., New York, 1945).

The following two works might prove helpful to students:
Farrell, Walter. *A Companion to the Summa [theologica]* (4 vols., New York, 1941–2).

Deferrari, R. J., Barry, M. I., and McGuiness, I. *A Lexicon of St Thomas Aquinas* (Catholic Univ. of America Press, Washington, D.C., 1948).

II

There are now a number of general histories of medieval philosophy available in English. Among shorter works are the following:

Copleston, F. C. *Medieval Philosophy* (Methuen, 1952).

Curtis, C. S. J. *A Short History of Western Philosophy in the Middle Ages* (Macdonald, 1950).

Hawkins, D. J. B. *A Sketch of Medieval Philosophy* (Sheed and Ward, 1945).

Leff, G. *Medieval Thought: St Augustine to Ockham* (Penguin Books, 1958).

Knowles, D. *The Evolution of Medieval Thought* (Longmans, 1962).

Larger works include:

Copleston, F. C. *A History of Philosophy* (Burns, Oates and Washbourne); Vol. 2, *Augustine to Scotus* (1950); Vol. 3, *Ockham to Suárez* (1953).

De Wulf, M. *History of Mediaeval Philosophy*, 3 vols. This work, of which the first two volumes were published in English by Longmans, has been republished by T. H. Nelson.

Gilson, É. *History of Christian Philosophy in the Middle Ages* (Sheed and Ward, 1955).

III

Of English works and English translations of foreign works on Aquinas one can mention the following:

Chesterton, G. K. *St Thomas Aquinas* (Hodder and Stoughton, 1933, 1947).

D'Arcy, M. C. *Thomas Aquinas* (Benn, 1931; 2nd edition, Dublin, Clonmore and Reynolds, 1953).

Grabmann, M. *Thomas Aquinas* (Longmans, 1928).

Patterson, R. L. *The Concept of God in the Philosophy of Aquinas* (Allen and Unwin, 1933).

Sertillanges, A. D. *Foundations of Thomistic Philosophy* (Sands, 1931).

And the following can be highly recommended:

Gilson, É. *Le thomisme* (2nd edition, Paris, 1952).

IV

For a fuller bibliography see Copleston, *A History of Philosophy*, vol. 2 (listed above). For considerably fuller bibliographies see De Wulf's *History of Mediaeval Philosophy* (mentioned above) and Ueberweg-Geyer's *Die patristische und scholastische Philosophie* (Berlin, 1928). Students who desire something more can consult:

Mandonnet, P., and Destrez, J. *Bibliographie thomiste* (Paris, 1921).

Bourke, V. J. *Thomistic Bibliography*, 1920–1940 (St Louis, Mo., U.S.A., 1945).

Index